PROPHECY AND POWER

Comparative Islamic Studies

Series Editor: Brannon Wheeler, US Naval Academy

This book series, like its companion journal of the same title, publishes work that integrates Islamic studies into the contemporary study of religion, thus providing an opportunity for expert scholars of Islam to demonstrate the more general significance of their research both to comparativists and to specialists working in other areas. Attention to Islamic materials from outside the central Arabic lands is of special interest, as are comparisons that stress the diversity of Islam as it interacts with changing human conditions.

Published

Earth, Empire and Sacred Text: Muslims and Christians as Trustees of Creation
David L. Johnston

Ibn 'Arabi and the Contemporary West: Beshara and the Ibn 'Arabi Society
Isobel Jeffery-Street

Notes from the Fortune-Telling Parrot: Islam and the Struggle for Religious Pluralism in Pakistan
David Pinault

Orientalists, Islamists and the Global Public Sphere: A Genealogy of the Modern Essentialist Image of Islam
Dietrich Jung

Prolegomena to a History of Islamicate Manichaeism
John C. Reeves

PROPHECY AND POWER

MUHAMMAD AND THE QUR'AN IN THE LIGHT OF COMPARISON

Marilyn Robinson Waldman

Edited by
BRUCE B. LAWRENCE
with
LINDSAY JONES and ROBERT M. BAUM

Published by Equinox Publishing Ltd.
UK: Unit S3, Kelham House, 3 Lancaster Street, Sheffield S3 8AF
USA: ISD, 70 Enterprise Drive, Bristol, CT 06010

www. equinoxpub.com

First published 2012

ISBN 978-1-84553-987-0 (hardcover)

British Library Cataloguing-in-Publication Data
A catalogue record for this book is available from the British Library.

Library of Congress Cataloging-in-Publication Data
Waldman, Marilyn Robinson.
  Prophecy and power : Muhammad and the Qur'an in the light of comparison /
Marilyn Robinson Waldman ; edited by Bruce B. Lawrence, with Lindsay Jones and
Robert M. Baum.
    p. cm. – (Comparative Islamic studies)
  Includes bibliographical references and index.
  ISBN 978-1-84553-987-0 (hb)
  1. Muhammad, Prophet, d. 632–Prophetic office. 2. Prophets–Comparative studies.
3. Koran–Criticism, interpretation, etc. I. Lawrence, Bruce B. II. Jones, Lindsay,
1954– III. Baum, Robert Martin. IV. Title.
  BP166.5.W35 2012
  297.6'3–dc23
                                                                        2011021804

Typeset by JS Typesetting Ltd, Porthcawl, Mid Glamorgan
Printed and bound in the UK by MPG Books Group

CONTENTS

PREFACE

When Marilyn Waldman died in July 1996, she was at the forefront of those comparativists who shaped the emerging field of Islamic studies. After earning her PhD from the University of Chicago, she joined the faculty at Ohio State University where she continued to teach, to administer and to goad others to do comparative labor, until her death at the age of 53. In her earliest monograph, titled *Toward a Theory of Historical Narrative: A Case Study in Perso-Islamicate Historiography*,[1] through resort to John Searle's notion of speech act, she did a literary analysis of the surviving portions of the History of Bayhaqi, a notable eleventh-century historian. Not only did she examine the significant tension between the explicit and the implicit values of this historical text, but she also showed how audience expectations and other contextual limits pervaded and shaped Bayhaqi's work. In the words of her colleague, Dick Davis, Marilyn demonstrated how "historical narratives function more as images and representations of the past than reservoirs of presumed historical realities." Her emphasis on "the essentially generic nature of medieval Islamic historiography, and the ways in which the conventions of genre dictate how material is presented," according to Davis, "have emerged as a lasting legacy to the field."[2]

As William Graham, dean of Harvard Divinity School, noted in his 1997 tribute to Marilyn, she had the singular ability "to set different cultures in mutually enriching conversation, trying insofar as possible to avoid labels altogether, in favor of more cumbersome multi-word formulations that recall the approximate nature of comparison and

---

1. Published by Ohio State University Press (Columbus, OH) in 1980, it was later translated into Persian as *Zamāna, zendagi, o ruzgar-e Bayhaqi* by Mansoureh Ettehadieh (Teheran, 1996).
2. For a full tribute to Waldman's initial work, see Dick Davis, "Marilyn Waldman," in *Encyclopaedia Iranica*, www.iranica.com/articles/waldman-marilyn (20 July 2005), accessed on 14 August 2010.

discourage reification." Graham was citing Marilyn's own words in order to work out his own mode of conceptualizing her project in new language that is at once multi-word and cumbersome, yet also non-reifying and inclusive.[3]

Marilyn's work remains fresh and vital, in need of iteration and application, over fifteen years after her demise. She allows us to revisit prophecy even while recognizing its conceptual limits. She requires us, and assists us, to rethink what has been the role of prophecy and prophets in the broadest sweep of Islamic civilization.

Marilyn was passionate, both about humor and hubris. Humor she displayed on every possible occasion, whether from her amiable Mulla Nasrudin or from some other source, while hubris she exposed and decried in every guise in which she detected it. Labeling was and is an academic hubris, even though non-academics also appeal to the quick and simple, increasingly so in the Internet age, where a sound bite too often substitutes for a subtle reflection, when multimedia communication resorts to labels as necessary hooks for would-be consumers.

Marilyn's project was to recognize the impossibility of destabilizing "prophecy" from either its academic or popular usage, while at the same time she was hoping to show just how elastic and productive a comparative enquiry into prophets and prophecy could be.

At the outset of her manuscript she declares that she "wanted to use the taken-for-granted category of prophecy to question the category of prophecy itself, in fact to question all categorical comparison." In her role as hostess she invited various prophets to come to her banquet table and to help her entertain comparisons—comparisons that were made possible because so many of them were present on the same occasion, the one that she uniquely had convened.

I would like to stress not only how odd (yet fitting) is the guest list at Marilyn's table, but also how strongly weighted with Islamic evidence is her resulting narrative. Islam *is* the religion of prophecy *par excellence*, with the creed itself establishing Muhammad's authority as the *rasūl* (prophet-messenger) of God's revelatory self-disclosure. Into that familiar domain Marilyn bursts with a whole new set of questions. She uses her special knowledge of Islam to attack general knowledge of Islam, but even more to undercut taken-for-granted conceptions of prophecy that exclude or reduce or misshape Islamic evidence.

---

3. William A. Graham, "Inviting Prophets and Entertaining Comparisons: Some Reflections of an Islamicist," 16 November 1997. My own reflections at this same American Academy of Religion panel in November 1997 provide the basis for some of the analysis offered here. It has not been previously published.

At every point of her carefully staged enquiry Marilyn establishes what she intends to do, while also qualifying her own role. On the one hand, we are told that "what we choose to include under Islam and the study of prophecy will greatly influence whatever definition [of prophecy] emerges," and yet she notes that "all beginning points are arbitrary, connected with anticipated outcomes and constructed contexts." If all knowledge reflects precommitment, then why should we bother? Will we not in our turn be contributing to "the large number of competitive and contradictory theoretical and conceptual frameworks" that already mark modern American and European scholarship on prophecy? Marilyn was painfully aware of how difficult it was to say anything new that could be projected beyond the Foucauldian net of a desire to know in order to control. After all, she laments, "the power struggle exists both between the scholar and the people she studies, and between the scholar and her colleagues, among others."

Despite these many well-placed qualifiers on her own labor, Marilyn did say something about prophecy within Islam that has seldom been heard beyond Islamic studies' circles. As a historian she was "always keeping one eye on change over time." Hence her major point about the Prophet Muhammad within the emergence of Islamic norms was the change between qur'anic evidence and later historical reformulations of his role. The decisive century was the ninth. For "Muslims of the ninth century had elevated Muhammad above other previous *nabīs* in a way that his own contemporaries had not. The Qur'an speaks as much about Abraham and Joseph and Moses as it does about Muhammad."

How this happened occupies much of her complex, always nuanced arguments about anticipating the outcome and constructing the context for Islamic prophecy. Several Arabic terms are subjected to intense scrutiny, among them *nabī* and *rasūl*, so that we are told these terms are not "mere" synonyms, even though both "connote someone who enunciates or delivers a message." Rather, "each one acts to supply what is missing in the other, or to control what is superfluous … What is involved is a translation from the biblical tradition to Muhammad's cultural context." While "*nabī* is necessary to link Muhammad with the cosmic history that included Abraham, Moses, and Jesus, it raised expectations that were inconsistent with Muhammad's role. *Rasūl* excludes the inappropriate things about *nabī*, without losing the desired similarities, but it also focuses on the loyal, consistent, clear delivery of a message created by the sender, not the messenger."

It was the use of extra-Islamic sources ("a translation from the biblical tradition to Muhammad's cultural context") that was needed to make clear how Muhammad was both *nabī* and *rasūl* in a way that underscored the finality of his prophetic mission. Far from undermining the "truth" of Islam, for Marilyn this process of "centering on Muhammad as norm," which dates back to the ninth century, was a way of answering a really big question that she asked but never had the chance to answer. Why do only such a small number of oppositional figures (aka prophets) have such extensive posthumous careers? Or, as she herself put the same question more directly, "Do foundational figures (of major religious traditions) really become powerful *only* through this posthumous process [of expanding their range of plausible roles and corresponding images]?"

In a close reading of Marilyn's analysis, we do find an indirect answer to her central question. She underscores the role of exchange and competition as decisive. Exchange and competition are decisive because they mutually reinforce the way that early Muslim communities understood both themselves and the Prophet Muhammad. Hence she looks at three kinds of evidence to move beyond the solitary qur'anic reference to Muhammad as *khatm al-anbiyā* or "the seal of the prophets." She explores "narrative accounts of his career (*sīra*), discrete reports of his exemplary nature (*Hadith*), and social movements formed around other kinds of 'final' leaders."

At the same time that Muhammad by the end of the ninth century is emerging "as an intercommunal norm beyond compare," the very constructedness of this model of Muhammad allows us, as historians of Muslim and other religious traditions, to see how the process itself requires us to undercut the terms used. We undercut them by qualifying them with multiple meanings, both overlapping and corrective, but we also decapitalize them in order to suggest how much broader they were in earlier contexts, and how much broader they may become, or were intended to become, in later contexts.

The effectiveness of this move is demonstrated when Marilyn can extrapolate from her comments about specifically Muslim evidence to expand the notion of what is human. The human as Muslim, the human as forgetful, the human as capable of ethical judgment, the human as gendered—all comprise one of the many tangents of analytic insight that Marilyn begins to generate in the analysis that follows.

The denouement of Marilyn's comparative zest and analytical genius is the collaborative chapter that she did with Robert Baum, a west African historian and her former colleague at Ohio State University. It is framed as Chapter 4 below. It provides a frame narrative for illustrating concretely several points about prophecy and Islam. Far from belittling the Prophet Muhammad, it illustrates graphically how Marilyn's proposed revisionist agenda can illumine the familiar, imbuing it with a freshness that conventional categories and taken-for-granted terms will always deny. It is difficult not to see something of Marilyn's wry humor in conjuring a twentieth-century Senegalese prophetess as the fitting partner in conversation with the seventh-century Arab prophet Muhammad.

But the outcome is far from funny; it demonstrates how critical the response of those opposed to prophetic exemplars is. As Marilyn observes:

> Because Muhammad was able to win over most of his opposition and Alinesitoué could not, Muhammad benefited more from the results of persuading people to accept what they had formerly opposed. And although both used their control of a unique form of privileging communication as a focal point for a new network of relationships, Muhammad's situation allowed him to benefit more from his unusual skill in forging the actual social alliances that allowed him to overcome opposition. Both individuals appear to have been especially sensitive, flexible, adaptive, and insightful into their own cultures, but Alinesitoué's integrative abilities were, by force of circumstances, expressed primarily in her teaching network, whereas Muhammad was free to establish broader kinds of alliances.

* * *

The benefit of Marilyn's work and her enduring insights would not have been possible without the generous labor and support of many people. First on the list is Loren Waldman, who helped in providing financial as well as moral support for more than a decade. Also enthusiastic in his engagement with this project has been Professor Robert Baum of the University of Missouri. Bob wrestled with the issues that mark the collaborative essay he did with Marilyn, and then he generously made time to update that essay in order to make it the capstone it now is in the current volume. Professor Bruce Lincoln of the University of Chicago also lent valuable, and much appreciated, support. The editorial challenge was met by a host of graduate students, beginning with Sarah Savant, Scott Kugle, Peter Wright, and Timur Yuskaev. They were aided by a number of gifted undergraduates, but principally Sandy Hernandez, Dania Toth, and most recently, with extraordinary commitment, Atif Mahmood. A 2009 graduate of Reed College, Samara Holub-Moorman, literally rescued the manuscript. Samara provided exemplary editorial help at a point when the project seemed too massive and too woolly to complete, and I want to extend to her my special appreciation. The

Postscript by Lindsay Jones came as the crowning point of the process, and he too deserves a special commendation for having put yet another dimension of Marilyn's legacy on record for all to imbibe and use.

These many supporters and laborers have collectively made the work of a gifted scholar accessible and provocative for the next generation of those concerned with prophets and prophecy, power and institutions, revelation and its lingering, unending controversy. Marilyn was a hostess and, in her own way, a prophetess of the art of comparison. We all remain in her debt; we all feast at her table.

Bruce B. Lawrence
Durham, NC

Prologue

INVITING PROPHETS AND ENTERTAINING COMPARISONS

A neighbor found Mulla Nasrudin crawling around under a street lamp. Asked why, the Mulla replied, "Because I lost my ring across the street."
"Then why are you looking under the lamp?"
"Because the light is better over here."[1]

Like the Mulla, I began my search where the light is better, in the comparative study of prophecy, one of the most well-worked categories in the study of religion. I looked there first because I thought I wanted merely to expand the study of prophecy by incorporating materials from the study of Islam.

I soon realized that what I was looking for was in the dark, on the other side of the street, or even on the other side of the tracks. Inspired by my experiences as a maverick in a marginal field, I found that I really wanted to use the taken-for-granted category of prophecy to question the category of prophecy itself, in fact to question all categorical comparison.

It was the very nature of comparison as an academic endeavor that attracted me to prophecy in the first place. I realized that certain "prophets" had initially been inviting to me because they and their followers had done something that I see myself doing as a scholar—inviting and entertaining comparisons, comparisons that generate legitimacy and power the more inviting and entertaining they are. I discovered that my understanding of Muslim experiences with "prophethood" had drawn me to the problem of politically staged comparison and its connection with leadership.

I did not, after all, want to squeeze more individuals into the category of prophecy. Rather, I wanted to compare instances of something that I

---

1. Idries Shah, *The Exploits of the Incomparable Mulla Nasrudin* (London: Picador, 1966): 26. The anecdote sometimes refers to a key rather than a ring, but the punch line is the same.—Ed.

had identified as interesting to me for a particular purpose in a particular context, something that could shed light on what I do as a scholar, on the particulars of the cases I study, and on the possibility of making useful generalizations that do not have to turn into categories or laws. In this instance, comparing uses of politically staged comparison has proved an ideal way to do all three.

I also discovered that the best occupational metaphor for my style of comparison is "hostess:" someone who knows how to invite guests who will entertain conversations that can lead to new guest lists and new conversations at future get-togethers. As a result of "inviting prophets" to my first rather plain and simple gathering, I had learned to entertain comparisons that have generated new questions rather than reinforce old categories. This book is the story of that transformation.

In pursuing my original objective, expanding the study of prophecy to incorporate Islamic materials, I considered two alternatives: stretch existing definitions of prophecy just enough to fit Islam, or experiment with a new definition of prophecy that uses Islam to both illumine and question the adequacy of prophecy as an analytical category. In choosing the latter, I felt like Mae West when she said: "When I'm confronted by a choice between two evils, I choose the one I haven't tried before." I knew I would not ultimately be satisfied with turnabout as fair play, but I did assume that turnabout might be a novel first step in the direction of a more even-handed framework for comparison. After all, in a truly cross-cultural approach to comparison, should a question like "What is the Muslim Bible?" continue to seem so obvious while one like "Who is the Christian Muhammad?" would continue to seem so unfair? For I was envisioning a style of comparison that would involve greater reciprocity, one that would not suppress differences in favor of the kinds of similarities produced by "universals" that were really just extensions of one group's point of view. By way of experimenting with Islam as a starting point, I will, in this first section of the book, lay out in a very selective fashion those things that had come to interest me about Islam and prophecy, loosely construed.

To claim that something "essentially" Islamic is guiding my presentation would be disingenuous. First of all, as a historian who always keeps one eye on change over time, I do not subscribe to timeless essences as the definers of religious traditions as experienced historically. Second, and more importantly, my interpretation of what stands out in Islamic history is to my mind a convergence of something Muslims have expressed and a series of interests that I bring to the subject. So before I turn to Chapter 1, a discursus on those interests is in order.

For most of my career, I have been dissatisfied with our failure to become truly comparative and cross-cultural. It is not surprising that the study of prophecy has not incorporated Islamic materials. The problem is much bigger than that. While it is now possible to review how so-called non-Western materials have been incorporated into multiple comparative cultural endeavors, much still needs to be done in the field of Islamic studies. There has also been a particularly noticeable ignorance of things Islamic in comparative work. For many years, American scholars of Islam have bemoaned the failure of their specialty to become common knowledge, either among fellow academics or among the general public. Some blamed the insularity of Islamicists themselves; others, the narrowness of non-Islamicists; still others, the indifference of the general public.

If the study of Islam, like most things "non-Western," has remained generally marginal to the comparative study of culture, it has remained particularly so in the academic study of religion. Most "experts" in Islam have insisted on a linguistic and technical mastery that most general scholars of religion do not possess. Furthermore, Orientalist language-based disciplines were already well established when the academic study of religion emerged about a century ago. However, that was not the only thing that put religion scholars at a disadvantage. They have often privileged categories, such as "myth," with which many Islamicists, especially Muslim Islamicists, feel uncomfortable, or, as we are seeing, they have used seemingly relevant categories like "prophecy" in such a way as to make Islamic examples seem deviant or aberrant.

This gap between special and general knowledge of Islam remained largely academic until the Iranian "revolution" brought its wider import home in a very urgent way. Between 1980 and now, world events have kept that window of opportunity open longer than we would have anticipated. At the same time, a domestic backlash against the many things classified as "multiculturalism," and now the pernicious effect of Islamophobia after 9/11, have threatened to close prematurely the window of opportunity for engaging Islam, perhaps more so within educational institutions than without.

Thus, in both public and academic forums, the need for new knowledge of the world competes with domestic political agendas and anxieties, putting the academic purveyor of such new knowledge in an ever-intensifying cross-fire, and redefining or complicating the political stakes constantly. As Aaron Hughes pointed out, there has been a conflicting tendency to either over-generalize about Islam, ignoring or failing to critique one's own assumptions, methods and agendas, or else the opposite tendency, to assume that specialized, local inquiry "solves" all the big problems, and answers all the glaring questions, about Islam.[2] For every expression of a desire to know, there seem to be many more expressions of a desire not to know, coming from the most unlikely bedfellows. Some do not want to know because they fear that understanding will equal approval or even advocacy. Others do not want to know because they fear a decentering of "our own" culture in the education system, or because they fear a decentering of the institutional commitments and investments in teaching "our own" culture. When such cross-cultural comparative knowledge is associated with new structures within universities, turf wars are even more likely. Still others attribute their not wanting to know to a post-modern, post-colonial insight: since the desire to know is always connected with an Orientalist–imperialist will to power, the only alternative is to resist the desire to know, especially when it privileges "non-native scholars" who have learned about other cultures as part of European or American educational enterprises. At the same time, for their own reasons, some domestic, some international "insiders" of "other" cultures often claim special privilege or knowledge over "outsider" scholars.

Like it or not, then, the claim "merely" to expand ongoing comparative study with new materials from other cultures is likely to be perceived as a competitive, power-seeking claim. The power struggle exists both between the scholar and the people she studies, and between the scholar and her colleagues, among others. My own location in this power struggle has had, like everyone else's, personal factors as well. As a first-generation American growing up Jewish in Dallas, I had never felt comfortable with conventional definitions of "our own" culture. Then, too, I had also chaired and advocated an academic unit dedicated to cross-cultural comparison, and in so doing had experienced the embattled nature of such work on a daily basis. I was drawn to a marginal field, I fought for it, I used what I learned to challenge convention, and these experiences obviously helped me to integrate an existential problem with an intellectual problem. Such a convergence, some say, produces the best work. But only when I realized that I was studying the kind of comparisons that I was trying to make did I completely understand my own location in the intellectual struggles of my day.

---

2. See Aaron Hughes, *Situating Islam: The Past and Present of an Academic Discipline* (London: Equinox Publishing, 2007).—Ed.

In Chapter 1, which deals with the career of Muhammad, I focus on the role of comparison in legitimating a leadership role that is oppositional to the status quo. That focus represents the convergence of themes that I believe are present in the sources with the interests that I bring to them; it also suggests what I hope others can learn with me about the nature of comparison as it applies to power and prophecy.

1

OPENING A BLACK BOX: RETHINKING THE COMPARATIVE STUDY OF PROPHECY

DAUGHTER: All right—but then what does explain gravity?
FATHER: Nothing, my dear, because gravity is an explanatory principle.

DAUGHTER: But didn't he [Newton] discover gravity? With the apple?
FATHER: No, dear. He invented it.

FATHER: ... There's no explanation of an explanatory principle. It's like a black box.
DAUGHTER: Oh.

DAUGHTER: Daddy, what's a black box?
FATHER: A "black box" is a conventional agreement between scientists to stop trying to explain things at a certain point.

DAUGHTER: So a "black box" is a label for what a bunch of things are supposed to do.
FATHER: That's right. But it's not an explanation of how the bunch works.[1]

Like most scholarly fields, the academic study of religion is full of such black boxes, "religion" foremost among them. Among the few scholars of religion who examine the nature of explanatory principles, some focus on their inventedness, while others treat them as native categories that must be approximated to indigenous perceptions, behaviors or expressions that have no universally suitable equivalent. In fact, most of the field's black boxes are a combination of the two; that is, native categories that have been *re*invented for scholarly purposes. This study argues against reinventing native categories for scholarly purposes. It proposes an alternative to the black box: a way to bunch things together

---

1. Adapted from Thomas A. Sebeok and Alexandra Ramsay (eds), *Approaches to Animal Communication* (The Hague: Mouton, 1969).—Ed.

that encourages comparison and explanation, but also trusts native categories. To do so it opens one very prominent black box—prophecy—
and, in the process, turns it into Pandora's box.

A scholar can advance knowledge in at least two ways: by going
where no other has gone, or by following the pack on the assumption
that where interest is concentrated, the problems are the toughest and
the stakes the highest. This work is of the latter sort, in that it tries to
say something fresh about the timeworn subject of prophecy by exploring its association with temporal power. Prophecy is inextricable from
power, and for that reason the study of prophecy has attracted extensive
attention in a variety of academic fields within the humanities, such as
biblical studies, Jewish studies, religious studies, Islamic studies, history and classics, but also in social science fields that bridge to everyday concerns, such as communication, anthropology, African studies,
sociology, and political science.

Despite the rapt attention to prophecy, there is little agreement about
it, either among those who follow it or among those who study it.
Like most human phenomena, prophecy is a messy business. The sheer
number of those deemed to be prophets is daunting. Muslims alone
count 124,000, but from an academic perspective that would be a con-
servative estimate. Given the large numbers, it is not surprising that
followers of prophecy disagree considerably about who is and who is
not a prophet. Many individuals who have been viewed as legitimate
prophets by some have been dismissed as false prophets by others, or
else relegated to some other category altogether. Muslims view Jesus
as a major prophet, for instance,[2] yet most Christians view Jesus as the
messiah and Muhammad as a false prophet. Manicheans viewed the
Buddha and Jesus as prophets, while Christians viewed Mani as a false
prophet and Buddhists viewed the Buddha as something other than a
prophet. Bahais view both Muhammad and Bahaullah as legitimate
prophets, yet Muslims view Bahaullah as a false prophet. While a few
Muslims have considered the Buddha and Krishna prophets, most have
not. Similarly, a few Jews have considered Muhammad a legitimate
prophet, but most have not.

Within any single community, variability of terminology and nomenclature compounds the confusion. For example, many English-speaking
Americans use the word prophet to describe anyone who predicts, especially if the prediction comes true, or to refer to anyone who receives

---

2. See Tarif Khalidi, *The Muslim Jesus: Sayings and Stories in Islamic Literature*
(Cambridge, MA: Harvard University Press, 2001).—Ed.

a vision. This looseness of terminology also applies to scholars. Even when English-speakers denote as prophet someone who has a certain kind of special relationship with God, they generally retain the focus on prediction, using three related words interchangeably—prophecy, prophetic, and prophesy—that entail an element of futurism. Although English has a separate word for the office of a prophet—prophethood— it is more common for Americans to use a single word—prophecy— both for the office and for the utterances of a prophet. At the same time, however, the gift of prophecy can be attributed to individuals who do not occupy the office of prophet, or to individuals who utter a prediction only once in their lives. Furthermore, while English speakers sometimes try to distinguish between such words as prophet, seer, and diviner, too often they use them interchangeably.

This slipperiness partly reflects the derivation of English usage from a convoluted process of translation, one that occurred from cognate and non-cognate languages without distinguishing between them. The Greek origin of the English word prophet seems clear enough: *pro*, meaning "for" or "forth," and *phonai*, "to speak;" thus, "to speak [forth] for another."[3] Yet speaking for another, even if the other is identified as extra-human, has assumed different meanings in different contexts. Among certain late first-millennium BCE Greek oracle cults, *prophutus* (m.), or *prophetis* (f.), was used interchangeably with *promantis* and *hypothutus* for "one who speaks in place of or on behalf of the god," usually at a special site.[4] Predicting was not generally what *prophetai* did; and they shared the power of augury with occupants of a related role, *mantis*; but not every *mantis* could be the direct mouthpiece of a god.[5] Nevertheless, the *mantis* could deliver non-oracular prophecies anywhere; they could also share a similar social function with the poet, just as the poet (*thespiodos*) could be responsible for poetizing the utter- ances of a *promantis*.[6]

The Hebrew Bible adds to the complexity of denotations for proph- ecy in English. It applies the word *nabī* both to various figures whose

3. Robert R. Wilson, *Prophecy and Society in Ancient Israel* (Philadelphia, PA: Fortress Press, 1980): 22.

4. David E. Aune, *Prophecy in Early Christianity and the Ancient Mediterranean World* (Grand Rapids, MI: William B. Eerdmans Publishing Company, 1983): 29.

5. *Ibid.*: 29.

6. Charles Segal, "Poetry, Performance, and Society in Early Greek Literature," *Lexis: Poetica, Retorica e Comunicazione nella Tradizione Classica* 2 (1988): 129, www.lexisonline.eu/images/archivio/2_lexis/segal_poetry.pdf, accessed 17 August 2010.

activities and writings appear therein and also to their "mistaken" competitors and precursors. It further seems to distinguish the *nabī*, who was called by God to speak out (sometimes in an ecstatic state, sometimes not), from the *ro'eh*, literally "see-ers," who inquired of God on request, and the *hozeh*, those who had visions of God. The biblical authors were succeeded in the third to second centuries BCE by Septuagint translators of the Hebrew Bible into Greek. Just as the biblical authors were themselves making their own retrospective sense of roles that had been changing continuously for many centuries, the Septuagint translators used the word *prophutus* to cover *nabī, ro'eh*, and *hozeh*, as well as, on one occasion, *mala'ik*, heavenly messenger.[7] That did not stop medieval European writers from using the Latin term *prophetae* for a large number of apocalyptic warners who led violent protest movements.[8] Thus, like contemporary American English-speakers, others have used the same word for different roles and different words for the same role, and have understood any given term as part of a system of related terms. The history of terminology is an unavoidable part of the study of the phenomena to which it refers, and modern scholars must address that history to give analytical value to their own labor.

As these examples illustrate, terminology and nomenclature vary not just within one community, but also from community to community. For example, one very common Arabic–Muslim usage shares the Greek and Hebrew emphases on speaking for a god, but with fundamental differences. There are two words in Arabic for figures who receive unsolicited communications from God: *nabī* and *rasūl* (as in the phrase, *rasūl Allah*, "Messenger of God"). Explanations of the relationship between these two has varied, but *nabī* commonly refers to a large number of individuals to whom God has communicated special messages, whereas *rasūl* refers to a much smaller number charged with founding and governing a community on the basis of God's communication.[9] The content may be termed *risāla* (literally message, related to *rasūl*); but the most common word for the office is *nubuwa* (literally, the capacity of being a *nabī*). Thus, the office and the content are related but not synonymous or interchangeable. The verbal root of the noun *nabī* has connotations of withdrawal, contradictoriness, and conflict. The verbal root of *rasūl*

7. Robert R. Wilson, *Prophecy and Society in Ancient Israel*: 23.
8. See Norman Cohn, *The Pursuit of the Millennium: Revolutionary Millenarians and Mystical Anarchists of the Middle Ages* (London: Maurice Temple Smith Ltd, 1970): 62–3.—Ed.
9. Willem A. Bijlefeld, "A Prophet and More Than a Prophet?" *Muslim World* 59 (1969).

can connote sending a message, as well as sending an imposition and/ or a blessing.[10] Neither focuses on prediction. Some Christians can imagine prophecy in individuals who do not specialize in it or share the messages with others, and instead use it only for their own guidance, but Muslims distinguish sharply between the messages a *nabī* receives and other forms of God's guidance to individuals. Christians and Jews focus on prophets who were not political leaders in their own right; Muslims privilege those who were.

In order to overcome this messiness and confusion surrounding the term prophet, modern American and European scholars have generated categories of their own. The result is a large number of competitive and contradictory theoretical and conceptual frameworks. Many of them assume that prophecy can be defined in such a way as to overcome its culture-specific connotations and the complex history of its usage. In effect, the classification systems of the modern researcher, in almost every instance, are privileged over those of the faith community.

The ways of defining prophecy display a staggering diversity. Some scholars treat prophecy within the context of religious phenomena only, while others stress the relationship between religious and non-religious phenomena. Some scholars recognize the interplay between prophecy and associated phenomena, but none of them focuses on it. Some focus on the history of prophecy, while others focus on its structure. The more historical approaches tend to stress the careers of individuals, the content of prophecy, and the impact of both on the formation of religious traditions. Those that foreground the structure of prophetic activity tend to be more interested in prophecy as a type of authority, in the settings in which prophets emerge and operate, in prophet as a role, or in the social impact of the person designated as a prophet.

The range of evidence in every case influences the resulting definition, and so it should be obvious that what we choose to include under Islam and the study of prophecy will greatly influence whatever definition emerges as "Islamic prophecy." Even if we liberate ourselves from existing scholarly definitions of prophecy, other interests will direct us in ways that will affect our findings. If the resulting definition were then projected as the basis of a universal category of analysis, certain things would be included and excluded according to the nature of the initial definition of prophecy used. My contention is that all beginning points

---

10. Mustansir Mir, *Verbal Idioms of the Qur'an*, Michigan Series on the Middle East No.1 (Ann Arbor, MI: Center for Near Eastern and African Studies, the University of Michigan, 1989): 145–7.

are arbitrary. Far being self-evident, they are inextricably connected with anticipated outcomes and constructed contexts. We could just as well begin this study with Abraham, the first Muslim *nabī* according to the Qur'an, if we wanted to convey one aspect of the qur'anic world-view, also advocated by some later Muslims. No definition of proph-ecy or any other segment of human experience can adequately cover all perspectives and all contexts. The crucial century, as will become clear below, is the ninth century CE, for by the ninth century Muslims had elevated Muhammad above other previous *nabī*s in a way that his own contemporaries had not; the Qur'an itself speaks as much about Abraham and Joseph and Moses as it does about Muhammad.

One must begin with the current state of scholarship on prophecy. The existing comparative approaches to prophecy are far from com-prehensive. If we survey the scholarly literature, we find at least five overlapping strategies that mark current approaches to prophecy. The following brief account of those strategies, culled from the vast litera-ture on prophecy, is indicative rather than exhaustive; it does no more than suggest the intellectual lineages that connect scholars with one another in time and space. Yet, by examining major reference works and their authors, one can, and should, highlight various strategies and the variety of fields from which they come.

STRATEGY 1. Selecting a particular kind of prophecy in Judaism and Christianity and identifying the same religious phenomenon in other traditions.
The entry on prophecy in the *Encyclopedia of Religion* states: "The term prophecy refers to a wide range of religious phenomena that have been manifested from ancient to modern times."[11] However, what the authors, G.T. Sheppard and W.E. Herbrechtsmeier, mean by "wide range of phenomena" takes as its norm a specific type of ancient prophecy: "Today comparativists use prophecy to describe religious phenomena in various contexts on analogy with the activity of ancient Hebrew prophets and other figures who had a similarly pivotal role in found-ing religions in Southwest Asia."[12] To be fully analogous, such fig-ures must be "divinely chosen messengers bearing a revealed message

---

11. Gerald T. Sheppard and William E. Herbrechtsmeier, "Prophecy: An Overview," *Encyclopedia of Religion*, vol. 11, ed. Lindsay Jones, second edition (Detroit, MI: Macmillan Reference USA, 2005): 7423, *Gale Virtual Reference Library*, http://go.galegroup.com/ps/i.do?id=GALE|CX3424502519&v=2.1&u=duke_ perkins&it=r&p=GVRL&sw=w, accessed 22 August 2010.—Ed.

12. *Ibid.*: 7424.—Ed.

to humankind," one that involves social criticism.[13] This definition implicitly excludes figures that are prophets only to their own people. Therefore it must interpret the biblical prophets, for example, as speaking not just to the Israelites but rather to humankind as a whole. For Sheppard and Herbrechtsmeier, the history of prophecy is the history of certain individuals and their subsequent impact. This kind of approach is less concerned with the sociological and anthropological setting of the phenomenon than with its impact on the formation of religious traditions. It is primarily concerned with the content of prophecy and the process of its canonization.

To construe a cross-cultural population, these authors foreground a trait that becomes apparent only after the lifetime of a prophet, who is also a founder, even though the various figures listed were founders in quite different senses. The Hebrew prophets, for instance, do not qualify as founders in any clear sense. The authors then focus on the commonalities among a limited number of founder figures: the literary prophets of the Bible, Zoroaster, Jesus, Mani, Muhammad, and, much later on, Joseph Smith and Mary Baker Eddy. Although others who have had a very close relationship with divine guidance or inspiration can be compared with founders, they are not deemed comparable. Such other individuals may be said to be analogous, yet qualitatively different: the ancient Greek *prophetai*, other founders who were sages and teachers (i.e., the Buddha, Confucius, and Mahavira), and Christian, Jewish, and Muslim mystical figures. To make that distinction, the authors must project onto the founder figures' lifetimes a special genius that is assumed to have informed their posthumous greatness. To draw parallels among them, the authors must in effect depend on the history of biographical representation as much as on evidence closer to the events in question.

Despite its less than rigorous use of evidence, this approach does manage to include within the cited cohort figures not generally identified as legitimate prophets by pious Jews and Christians or by many scholars who study prophecy from a background in Jewish and Christian studies. If it does not extend its category to cultures east of Iran, it does at least extend it to modern times. In its distinctions between prophets and others, this approach also tries to take seriously the distinctions traditions themselves make among different kinds of roles, and it manages to appreciate the competition among those roles within a given tradition. For example, the authors write that although a mystical figure's

---

13. *Ibid.*: 7426.—Ed.

experience may be comparable to prophetic experience, in no instance "could visionaries or mystics claim for themselves a mediational status equal with the founding prophets without subverting revealed canons and the traditions that rested upon them."[14] However, when the authors then go on to identify Jesus, Mani, and Muhammad as just such individuals, they undermine their own distinction, and have to add quickly, "Otherwise prophetic and mystical vision was subordinated to the revelation that had already been canonized."[15]

In addition to the problem of identifying figures as the very individuals from whom they are being distinguished, another problem arises from assuming that mediational status has a constant meaning or is always the criterion by which traditions themselves distinguish competitive roles. One immediately thinks, for example, of Jafar al-Sadiq's account of the Imams of the Imami Shi'is: according to him, they were of equal meditational status to the *nabīs* and had the ability to interpret, but not bring, *qur'an,* that is, the Revealed Word. He interpreted them in this way precisely to keep them within the limits of Sunni Islam and to prevent them from forming a separate tradition.

STRATEGY 2. Generalizing a meaning of prophecy in Judaism and Christianity so that it can be said to refer to a very widespread or even universal religious phenomenon.
Another author, W. Ahlstrom, begins his entry on prophecy in the *Encyclopaedia Britannica*[16] in this manner:

> Prophecy: in religion, a divinely inspired revelation or interpretation. Although prophecy is perhaps most commonly associated with Judaism and Christianity, it is found throughout the religions of the world, both ancient and modern. In its narrower sense, the term prophet (Greek *prophetes*, "forth-teller") refers to an inspired person who believes that he has been sent by his god with a message to tell. He is, in this sense, the mouthpiece of his god. In a broader sense, the word can refer to anybody who utters the will of a deity.[17]

It is odd that the parenthetical remark implies an association between ancient Greek usage and his "narrower sense" of prophecy, since many who delivered Greek oracles were not sent by a god with a message to tell, but chosen and appointed to speak for a god in a controlled

---

14. *Ibid.*: 7427.—Ed.

15. *Ibid.*: 7427.—Ed.

16. "Prophecy," *Encyclopædia Britannica Online,* http://proxy.lib.duke.edu:2292/eb/
article-9109409, accessed 5 August 2010.—Ed.

17. *Ibid.*

ritual setting.[18] Thus they did not correspond to a biblical notion of a figure called and sent to deliver an urgent message. It would seem that Ahlstrom's broader sense of prophecy would better include the Greek *prophutus*, except that when he fleshes out this broader sense his first step is to establish as a "primary characteristic of prophetic self-consciousness" an "awareness of a call, which is regarded as the prophet's legitimation."[19] To be sure, he goes on to include all sorts of religious specialists from various times and places, yet many of them, like many of the Greek *prophetai*, do not share that primary character-istic. Thus his broader sense does not manage to transcend his narrower sense completely, even if the figures he treats transcend both.

As a consequence of these tensions, Ahlstrom privileges his sense of these figures as prophets over their own self-conception, even when their self-conception depended on not being a prophet. For example, in a section on Muslim figures after Muhammad he writes: "Some proph-ets [among the Muslims] claimed that they were long-awaited saviour-deliverers (*mahdi*, 'restorer of the faith')."[20] In fact, *mahdi* figures had to claim not to be prophets (in the Muslims' sense of *nabī* or *rasūl*) if they had any hope of being accepted as *mahdi*s. Despite such unneces-sary confusion, Ahlstrom's approach does suggest that whatever mean-ingful distinctions are to be made among roles ought to emerge out of a considerably enlarged universe, in his case, all individuals who utter the will of a deity.

If Ahlstrom shows somewhat more interest than Sheppard and Herbrechtsmeier in the setting of the prophet, Thomas Overholt brackets the content and history of prophecy in order to focus primarily on one particular aspect of the prophet's setting: the communication process among the prophet, his source, and his audience. Building on biblical accounts of prophecy, Overholt develops a model of the social dynam-ics of prophetic communication that is theoretically applicable to a very wide variety of religious specialists, because "What makes practitioners of these distinct yet overlapping roles comparable is that their chief function is to communicate messages or information from the world of the spirits to the world of humans."[21] Broad as this approach may seem,

---

18. Aune, *Prophecy in Early Christianity and the Ancient Mediterranean World*: 28–9.
19. "Prophecy," *Encyclopædia Britannica*, http://proxy.lib.duke.edu:2292/eb/article-34059, accessed 5 August 2010.—Ed.
20. *Ibid.*—Ed.
21. Thomas W. Overholt, *Channels of Prophecy: The Social Dynamics of Prophetic Activity* (Minneapolis: Fortress Press, 1989): 4.

it too carries three significant limitations that undermine a full account of the very interpretive context he has chosen: communication.

First, by focusing on figures whose chief function is a certain kind of communication, and by focusing on that communication to the exclusion of other activities, Overholt cannot give a rounded account of the prophet nor consider seriously the prophet's relationship to other figures that engage in, but do not specialize in, the same kind of communication. For example, Overholt's model would exclude a phenomenon in South African independent churches, in which dream testimonies by ordinary church members have an important effect on the authority of the prophet who specializes in communication from God.[22] He also excludes those who receive personal guidance from an extra-human source, as in dreams or through prayer, but do not communicate it to others. Overholt would find it difficult to find illustrations of his model in societies where no one really specializes in this type of prophetic communication. Similarly, by focusing so sharply on the occasions when the prophet engages in prophecy, he is not able to give a rounded picture of all of the prophet's roles.

Second, "world of spirits" implies that a realm, rather than a being, is the source of the communication, and could exclude ancestors not thought of as in another realm. If Overholt is seeking to use neutral and generic terms, "extra-human source" might be preferable to "world of the spirits." The latter could also unnecessarily exclude monotheistic systems that try to restrict communication to one being only, and even "extra-human source" makes it difficult to include the Buddha and Confucius comfortably.

Third, "messages or information" is neither broad enough nor explored deeply enough. In many cases, information is sought from a being that is not trying to communicate, is not initiating communication, or who does not respond. And in many instances what is communicated is not so clear or comprehensible as messages or information would suggest, and has to be interpreted by someone other than the person whose chief function is the actual communication. However, if one does want to focus on the delivery of messages, one needs to take account of the relationship between divine messengership and human messengership.[23]

---

22. Bengt Sundkler, *Bantu Prophets in South Africa* (London: Oxford University Press, 1961).
23. Samuel A. Meier, *The Messenger in the Ancient Semitic World* (Atlanta, GA: Scholars Press, 1988): 206.

Overholt himself underscores these uncertainties about the breadth of his own definition by writing, "If we were to follow a recent author in defining prophecy as 'the proclamation of divine messages in a state of inspiration,' we would have little trouble in speaking of any of these figures as prophets."[24] If "world of the spirits" could be construed to exclude, for example, ancestors, "divine" definitely does. If "communicate messages or information" implies initiative on the part of the extra-human source, "proclamation of divine messages" seems to entail it. Furthermore, extra-human communication conceived of as broadly as possible would not be limited to persons in a state of inspiration, since in some societies some of the most important information comes in dreams, or a figure who at first must be in a state of inspiration gradually acquires the ability to "receive" in a not-so-altered state of consciousness. Indeed, Overholt himself focuses on prophecy among the Israelites and other tribal societies, especially among the North American Indians, excluding Islam and many other Asian religions almost entirely.

Beyond problems of scope and definition are problems of method. Overholt advances his model of communication without a clear explanation of the way in which it has been developed, although biblical materials seem to have been an important empirical source. He then uses Wovoka, Jeremiah, and Handsome Lake to illustrate three things: his model of the prophetic process, the application of his model, and the prophetic process itself. In not distinguishing these three things from each other, Overholt raises crucial questions about the objectives of comparative study and the ontological status of interpretive strategies and the phenomena they purport to describe. Saying that one is illustrating a model implies that models have some importance and utility beyond the materials they help to organize for purposes of comparison. Illustrating the application of a model, however, reflects a sense of the model primarily as a device to shed light on the particular materials to which it is applied. Illustrating something called "the prophetic process" by applying a model of the prophetic process implies that the phenomenon is a reification of the model. Those three choices leave aside the question whether comparison is intended to improve understanding of specific cultural situations beyond what would be learned from studying them in isolation from each other.

When Overholt evaluates the outcome of the application of his model, he underscores the importance of making such distinctions:

---

24. Overholt, *Channels of Prophecy*: 4.

All of these figures ... have been called *prophet* by those who have studied
them. Still, words can be slippery. We want to know to what kind of activity
the term *prophet* refers and whether sufficient similarity exists among the
three cases to warrant its application to all of them. Are all three prophets?
  The discussion has shown, I believe, that the data available about these
three figures fit the model well; the three really are comparable. We can
therefore say that the model works cross-culturally: it provides us with a tool
for comparing the activity of intermediaries that is not unduly prejudiced by
the obvious differences in their historical and cultural situations.[25]

Overholt has in fact found them comparable without comparing them
with each other, at least not for the reader. Rather, he has compared
each figure with a model that has been abstracted from similar cases,
and, finding that each can be discussed in the language of the model,
he makes the familiar move of saying that the three separate figures are
comparable with each other. Even that would have been all right had
he explicitly acknowledged that their comparability resulted from his
model, and that he used not all of the data available on these figures, but
all of the data that illustrated the model. Instead, however, he oscillates
between transcending the limitations of culture-specific terminology
and succumbing to them in his quest for the constant to which the word
prophet "refers," and between recognizing interpretive strategies as
constructions and reifying them into phenomena. In the end, he has
redefined prophet as someone who engages in the kind of communication acts he has modeled, even though he himself has stressed that
communication is just one aspect of prophecy. In the end, his model
of the prophetic process has been generalized, like Ahlstrom's, from a
particular view of biblical prophecy.

  Despite all of these problems, however, Overholt's emphasis on
communication is very promising, since it encourages the analysis of
an individual within a historical setting and makes a central place for
the role of the audience. By stressing cross-cultural commonalities in
the dynamics of certain kinds of communication, Overholt is able to
compare figures whose differing content might otherwise discourage
comparison. But if the best insights of historians and social scientists
are to be combined, such commonalities should not be bought at the
price of relegating historical and cultural differences to the background.
Using cases as illustrations can be enriched by comparing cases with
each other in a detailed and extended manner.

---

25. Overholt, *Channels of Prophecy*: 66.

STRATEGY 3. Subsuming a more limited definition of prophet, along with various other religious roles, into a larger religious category intended to be less culture-specific, and thus more neutral and generic. Under the influence of sociological and anthropological approaches, Robert R. Wilson has recently experimented with the concept of "intermediary," which he uses in order to be able to "embrace" a narrow or broad variety of religious figures "characterized by the fact that in some way they serve as intermediaries between the human and divine worlds."[26] For the activity of such intermediaries, he uses the term "intermediation." In his choice of an umbrella rubric, Wilson echoes Overholt's concern with the setting of prophecy, but in his application of the concept, he focuses on social function and location rather than on the communication process.

Although "intermediation" is potentially very broad, Wilson imposes significant limitations on his own uses of it. Unlike Overholt, he does not concentrate only on specialists, individuals whose primary role is intermediation, nor on intermediation to the exclusion of the other roles intermediaries might also play. Among all possible religious specialists, Wilson identifies a small number of social roles that have been synthesized from a variety of cross-cultural evidence and that he wishes to include in his own study of intermediation: prophet (used only as a translation for Hebrew *nabī*), shaman ("master of the spirits"), medium (channel of communication), diviner (seeker of hidden information), and witch/sorcerer. He defines witchcraft and sorcery as related uses "of an innate power to cause harm in other people," despite the many prominent examples of their benevolent use.[27]

Wilson excludes a number of figures that very easily might have been included on his list. The mystic is left out because, according to Wilson, it is not a social role. Yet the literature contains important examples of mystical figures that, like the shaykhs of Sufi *tariqa*s, are clearly intermediaries with a prominent social role. He also excludes the priest, defined in Weberian terms as a cultic specialist,[28] because even though it is a social role and an important form of intermediation, "in most societies, including Israel, priests have many unique functions that must be the subject of separate investigation. To treat the priest along with the other specialists does not take sufficient account of his [or her?] uniqueness."[29] The exclusion of the priest seems questionable

---

26. Wilson, *Prophecy and Society in Ancient Israel*: 28.
27. *Ibid*.: 25.
28. *Ibid*.: 26.
29. *Ibid*.: 28.

a priori, because other roles can be shown to be just as institutionalized or to have unique functions, as Wilson himself notes,[30] just as some societies have no institutionalized cultic specialists, or have their cultic functions performed by individuals who are not specialists in intermediation.[31] The exclusion is further challenged by one of Wilson's own observations—namely, that:

> prophets, shamans, witches, mediums, and diviners can also be priests if they have regular cultic roles in their societies. In turn, priests can on occasion function as diviners, prophets, or mediums. ... the fact that priests sometimes have other religious functions prevents sharply distinguishing the priest from other religious specialists."[32]

In addition to the roles and figures that Wilson explicitly excludes, one major form of intermediation, "cosmological kingship" is not considered for inclusion at all. To be sure, Wilson does briefly explore the "prophetic legitimation" of Israelite kings like Samuel.[33] However, he does not acknowledge the frequency with which other types of rulers have served as important intermediaries between the "divine and human worlds" even though they can in no way qualify as religious specialists.

Despite Wilson's decision not to carry his own concept to its logical limits, his approach has important advantages. He reminds scholars to remember that religious specialists exist within culturally defined roles and social structures. He shows a subtle understanding of how roles and their associated titles overlap, and how one individual can, by fulfilling a variety of social functions, be perceived under overlapping rubrics. Seen in the light of the subtlety of his grasp, and the breadth of his umbrella concept, his own unnecessary limitations and exclusions are also a warning about the ease with which the study of prophecy can revert to unquestioned categorical thinking.

STRATEGY 4. Typologizing religious roles, including prophet as one type, and, sometimes, typologizing different kinds of prophets.
In the academic study of religion, one of the best-known and most influential examples of this strategy occurs in Joachim Wach's *The*

---

30. *Ibid.*: 27.
31. Robert M. Baum, *Shrines of the Slave Trade: Diola Religion and Society in Precolonial Senegambia* (New York and Oxford: Oxford University Press, 1999): chapters 2–3.
32. Wilson, *Prophecy and Society in Ancient Israel*: 27.
33. *Ibid.*: 154.

Sociology of Religion.[34] At the end of that work, Wach classifies types of religious authority according to a small number of religious roles, which, like those of Wilson, have been synthesized from a plethora of specific cross-cultural materials. Unlike Wilson, however, Wach arranges roles hierarchically, in terms of degree of authority, which is then associated with degree of creativity and intensity of experience. Since typologizing remains so popular in the comparative study of religion, it is valuable to provide at this point at least a thumbnail sketch of Wach's scheme of classification. Although Wach, like most authors, did not use gender-inclusive language in his description of the roles, the following account does, to reflect the fact that all of them have been occupied by men, women, and even androgynes of one sort or another.

- *Founder:* According to Wach, this is the foremost type of religious authority. Unlike Sheppard and Herbrechtsmeier, Wach does not limit himself to founders who were messengers of a deity, and thus includes such figures as the Buddha, Confucius, and Lao-tze. However, as Wach is interested in the "sociological effect of their activities,"[35] he, like Sheppard and Herbrechtsmeier, uses a posthumous criterion to configure this particular category, which becomes the norm by which to evaluate all "lesser" forms of religious authority.[36] Although he finds it difficult to generalize about their sociological effects, he is able to draw parallels from their biographical images, which he assumes can be projected back into their actual careers.[37]
- *Reformer:* These are leaders who emerge in times of stress. They are neither of the same status as founders nor does their religious insight and creativity qualify them to be founders. Although in their power, magnetism, energy, and endurance, reformers somewhat resemble founders, "the sociological effect of their activity cannot be compared to that resulting in the emergence of the great faiths."[38] Many reformers may be called prophets, but they should not be, since "reformers differ from prophets psychologically, sociologically, and theologically." Whereas Sheppard and Herbrechtsmeier allow that

---

34. Joachim Wach, *The Sociology of Religion* (Chicago, IL: University of Chicago Press, 1944).
35. *Ibid.*: 341.
36. *Ibid.*: 341.
37. *Ibid.*: 341–3.
38. *Ibid.*: 344.

other figures can be compared with founders, even if they are not
ultimately comparable to them, Wach says that they cannot even be
compared.[39]

- *Prophet:* Wach purposely does not limit his use of this term to *nabī* in
  the Hebrew Bible, as Wilson does, but his definition certainly resembles it: "The prophetical charisma seems to be the chief religious
  gift."[40] His definition of prophet implies immediate communion
  with the deity, the "intensity of which is more characteristic than its
  continuance. The mandate which the prophet receives is essential."[41]
  The authority of the prophet is secondary to that of the founder,
  but, like the founder, the prophet has "unusual sensitiveness and
  an intense emotional life."[42] The prophet is like the seer but unlike
  the magician or augur, since the messages the prophet receives are
  not induced but are spontaneous and passively received. In leading
  an ascetic life, the prophet is also distinguished from the diviner.[43]
  The prophet is archaic in speech and politically active, often an
  antagonist of the priest. Although Zoroaster might come to mind as
  an example of a priest who became a prophet, that would not present
  Wach with a problem, since Zoroaster is classified as a founder. It
  is also no problem that the Buddha, Confucius, and Lao-tze could
  not be prophets by this definition, because they too can be contained
  under the same founder rubric.
- *Seer:* The precursor of the prophet, the seer has less pronounced
  authority and is less active. "His charisma ... is derived from a
  genuine but less creative religious experience."[44] Unlike the prophet,
  who receives from the gods, the seer intuits them. Unlike the augur,
  he does not engage in methodical interpretation of external objects.
- *Magician:* The magician is not connected with cultic activities, but
  rather has "command of power due to communion with the unseen
  or the spirits."[45] The main task of the magician is to fulfill the expectation of clients. The possibility that any of the other roles might do
  the same thing is not considered in Wach's framework.
- *Diviner:* Like the founder and the prophet, the diviner's charisma may begin as "personal but easily and regularly becomes

---

39. *Ibid.*: 344.
40. *Ibid.*: 347.
41. *Ibid.*: 347.
42. *Ibid.*: 347.
43. *Ibid.*: 347.
44. *Ibid.*: 351.
45. *Ibid.*: 354.

institutionalized."[46] Essentially passive, like the seer, the diviner relies on the manipulation of divinatory objects in ways that the other roles do not.

- *Saint:* The saint is recognized as a holy person on the basis of intrinsic qualities. His or her authority is inferior to that both of the founder and the prophet, but he or she is less different from the prophet than from the founder. The saint's authority depends not so much on achievement as on personal qualities, and he or she is generally less vigorous than the prophet in the degree of influence. According to Wach, this role rarely appears in "primitive" societies because "a higher degree of civilization appears necessary to produce a 'saintly' character and life."[47]
- *Priest:* This is the role that depends (most) on "the charisma of office," which involves performance of cultic activities. Instead of a call, the priest has a calling. Though he or she maintains ongoing communion with a deity or deities, his or her experience is less spontaneous than that of the founder or prophet, and he or she is required to receive "more preparation and education for the role."[48]
- *Religiosus:* The least formal of all of these roles, Wach includes it to acknowledge the prevalence of "men and women who have been compelled by their religious experience to live a life of closer communion with God than that of ordinary people."[49] The presence of this last, catch-all category, reminds us that, like a well-run home, a typology must maintain a place for everything and everything in its place. This last category also demonstrates how difficult it is to establish an exhaustive set of types according to consistently applied criteria. Some of the categories rely on developments after the lives of the individuals in question, which are then projected back into their lives, while other categories are formed from an evaluation of their lives without respect to their historical impact. This is the case even though Wach recognizes how much of a founder's influence comes from the appropriation and elaboration of their images after their deaths. The most prominent criteria of comparison Wach uses is degree and type of authority, but one category, founder, sets an absolute standard against which all others are measured. This final category, "religiosus," is defined by a kind of moral authority, which

---

46. *Ibid.*: 356.
47. *Ibid.*: 359.
48. *Ibid.*: 360–62.
49. *Ibid.*: 369.

is rather different from the more sociological authority of the other roles.

Some would argue that the only valid critique of a generalization is a better generalization, not an exception. However, when a large number of exceptions instantly leap to mind, one wonders whether the generalizations have been based on enough data. Even if they have, each category has to be something like an average, and like any average of a given population, there may be no one individual in the population who fits that profile. Although the most sophisticated typologizers recognize that the types are not isolated from each other, and that one individual can occupy more than one category, the mere act of establishing static categories requires that they be overcome to explain such overlaps. Thus, someone who naturally and easily integrates related traits that fall into different scholarly categories inevitably must appear to be a hybrid of separate traits. This designation of "hybrid" emerges from a categorical approach, and minimizes the originality of a particular individual, preferring to interpret him or her as a combination of pre-existing categories.

    Although these criticisms of typological approaches have been made before and better by others, it is rare to have attention called to the practical consequences of typologizing for the comparative study of human phenomena; they do not often promote extended and detailed comparisons. Rather, human phenomena such as prophecy tend to promote an analysis of a single case, or a collection of cases, identified a priori as belonging to a particular category, and analyzed according to the expectations set for the category.[50]

STRATEGY 5: Subsuming a restricted definition of prophet into a larger category not limited to religious phenomena.
A.F.C. Wallace's concept of revitalization is a version of this strategy that sets prophecy in a very broad social and cultural context. Wallace uses the phrase "revitalization movement" to denote "any conscious, organized effort by members of a society to construct a more satisfying culture."[51] This very broad rubric allows Wallace to be truly global in

---

50. Ann Ruth Willner, "The Neotraditional Accomodation to Political Independence: The Case of Indonesia," *Cases in Comparative Politics: Asia*, ed. Lucian Pye (Boston. MA: Little, Brown, 1970): 248–51.

51. Anthony F.C. Wallace, *Religion: An Anthropological View* (New York: Random House Inc., 1966): 30.

his scope, and to be able to use examples from all times and places, religious and political, among which no invidious comparisons are made, except in the eyes of those who would find it inherently invidious to put the founding of so-called great faiths on a level with local American Indian movements and the German National Socialism of Hitler. The approach is a strong corrective to two popular approaches to religion that focus on individuals or focus on conservatism. Wallace subordinates individual figures to the movements they lead, or, in his terms, merely help to formulate. For him the individual leader must be seen as part of a collective effort. He grants that the code of a movement may be formulated by one individual, either in hallucinatory revelation, as is characteristic of religion, or in a set of laws, as is characteristic of politics, but sees such individuals merely as sensitive to widespread cultural distortion that is already in the air. He would, however, find it difficult to go much further in explaining why one individual and not another. He undermines the association of religion with conservatism and resistance to change by stressing the radical, destructive, and anti-traditional nature of such movements, which arise, according to him, in response to widespread awareness of stresses brought on by a variety of factors. Wallace's desire to emphasize the radical side of religion shows when, after observing that, though not limited to religion, revitalization is nevertheless central to it, he says that "it is attractive to speculate that all religions and religious productions, such as myth and rituals, come into existence as parts of the program or code of revitalization movements. Such a line of thought leads to the view that religious belief and practice always originate in situations of social and cultural stress."[52]

Using organic, biological, and even neurological metaphors for society, Wallace holds that revitalization movements go through five predictable phases: the steady state, the period of increased individual stress, the period of cultural distortion, the period of revitalization (which has six sub-steps), and the new steady state. Although revitalization movements are not set into a typology of movements in general, Wallace does typologize different types of revitalization movements. Aiming to focus on disequilibrium rather than equilibrium, this remains an equilibrium model in that, rather than see society as always suffering from a degree of flux, disorganization, and stress, Wallace sees it as cycling between periods of steadiness and periods of disorganization.

Well done as this work is, it cannot completely escape the problems of circularity already noted in Overholt's work. The model is in some

---

52. *Ibid.*: 30.

sense a summary of data, an extraction of common denominators, and the mode of exposition is illustration, case study, and implied comparison rather than extended comparison. It is, after all, not surprising that "examples of revitalization are easy to find,"[53] since the criteria of revitalization have been drawn from many of its examples. But is an example of Wallace's model of revitalization the same as an example of revitalization itself? Like Overholt, Wallace understands that models are heuristic devices, yet there is always the tendency, if a case proves not a good example of the model (which often means "cannot be discussed in the language of the model"), to say that the example doesn't fit the model rather than that the model doesn't fit the example.

Nevertheless, despite what might be the inescapable problems of the modeling method, Wallace's concept has important advantages, largely as a corrective to a certain narrowness of vision among many who specialize in the academic study of religion. His approach resists a sharp distinction between religious and non-religious movements as social phenomena. It insists that individual leaders be analyzed as part of a collective enterprise. It understands the relationship between religious change and social change. Because it doesn't focus so much on classifying individuals into synthesized roles, it avoids the confusion of trying to restrict or expand the definition of prophet and similar terms.

Max Weber was an even more influential figure who realized that no single indigenous system of nomenclature, not even his own culture's, could yield adequate categories for comparison. Therefore, he abstracted meta-categories, or more properly, ideal types, that could cut across the cultural and linguistic boundaries established by individual societies. Prophets are one important type under his well-known rubrics of charisma, charismatic authority, and charismatic leadership. That category also includes other types of religious figures, and certain military and political heroes as well. For Weber, the charismatic leader acquires followers not through occupying an office but through the audience's recognition of his or her exceptionally compelling personal characteristics, which include a convincing claim to be fulfilling a mission and the ability to provide extraordinary proof. In religious leaders, that often involves divine commissioning and the performance of miracles. Charismatic leaders tend to emerge in times of stress, and their authority is quite transient and unstable unless routinized into another type of authority. Since they aim to transform the status quo into something new and better, they are revolutionary.

---

53. *Ibid.*: 31.

Like Wallace, Weber had, then, to override indigenous classification systems, none of which had generated his charismatic array. In so doing, however, he also had to ignore the ways in which specific communities had themselves aggregated portions of his cohort, often in competitive and mutually exclusive ways. Many figures that would fall into Weber's charismatic type were recognized as legitimate by some traditions and not by others. Many were viewed as part of one special category by one group and as something else (sometimes positive, sometimes negative) by others, even within the same community. Sometimes, several individuals have claimed to occupy the same special role and competed with each other or with figures recognized to be fulfilling other roles. Figures given a special label by one group could be held to operate in a very different manner from figures called by the same label by another group.

By treating charismatic authority as a separate type, Weber was also naturally led to contrast charismatic and non-charismatic figures. In treating prophets under the heading of charisma, he had to finesse the fact that sometimes prophet and cognate or related words, such as Greek *prophetis* or *promantis*, are used for figures who are not charismatic in his sense of the term. That is, they do not acquire authority and followers by recognition of their extraordinary personal characteristics, and they are not oppositional.[54] By attributing no significance to the close relationship suggested by this terminological slipperiness, he was led to treat prophets as naturally antithetical to related figures, writing that, "As a rule, the prophet or savior has stood in opposition to the traditional hierocratic powers of magicians or of priests. He has set his personal charisma against their dignity consecrated by tradition in order to break their power or force them to his service."[55]

Although Weber, then, did try to analyze one form of authority within a system of types of authority, in his efforts to delineate their differences, he made a very important distinction between oppositional figures and non-oppositional related figures, but then exaggerated it. Bryan Turner's corrective to this exaggeration is particularly efficient: "Religious experience can only provide evidence for things which are already known or believed in ... the term 'breakthrough' which is normally associated with charismatic movements must be an

---

54. See Wilson, *Prophecy and Society in Ancient Israel*, 56–58. An excellent account of such overlaps can be found in Aune, *Prophecy in Early Christianity and the Ancient Mediterranean World*.

55. Max Weber, *From Max Weber: Essays in Sociology*, trans. H.H. Gerth and C. Wright Mills (London: Routledge & Kegan Paul Ltd., 1948): 328.

exaggeration. Charisma must be far more a matter of re-interpretation of known facts and *Weltanschauung*."[56] This suggests that Weber's approach would be more explanatory of on-the-ground experience if it could be restated in a more interactive way. Obviously, Weber's approach has many of the same advantages as Wallace's, but in giving slightly more weight to the need of the oppositional leader to be self-proving if he or she is to be successful, Weber's model, if restated more interactively, could lead someone with a thorough grasp of the historical material to predict the factors, circumstantial and personal, that might make one oppositional figure more successful than another.

DISTINGUISHING NEW COMPARATIVE
APPROACHES FROM OLD

The design of the present study combines the strengths and resists the limitations of these five strategies. First, it entails a radical reconsideration of the comparative study of prophecy, and of religion more broadly, as a definitional, and indeed definitive, enterprise. As the preceding overview has illustrated, comparativists in human studies have tended to emulate physical and biological scientists in their search for universal classification systems, and for the best definitions of classes. In the case of prophecy, and of many other topics, this search has taken two forms: first, remaking one's own culture's terms and concepts into allegedly universal vehicles for cross-cultural comparison and second, deducing or inducing meta-categories that can subsume all local phenomena under one allegedly universal umbrella. In both of these forms, the definitional project has introduced new contradictions and inconsistencies, and in both cases, scholars of prophecy have retained the followers' concern with inclusion and exclusion.

---

56. Bryan S. Turner, *Weber and Islam: A Critical Study* (London: Routledge & Kegan Paul, 1974): 26–7. In compensating, Turner becomes too categorical in the other direction: "Weber's theory is modified in that, rather than considering charisma as erupting in socially marginal positions, we now view charisma as erupting within highly traditional and central social institutions" (28). As this chapter shows, opposition emerges wherever space is available at a given point in time and space. Some oppositional figures distinguish themselves minimally from similar figures, some maximally. Cf. Rodney Stark, "How New Religions Succeed: A Theoretical Model," *The Future of New Religious Movements*, ed. David G. Bromley and Phillip E. Hammond (Macon, GA: Mercer, 1987): 14–15. Stark well appreciates the need to work from the familiar, but does not account for the appearance of the unfamiliar.

Nevertheless, in the course of this search, comparative frameworks have become more comprehensive and more cross-cultural, but they have done so by subordinating indigenous systems of comparison and classification to those of the academic, relegating full appreciation of the inner workings of specific cultural systems to specialist studies. Thus, the comparativist's primary mode of exposition shows a marked preference for implied comparison—that is, for applying or illustrating a comparative strategy rather than developing it through detailed and extended comparison. This study, however, treats comparison as heuristic, not definitive. It views academic comparison as an extra language, not a substitute language, for promoting conversations among indigenous systems of comparison and classification. Therefore, it employs a mode of exposition that uses comparison itself as a vehicle for generating more flexible and variable comparative strategies, and more numerous comparisons.

Many of the authors of the strategies listed above assume that prophecy can be defined in such a way as to overcome its culture-specific connotations and the complex history of its usage. Still, for most of these scholars, issues of inclusion and exclusion are as important as they have been in confessional circles. Although most of them accept the value of comparison through typologizing or classifying, virtually none of them privileges indigenous classification systems over those of the modern researcher. Most of these strategies are essentially definitional enterprises. This study aims to overcome two major lines of divergence revealed by the foregoing overview. Some approaches treat prophecy within the context of religious phenomena only; others stress the overlap between religious and non-religious phenomena without trying to distinguish them. This study tests the distinction between the two. Some approaches focus on the history of prophecy, whereas some focus on its structure. The more historical approaches tend to focus on the careers of individuals, the content of prophecy, and the impact of both on the formation of religious traditions. Those that focus on the structure of prophetic activity tend to be more interested in prophecy as a type of authority, in the settings in which prophets emerge and operate, in prophet as a role, or in the social impact of the prophet. This study responds to J.Z. Smith's call for "the integration of a complex notion of pattern and system with an equally complex notion of history."[57]

---

57. Jonathan Z. Smith, *Imagining Religion: From Babylon to Jonestown* (Chicago, IL: University of Chicago Press, 1982): 29.

Therefore, the comparisons in this book aim both to shed light that would not be shed on specific situations if they were analyzed in isolation, and to raise and address general questions. As much as possible, then, it tries to situate particular information in a historical and cultural situation in order to develop generalizations that can be tested on those situations and can stimulate further exploration of historical and cultural particulars. To maintain this balance, this work prefers to compare situations rather than individuals or any other single elements. It makes particular use of the study of roles, since roles involve attention to actor–audience interaction, and to the transmission of historical traditions for recognizing authority and legitimacy. Because it tries not to telescope history in pursuit of simplified comparison, it tries as much as possible not to use posthumous developments to explain or classify prior developments.

Comparison as heuristic

This study views comparative strategies not as definitive but as heuristic—that is, as aiding or guiding discovery, inciting to find out, leading a person to investigate further. Comparative strategies that are heuristic resist reification in order to remain flexible and variable. As such, they expand, rather than limit or restrict, the number of comparisons that are actually made. The advantages of a heuristic method are measured against the investigator's stated purpose. Although that purpose necessarily entails a certain perspective, at its best it is the perspective of a sculptor who comprehends an object in the round, rather than that of a painter, who must adopt a line of vision.

When comparison is viewed as heuristic, similarity and difference do not seem so self-evident or uncomplicated as common sense would have it, especially in their relationship to something called "comparability." Neither does the relationship between perceiving similarity and difference and stressing similarity or difference so as to enable a judgment of comparability or non-comparability. For non-academic purposes, it is natural to let taken-for-granted taxonomies make the perception of similarity or difference seem obvious. However, if academic comparison is to distinguish itself and make a distinctive contribution, it will need to challenge conventional wisdom on these points. Despite rare and valiant efforts to raise scholars' consciousness about comparison, lack of clarity persists, especially about the relationship between academic inquiry and the taken-for-granted taxonomies of the inquirer's own culture.

Once again, a quirk of English usage both reflects and encourages the confusion. Not only are there two dictionary meanings of "compare," but the variants of each entail positions that are not in fact interchangeable. Put simply, one meaning makes "compare and contrast" a redundancy whereas the other does not. The definition of "compare" that usually appears first is, according to one dictionary, "To represent as similar; to liken,"[58] and in another, "To consider or describe as similar, equal, or analogous."[59] This first definition, therefore, would associate "comparison" with demonstrating likeness, and it would make "comparable" mean "alike" (whether really alike or representable as alike). In practice, that is the most common usage of "comparable."

The meaning of "compare" usually listed second has variants that reflect differing degrees of tentativeness. According to the first dictionary quoted above, "compare" means: "To examine the character or qualities of, for the purpose of discovering their resemblances or differences." According to the second dictionary, it means: "To make a detailed analysis of points of similarity and difference." "Discovering" plays down the investigator's role in structuring the outcome, at the same time that "character and qualities" (which require prior judgment) plays it up. "Making a detailed analysis of the points of similarity and differences" implies greater comprehensiveness, as well as greater neutrality, without specifying the purpose that necessitates both. Both variants imply that similarities and differences suggest themselves; however, the first is not only more purposeful than the second, but in using "or" rather than "and" it implies that the comparer might have a reason for making a choice between discovering resemblances or discovering differences. The more tentative and approximate the construct, the more emphasis there is on the constructive role of the agent of comparison. The second definition also has different implications for the meaning of related words. "Comparison" would somehow take account of similarity and/or difference, not just likeness. More important, "comparable" would mean any two things that can be analyzed in terms of similarity and difference. But then everything would be comparable with everything else, which common usage rarely (if ever) allows.

---

58. *Merriam-Webster's Collegiate Dictionary*, *Encyclopædia Britannica Online: Academic Edition*, http://search.eb.com/dictionary?va=compare&x=0&y=0, accessed 17 August 2010.—Ed.

59. *The American Heritage Dictionary of the English Language*, fourth edition, www.thefreedictionary.com/compare, accessed 22 August 2010—Ed.

Even if common usage would not allow that possibility, the academic engaged in heuristic comparison does. For if anything can be compared with anything else, works themselves are things that are similar in fewer ways than they are different in many more. Furthermore, for purposes of a comparison that integrates structure and history, similarity cannot be said to lie behind difference, for this at its extreme becomes perennialism, nor can difference be said to invalidate comparison, for this position can lead to historicism.

Thus for an academic engaged in heuristic comparison, no comparisons are more natural than others, and no two things are inherently more comparable than any others. Any comparison can be useful if the questions that generated it are specified and if the limits and advantages of the chosen comparative strategy are understood. Bad pun though it is, one can make fruitful comparisons between apples and oranges, especially if one is interested in small round objects with seeds. There is no inherent limit to comparison, just limits to the factors that make a comparison interesting, and comparisons are better or worse only in terms of their appropriateness to the objectives for which they have been undertaken. The debate that should engage any comparative field should not, then, center on what things are or are not comparable, but rather on which questions are most worth asking that can be answered only through comparison.

The more common meaning of "comparable"—that is, "alike"— would also be useful as long as it means "alike" in terms of clearly stated objectives. The scholar of prophecy is like the follower of prophecy in the sense that the ultimate judgment of similarity or difference depends on a perspective. The academic, however, need not be bound by the perspectives and taxonomies that structure confessional communities. Rather, she is free to test and stretch her culture's conventional limits of classification through cross-cultural exploration in order to multiply the number of conceivable frameworks. However, even if scholars are not bound by any one community's limits in designing their own frameworks, they are bound to account for differing systems of thought. Scholars, in the end, offer an alternative point of view, not a substitute point of view. This study aims to design a framework that allows for conversation among various communities' cultures, while avoiding the role of the omniscient social scientist who assumes that his classification system is more explanatory and truer to the real facts than the self-presentation and classification of the people who are studied.

Comparison as extra language

The approach used in this study amounts to the creation of an extra language (not a substitute language) that will allow speakers of different languages to converse with each other in new and flexible ways. A story might best convey this point, a story told by the late Alford Carleton, who spent most of the interwar years in Palestine as a representative of the World Council of Churches. One day, crossing the Bosphorus on a ferry, he became friendly with a Turkish Muslim passenger. Both wanted to talk, but one spoke no Turkish and the other no English. However, both knew French, and so began to converse in that language until the Turk, finding Carleton more and more *sympathique*, used the phrase *nous musulmanes*. Fearing the results of complicity in this misperception, Carleton interrupted to say, "I'm sorry to have to tell you that I'm not a Muslim."

"Then what are you?"

"I'm a Christian."

"That's funny, you don't look a bit Armenian."

Two individuals who could not speak each other's primary language conversed in another language that belonged to neither. The resulting conversation exposed their differences without reducing them, but it also made it possible for them think about their cultural assumptions in new ways.

The limits of conventional vocabulary

This study's extra language is not a reworking of the conventional terminology of any group being studied. Words like prophecy will always carry their various colloquial connotations, even if academics stipulate restricted or expanded technical meanings for them. It is even more difficult to stipulate a meaning that is totally unrelated to conventional usage. Terms like prophecy also obscure the scholar's role in constructing objects of study, because they seem naturally or self-evidently to mean something at once particular and general, and thus to point to a pre-existing class of things. Such usage easily becomes mythic in Roland Barthes's sense of the term—namely, "a way of understanding the world that is not problematic, that we are not fully conscious of, that seems, in a word, natural. A myth is a way of thinking so deeply embedded in our consciousness that it is invisible."[60] This manner of thinking is what makes "Who is a Muslim prophet?" sound like a proper question and "Who is a Christian *rasūl Allah*" or "Who is a Jewish Buddha?" sound funny to us.

In this study, a word like prophet is useful only as long as it is not generalized—that is, when it is used to explain what one group takes for granted vis-à-vis what is made to seem natural by "comparable" words used by other groups. Therefore, this study treats prophecy and related words as particular groups' and languages' way of conceptualizing and segmenting a larger range of activity that the scholar has identified for heuristic purposes, that is, for holding the world still long enough to think about it. This approach allows for the history of each word and system, and of each word's place in a system. The history of usage would itself become part of our subject matter. Indigenous usage of such special labels has had a complex history, and has often made rather slippery distinctions. Insiders can, for example, attribute continuity, and the same special label (e.g., *prophetis*) to figures who appear to us to be very different from each other, or whom we would like to think of as very different. Conversely, they can insist on an essential difference between figures that appear to outsiders to be quite similar.

This mode of inquiry does not, then, assume that a term can be used as the basis for its own study, or that any group's special terms can be used across languages, even languages that have clearly cognate words. It would not, for example, assume that the interchangeability of prophecy and prophet in English is transferable to groups who do not take role and content to be identical, or even that an Arabic-speaking Muslim who has learned English uses the word prophet exactly the same way he uses the term *rasūl Allah*. Setting different cultures in mutually enriching conversation may even benefit from avoiding labels altogether, in favor of more cumbersome multi-word formulations that recall the approximate nature of comparison and discourage reification.

"Privileging communication" as a conversation space

If any one culture's terminology is inadequate to the conduct of such cross-cultural conversations, it can nevertheless suggest the space in which they might take place. Like Wallace's "revitalization," Weber's "charisma," Wilson's "intermediation," and Overholt's "prophetic

---

60. Neil Postman, *Amusing Ourselves to Death: Public Discourse in the Age of Show Business* (New York: Penguin Books, 2006): 79.

process," the English term "prophecy," in all of its many uses, has something to do with communication that has been privileged by its audience as being "special" in one way or another. "Privileging communication" has been coined for this study in order to indicate communication that becomes capable of rendering itself, its source, its carrier, and/or its audience special when it is recognized as "privileged" in a particular social and historical setting. The more common phrase "privileged communication" is avoided because it implies an inherent privilege independent of a social setting. "Privileging communication" reinforces the role of actor and audience in actively privileging the communication.

Communication associated with privilege is, of course, very common, and most human beings engage in it at some time or to some extent. Some individuals engage in it much of the time, especially those who occupy roles that require extensive communication, such as "parent" or "teacher." Some individuals who occupy privileged roles have privilege attributed to communication made apart from those roles. Other individuals who have privileging communication attributed to them without claiming it do not occupy a privileged role. Still others intend to deliver privileging communication but are not recognized as doing so. Of necessity, most people who engage in privileging communication do not engage in it, or a role with which it is associated, all of the time, and it's not always easy to tell when they are and when they are not engaging in it.

Most privileging communication does not make reference to an extra-human source. Still, the sense of access to an extra-human source has been widely distributed in most societies, and has taken all sorts of forms. Most broadly construed, it includes what anthropologists and psychologists call possession, much of what moderns call madness, and all cases in which something or someone extra-human appears in dreams or visions. Although recourse to the extra-human is usually taken by scholar and non-scholar alike as distinctively "religious," there are many figures who present their communication as privileged because it is inspired by an extra-human source, and yet do not occupy roles conventionally considered religious. Poets and nationalist leaders are two prominent examples. Still others, like Joan of Arc, begin as one and end up as another. Other figures that do not posit an extra-human source nevertheless share many traits with those who do. Still other figures, like the Buddha, have not appealed to an extra-human source in the narrow sense, but have engaged in privileging communication considered to be religious.

A conversation space in this sense is neither native nor universal. It is, rather, a way of occasioning a particular range of questions about how groups themselves aggregate complexes of human thought and action, and make distinctions within them. Just as different cultures organize in different ways, so do different academic fields. And very seldom do the societies being studied organize human phenomena the way their studiers do. For example, scholars of religion must group together all instances of interaction with extra-human phenomena to imagine something called religion, but cultures themselves rarely have occasion to do so, or they might have a way of aggregating part of that complex with other things that do not have extra-human connections. As broad and encompassing as privileging communication appears to be, it too, is not an organizing principle for any society, as far as is known. The advantage of this particular conversation space is that it elicits native categories and promotes their comparison, allowing us to overcome modern distinctions that obscure roles such as prophet–poet, prophet–king, and prophet–healer. For this method to work, we have to be aware of all the relevant ways that these categories resist scholarly reification and comparison to other categories.

A particularly effective example of the variability of aggregation, and especially the importance of aesthetic association, is Ruth Finnegan's account of the Limba of Sierra Leone.[61] It is particularly interesting that her observations were occasioned by her attempt at cross-cultural application of another problematic category: oral poetry. To try to find the Limba "equivalent" of oral poetry, she cautions that "the way Limba culture—and no doubt others—divided up artistic-literary action does not at all fit our own literary practice." Her methodological response is two-pronged. On the one hand, she tries to render problematic the concept of "poet" by studying the Limba's different categories of artists and trying out our term "poet" to designate these artists, shaking up and extending our views of what it is to be a poet. On the other hand, closer to the emphasis of this study, she identifies a network of roles and forms of privileging communication, part of a larger complex known as *malimba ma*, "Limba times," or less literally, "Limba ways." Among artistic expressions, the Limba held in highest regard three that were themselves interrelated: music, dance, and song ("poetry" in the sense in which it is applied to the ancient Greek bard). Everyone in the society could participate in all three, but there were also specialists, some

---

61. Ruth Finnegan, "The Poetic and the Everyday: Their Pursuit in an African Village and an English Town," *Folklore* 105 (1994): 3–11.—Ed.

gender-specific, in each, and particular forms for particular occasions. This reminds us that specialists in privileging communication often don't monopolize the skills required, or perhaps more importantly, that a widely distributed activity can become privileging communication on special occasions, in special forms, or in special hands. However, in the Limba context, even ordinary performance ability was taught and mastered over an extended period of formal and informal education.

Nonetheless, unlike ordinary performers, the specialists were regarded as a handful of people who handled wild and dangerous things, whereas ordinary human beings belonged in a sphere where humans were clearly in control. In this respect, these artistic specialists were classed with others who were not master performers and whose roles sometimes involved privileging communication, but did not always focus on it, such as diviners, smiths, and hunters. All of these had special and exceptional powers, beneficial and necessary for society, but at the same time possibly dangerous to others and to themselves. All of "these special talents were sometimes explained" by saying that exceptionally gifted individuals had been "helped by a 'spirit' (*wāli*)."[62] By interacting with the non-human, such individuals could become partly non-human themselves. Some singer–poets were said to have four eyes (i.e., doubled or special vision), to see into human hearts and also beyond the mundane and material human world.

Access to an extra-human source is viewed paradoxically—it is necessary for social stability, but also threatening to it if not domesticated by exceptional individuals. However, possession of a talent (through the help of a *wāli*) is not necessarily associated with a role that is dependent on it, and any given role may be classed in different ways depending on which aspect is foregrounded.

> For some purposes, all performers may be classed together; for other purposes, it may be all individuals who go "where the wild things are," which may include smiths and hunters as well as singers. Story-tellers and orators were also valued performers, classed among Limba artists, but they were not associated with wild and mysterious things. Unlike music, dance, and song, the mastery of oratory was achieved through the normal process of socialization, and by the need to carry out certain social roles, rather than by supernatural and individual gifts.[63]

---

62. *Ibid.*: 5.—Ed.
63. The reference may be Ruth Finnegan, *Limba Stories and Story-Telling* (Oxford: Oxford University Press, 1967) or Ruth Finnegan, *Oral Poetry: Its Nature, Significance and Social Context* (Cambridge: Cambridge University Press, 1977), but the exact quotation could not be located. Consult both books for a better understanding of Limba culture.—Ed.

This classification system of the Limba shows how many different roles can share the same place in complementary ways even though they are potentially competitive.

Lest one think that such complexities are peculiar to Africa or some other non-Western setting, consider ancient Greece, where different aesthetic forms could share the same social functions and locations, and related aesthetic forms could have different social locations and functions. Of course, the association between inspiration and special speech patterns was a very old one in much of the Mediterranean world.[64] However, one of the words now used in English for one such individual, "poet," has such a secular connotation that it obscures the connection to extra-human inspiration. It also implies an inherent rather than circumstantial distinction between one form of special speech and another. The word "poet" has also become so closely associated with writing that its ancient association with speaking, chanting, reciting, and singing has been obscured. The spoken or sung aspects of the role give more vivid significance to the poet as the voice of the gods, muses, or ancestors.[65]

The distinction we now make between poetry and prophecy has not always been so clear-cut. Material from early Greece shows that overlaps and distinctions are situational and need not lead to competition. In *The Iliad* and *The Odyssey*, as viewed by Charles Segal, as with the Limba, "poetry is envisaged as part of a performance, as the living voice of song ... [and] belongs to a social occasion and is almost unthinkable outside of that context."[66] And the singer–poet, the bard, is a social role. Furthermore, similar to the Limba, his song is a "mysterious gift from the Muses which, when it comes, bestows a flow of words as sweet and rich as honey."[67] The good song–poem is a kind of healing, and combines aesthetic, sensual, and moral gratification. Using a recognizably different verbal form is the *mantis*, who specializes in delivery of inspired and visionary predictions on certain occasions. In fact, *The Odyssey* has both an *aoidos* and a *mantis* performing at banquets to which they are invited as guests. According to Segal, the two

---

64. See David E. Aune, *Prophecy in Early Christianity and the Ancient Mediterranean World* and Michael Zwettler, *The Oral Tradition of Classical Arabic Poetry: Its Character and Implications* (Columbus, OH: Ohio State University Press, 1978).—Ed.

65. See James L. Kugel, *Poetry and Prophecy: The Beginnings of a Literary Tradition* (Ithaca, NY: Cornel University Press, 1990).

66. Segal, "Poetry, Performance, and Society in Early Greek Literature": 124.

67. *Ibid.*: 123.

resemble each other in that each "has a marginal relation to the society, is dependent on the good will of others for support and food, is an itinerant craftsman ... and stands in a privileged relation to the gods, from whom he has a skill hidden from other mortals."[68] Even more interesting in light of the Limba case, the *aoidos* and the *mantis* are grouped together with the healer and the ship-builder as strangers who must be called in to a wealthy house because "the small, self-sufficient, agrarian community does not generate the special skills which these 'strangers' possess and offer."[69] This reminds us of the relationship between ecology and social position, since by way of contrast, the Limba have among them as insiders a range of skills that might be possessed only by outsiders in another case. Such considerations become particularly crucial in an analysis of individuals who might acquire power through occupying such roles.

Consider Hesiod's *Theogany*, where the use of analogy is at once original and decisive. In the poem, according to Segal:

> Hesiod implies an analogy between the honeyed speech with which the king holds the awe of the crowd and his own gift from the Muses ... Both king and singer are recipients of "the holy gifts of the Muses to men" and are "beloved" by the Muses. Although "kings are from Zeus," they, like the poet, depend on the Muses for the all-important power of words.[70]

Just as the king acts on behalf of gods, the poet often claimed to sing not only for men, but also for the gods.

Another important distinction in ancient Greece, as with the Limba, hinges on how special skills were acquired. Segal cites the case of Phemius in the Odyssey, who associated being self-taught (*autodidaktos*) with the presence of God's breath, saying "I am *autodidaktos*, and a god breathed into my breast songs of every sort."[71] In this way, he contrasts learning from himself, which involves having his own powers augmented by divine breath, to "repeating what he has acquired from a specific human teacher or model."[72] In the Limba case, this corresponds to a distinction between masters and ordinary performers. Central to this distinction between tutored and untutored experts is the question of the acquisition of power, specifically, the source of the power or

---

68. *Ibid.*: 129.
69. *Ibid.*: 129.
70. *Ibid.*: 130.
71. *Ibid.*: 136.
72. *Ibid.*: 137.

skill. If the singer conceives of the special words that come in part from outside the self, then the words can be conceived of as beyond "individual talent and indeed beyond his individual life."[73] Thus he is a performer of "supra-personal poetry and the vehicle of ancient wisdom."[74] It is important to know the relationship between inspiration and human instruction in the particular society being studied in order to understand, for example, why figures like Muhammad or Moses are described as upsetting people by displaying skills without any evidence of preparation. We have to know the degree to which certain skills are generally tutored or untutored, and the accepted forms of inspiration or extra-human contact.

As long as privileging communication is recognized as only one aspect of the situations and figures it helps to compare, creating this larger conversation space has a number of advantages. It makes it possible both to blur and to test the distinction between religious and non-religious activity in interesting ways. It sees religion as ordinary rather than exotic, that is, as a variant of some generic human activity. It lets societies themselves demonstrate how they locate, define, and segment the field in which various types of extra-human communication occur. In so doing, it pays attention to indigenous classification systems, titles, labels, terminology, and nomenclature as an important part of comparative study. Different systems can then be compared without trying to align their elements perfectly. It can take account of the messiness and slippage within and among systems, not as something to be overcome, but as something to be studied in and of itself as a window into how cultures work.

It recognizes these as systems of alternatives and as comparative strategies in their own right. When, for example, a Muslim views a figure as a *nabī,* that is not a label in isolation, for it both puts that figure in a class with other *nabīs*, including Muhammad, and also explains how *nabīs* are both similar to and different from each other. It also entails a statement of what *nabīs* are not: *mahdis*, imams, and so forth. What appear to be separate phenomena are often parts of sets of alternatives, and the one adopted entails the one rejected. This reminds the scholar to try to develop an interpretive framework as subtle and complex as those it claims to interpret.

Whether the focus is on privileging communication more broadly, or more narrowly on privileging communication from an extra-human

---

73. *Ibid.*: 137.
74. *Ibid.*: 137.

source, it is clear that most societies have specialized roles based on this type of special communication. It is also clear that we can compare the ways in which different human communities have distinguished among the various ways in which people claim or appear to be receiving communication from an extra-human source, and that a vocabulary for such comparison would be suggested by the kinds of distinctions the cultures themselves make, for example, whether the individual solicits the communication or not, whether the communication makes claim to momentary or lasting significance, whether it occurs once or in an ongoing way, whether it is accidental to some other role or the basis of a special role, whether it is used for one's own guidance or for the guidance of large numbers of people, or whether it is falsifiable or not.

From categories to catchments

Within the space opened up by privileging communication, these distinctions among situations can be arranged in multiple patterns that can in turn generate many arrays for comparison, given the questions one wishes to pursue. Rather than let "a set of things just fall together" as a result of some conventional taxonomy, this approach precipitates comparable arrays out of a self-consciously designed space. It is as if one had an amorphous pile of metal bits, varying in color, shape, weight, and size, and could design a series of magnets that could temporarily configure items in varying ways, by any single trait, or, preferably, by any constellation of traits. Comparative frameworks are, in this view, better or worse only in relation to a particular aesthetic. The same subject matter can, therefore, be usefully studied in many different comparative frameworks. In fact, data can be as fully understood as possible only inasmuch as shifting frames of reference reveal their multiple dimensions and interrelationships.

Instead of taking phenomena as given or inferable from particular terms already in wide and special usage among those being studied, the third strategy assumes that nothing naturally falls into the categories of prophet and prophecy, no matter how much we expand or refine them. Rather it argues that we can design a number of possible patterns that are related to that word in different ways and that can shed different kinds of light on different kinds of fundamental questions that can be imagined in the comparative study of religion. Ideally, these patterns should generate overlapping arrays by foregrounding different issues for different purposes. This approach encourages the scholar to construe the same materials in terms of different phenomena rather than to look at the "same" phenomenon from different perspectives.

This is comparison by catchment, not by category. "Catchment" makes a good label for this approach because all three of its meanings are equally applicable:

- *The act of catching*: reminds the scholar of her role in generating comparability.
- *That which catches*: designates the combination of features, traits, or elements that configures a population for the purpose of comparison, and the questions that have suggested them.
- *That which is caught*: reminds us that when we let go of the configuration we are considering, our population "gets away from us" and becomes available for other purposes.

Unlike many types of comparative categories, rubrics, or umbrellas, catchments are designed and stipulated, and they are intended to overlap. They are justified in terms of the investigator's stated purpose and not drawn directly from any particular data. However, even though this approach treats comparative phenomena as constructed, it relies on terms that we take for granted, and on data, to suggest comparisons. When the approach remains fluid and tentative, it can frame overlapping sections from a pattern that the investigator has defined, so as to allow different cultures' systems to converse with each other. They are used to compare and to suggest further comparisons, not to summarize the results of comparison or to illustrate a comparative model. Different catchments have different understandings of the same material. All situations and figures that fall into a given catchment are comparable in the broad sense, in that any two things may be compared. Comparability in the narrower sense is a product of the actual comparison. However, whatever catchment is in use should recall others.

The catchment of oppositional figures

In many cases, communication seen as privileged has little to distinguish it from everyday communication except that it comes from a person in a privileged role or position. When, however, human beings are perceived to have access to an extra-human source, the resulting communication is usually in and of itself recognized to be other than everyday, and to be ultimately beyond their control. In some cases the perceived specialness of the communication is taken to reflect and reinforce a recognized and institutionalized role. In others, however, the perceived specialness of the communication plays a major role in the acquisition of authority and legitimacy by the individual who initiates it, and even by the audience that accepts it.

For whereas the communication of many of these figures operates within the status quo, the privileging communication of others serves as the basis for opposition to it, and opposition is frequently associated with figures who have not previously occupied institutional roles. Oppositional figures that rely on extra-human sources are often referred to as prophets in English, and by other words in other languages. Some of those words are cognates, such as French *prophetesse*, or Latin *propheta*. Some are related in more indirect ways, for example, Hebrew *nabī*, Arabic *nabī* and *rasūl*, and Persian *payghambar*. However, sometimes such figures are referred to by different words altogether, such as English "messiah" or Arabic *mahdi*. The fact that both uses of privileging communication often inhabit the same semantic field reminds us that they are often found in competition with each other, and can in fact turn into each other or take turns in the same individual. It also warns us not to make categorical distinctions between them.

Whereas Weber assumed that it is easy for a prophet to be differentiated from other related figures, I do not. For me the central question is: "How does a figure who emerges within an institutionalized system of privileging communication manage to be different enough to make a difference?" Any study of "oppositional privileging communication" would therefore need to focus on a dynamic of change that is often slighted or neglected—namely, the competition between a given oppositional figure and any other figures who must be co-opted, defeated, or otherwise displaced if the oppositional figure is to succeed. Authority based on oppositional "charisma," as Weber properly observed, is often very fragile and ephemeral, but can also generate extensive and durable ramifications. We must examine the nature of this competition in order to understand the variation in strength and duration of movements based on privileging communication. This is a particularly difficult approach to pursue; since history is the record of the winners, scholars have reflected most often on the "successful" figures, with a relative lack of attention to the ones who didn't make it.

Examining the competitive situation further focuses our attention on the ways in which the attributes of a given figure's role, and not just the content of his or her message, are shaped by that competition. Oppositional figures that engage in privileging communication must often face a number of other authoritative figures whose roles and functions are better institutionalized, some of whom make no claim to an extra-human source, some of whom make the same claim to an extra-human source, and sometimes make a claim to the same extra-human source, but in the name of the status quo. In situations where other, more "normal" or conventional forms of privileging communication are taken for granted, these oppositional claims represent an unexpected and not always welcome eruption of less controllable communication. Usually the burden of proof is on the oppositional figures, who must often identify themselves with a more vaguely understood or less commonly occupied role in order to legitimate themselves within the society's structure. Sometimes, numerous oppositional figures exist at the same time, the most successful of whom may even shift during his or her lifetime from opposing the status quo to defining it.

The need to be self-proving can require oppositional figures to define their roles over and against well-established definitions of similar roles. Where objective measures of oppositional legitimacy are lacking, legitimacy depends on the ability to compel and maintain recognition by an audience. The need for proof also implies the possibility of falsification. At the same time, to successfully overcome an audience's doubt and resistance could be an enhanced source of strength over more conventional sources of authority. In the process of competing with other intermediaries and constructing identities that must oscillate between the familiar and the unfamiliar, these oppositional figures often co-opt and recombine features foregrounded by their competitors. Frequently the act of competing and co-opting involves a claim to be recovering some kind of original and authentic prior practice, which often allows, ironically, for the refurbishing of existing practice.

The competitive situation introduces or emphasizes many disjunctions, the overcoming of which is a major source of power for the successful actor. In the words of an insightful sociological account of prophethood, "the first step in the acceptance of a totally alien idea is to attack it. ... The only way to resist an alien idea is to ignore it."[75] Often the very existence of opposition, resistance, rejection, or hostility comes to be seen as the ultimate proof of legitimacy. The saying, "A prophet is never welcome in his own country" is one popular way of turning necessity into virtue.

---

75. Philip Slater, *Earthwalk* (Garden City, NY: Anchor Press/Doubleday, 1974): 72.

The focus on the dynamic of competition suggests a series of questions to be asked of any particular historical situation in which such oppositional figures have emerged:

- Who else is claiming to have access to privileging communication? How strong are their claims?
- What frameworks and categories exist for understanding privileging communication, especially when used for oppositional purposes? What terms exist for describing various forms of privileging communication?
- How skillful is the oppositional figure in competing with and co-opting others?
- Does the oppositional figure successfully exhibit the traits expected of someone in his or her position?
- Is communication automatically privileged by a figure occupying a particular authoritative role? Or is the nature of the communication itself important in authorizing the role?

These questions can also be used to compare "oppositional privileging communicators." Given these possible combinations of traits, my catchment potentially includes all those individuals whose claims to have received unsolicited communication from an extra-human source have promoted opposition to the status quo and, occasionally, a new social order. But this catchment has particular advantages because it stresses the competition among roles, and the way in which it is a comparative strategy itself. If extra-human communication is a slippery field, the oppositional situation blurs the boundaries among roles even further. I want to know especially how some of these individuals promote opposition/critique while most don't, and within that, why a few of them achieve much greater influence as oppositional figures than most others. At the beginning of this chapter, I stated my intention to integrate material about what we mean by prophecy with Islamic examples. The central question is inspired by a feature of Islam that has tended to make it aberrant in the study of prophecy: the association of communication from an extra-human source with wider leadership and power. Therefore, we want to examine the circumstances and personalities that make it possible for extra-human communication to lead to extended leadership.

Focusing on oppositional situations foregrounds the relationships among roles. Ideally, this approach should reveal the most about how privileging communication from an extra-human source works, and how slippage allows certain kinds of change and the power required to generate it. The oppositional situation is also a comparative strategy in its own right, an ideal way to understand how societies themselves make distinctions among various extra-human communicators, and how such figures might best be compared with each other. Instead of using categories to oversimplify, this approach makes a messy situation messier. We don't want to override or neaten indigenous systems, because in doing so we lose our sense of how privileging communication is organized and how it is slippage that allows for certain kind of change to emerge. Sometimes it is better to be messy and complex than tidy and simplistic.

2

COMPARATIVELY SPEAKING: QUR'ANIC COMPARISON AS A MODALITY OF CHANGE

And these likenesses we strike for people,
so that they might recollect.
(Qur'an 59:21)

The representation of Muhammad as someone who defined himself in part by inviting comparisons can be largely derived from the Qur'an itself, with minimal reference to other sources. Despite non-Muslim scholarly controversy over its provenance, the Qur'an remains the earliest Muslim source for Muhammad's career. According to Muslims, Muhammad's recitations, *qur'ans*, from the one God, known in Arabic as Allah, were assembled into what is now known as the Qur'an within two decades after his death in 632 CE, specifically during the caliphate of Uthman (644–656 CE). The Qur'an is a source for Muhammad's career in two senses. It makes specific reference to his activities and to his role, which it compares with others, and it offers its special forms of communication—its poetic and inimitable language—as proof of his authenticity.

The next earliest surviving Muslim texts were written much later, in the ninth century, although they contain references to and quotes from eighth-century texts. These later texts elaborate on more cryptic references from the Qur'an, and it is from them that our fuller biographical image of Muhammad comes. Syriac Christian texts about Muhammad and his relationship to biblical figures and Jesus have survived from the eighth century. We also have convincing analyses of pre-Islamic Arabic poetry and its relationship to qur'anic languages, as well as the relationship of poets to Muhammad.

In using the Qur'an as the earliest—indeed, contemporaneous—reflection of Muhammad's career, we need to concentrate on the flexible, ad hoc character of its production: it is a collection of individual recitations. The Qur'an is first and foremost a series of *qur'ans*. It is itself an emergent document, accumulated over time in interaction with Muhammad's experiences and also with the reactions of his audience. Unfortunately, we cannot know for sure what order to follow. Muslims divide materials between Meccan and various Medinan phases; non-Muslim scholars have proposed chronological orders that contradict each other directly. Whichever order we follow, we must always remember that any particular qur'anic passage represents a moment in Muhammad's experiences, and is not a cumulative product of them. And so the question to ask, and to ask insistently, is the same question that loomed large for the *mufassirun* ("exegetes"): what moment might have been behind each *qur'an*? In this text, "Qur'an" will refer to the text as a completed whole, whereas "*qur'an*" will be used to describe the recitations of Muhammad that unfolded over a period of time through a process of interaction and revelation.

How did Muhammad's career, as reflected in the Qur'an, differ from "prophecy," as it is frequently construed in popular, as well as scholarly, English usage? One important difference lies in the fact that the English word "prophet" rarely coincides with the role of "leader;" however, this combination was crucial to Muhammad's success. Jeremy Silver noted this difference between approaches to the category of prophecy: "In our Freudian age we study prophecy under the heading of abnormal psychology and/or religious experience. Muslim scholars studied prophecy as a phenomenon associated with leadership."[1] Muhammad asked for more than having his messages heeded: he asked to be followed as the leader of a politically established and sovereign community.

Like many other prophets, Muhammad criticized the status quo in his messages, but he also opposed the status quo as a leader in his own right, and ultimately became the status quo himself. Unlike most other prophets, the roles that Muhammad occupied were not limited to his gift of distinctive speech, and the ones that he claimed were associated with his gifted speech did not have clear-cut cultural guidelines; they seemed to be fashioned out of, and compared with, other roles. Nor was he limited to prophesying the end-times—even though he did warn that the world would end dramatically, apocalyptic prediction did not dominate his communication. In other words, Muhammad's work extended beyond the message: he was not merely a warner, a prophesier of apocalypse, or an attacker of the status quo; building a new order was as important as calling an end to the old order. Because of this, he

---

1. Jeremy Silver, *Images of Moses* (New York: Basic Books, Inc., 1982): 281.

had to understand his community's needs, and could not occupy the same types of roles or exhibit the same behavior as, for example, some of the more apocalyptic Hebrew prophets. While a disheveled, idiosyncratic prophet might be able to captivate an audience with certain types of messages, such as the decrying of governmental corruption or the making of eschatological predictions, other types of messages, such as the calling for the creation of a new legal system, are less likely to be heeded from such a figure. Audience expectations play an important role in the delivering of public messages, and in order to be successful, the messenger must understand the expectations surrounding the particular type of message he is attempting to deliver.

In many ways, followers' expectations precede a leader's leadership style and help determine a leader's ability to lead. Yet the audience of the qur'anic Muhammad did not necessarily know what to expect when he first started delivering his messages. They also had varying criteria of identification. And none of his contemporaries could quite figure out how to classify him. In the Qur'an, Muhammad is presented as constantly having to overcome skepticism about his authenticity. He has to prove himself as a leader who should be obeyed because he is receiving unsolicited messages from Allah that are unwelcome to many hearers. He criticizes the status quo on the basis of these messages from Allah, and yet claims not to occupy any of the current roles known to specialize in such communication. Even so, he has to define himself in relation to better-established roles, and in relation to others who claim to deliver different messages from the same Allah, in order to create a distinctive and powerful role for himself.

How did Muhammad survive this identification crisis, and how did he turn it into an identification opportunity that fused gifted speech, opposition, and leadership? The answer to this crucial question goes beyond audience expectations. Its answer requires comparisons; not comparisons of others with Muhammad, but rather how Muhammad himself used comparisons to shape his emergent role in a fluid situation. Muhammad legitimated himself partly by inviting comparison, not always intentionally, with others in more recognizable roles, and by being more inviting, in both a literal and figurative sense. Being more inviting meant striking just the right balance between similarity and difference, likening himself to some while distancing himself from others, and enticing the audience to entertain new comparisons. As these comparisons became more and more inviting, Muhammad was able to co-opt the authority of those with whom he invited comparison. Since many of those from whom he wished to distance himself also claimed the gift of out-of-the-ordinary verbal utterances, the evolution of his special utterances, or *qur'ans*, and their incomparability, played a central role in his increasing attractiveness. These special utterances eventually became the Qur'an, but in the Meccan and also, later, the Medinan period, they were discrete utterances, each a *qur'an*, collectively a set of *qur'ans*. As these *qur'ans* were forming, Muhammad continued to be rejected by many others, which furthered the need for his oppositional stance. At this point, increasingly strong comparisons began to emerge between those who found him inviting and those who did not. His *qur'ans* also contained narrative comparisons between himself as a bringer of Allah's messages and others who had performed similar tasks in the past. These comparisons were presented as both intellectually convincing and entertaining. Because of that, the *qur'ans'* hearers were enjoined to entertain them as possibilities. Muhammad's role remained dynamic in its early stages of formation, perpetually having new light shed upon it by comparisons with known figures. Muhammad's distinctive role was, in many ways, created out of a series of tableaux with prior individuals and contemporaneous roles. He claimed to be like previous prophets and messengers, like Moses and Jesus, but to be categorically different than figures like sorcerers, poets, and soothsayers.

This complex and subtle process of politically staged comparison was an important part of Muhammad's fashioning of an oppositional strategy, and as his reception of discrete *qur'ans* increased, the strategy evolved into a social role, one that was subsequently institutionalized. In order to understand the process of politically staged comparison, we must pay special attention to emergent roles and role labels as systems of alternatives and as comparative strategies in their own right. Much of becoming "entitled" to lead depends on first fulfilling certain audience expectations, and then acquiring and controlling the right titles. We also must consider that the audience of that particular time and place may have had expectations and made comparisons that are not be obvious to us, here and now. When, for example, the Qur'an calls Muhammad the "messenger of Allah," the audience may well have considered what it knew of messengers in general. When the Qur'an presents Muhammad as a *nabī*, or (loosely) "prophet," it both puts him in a class with other *nabīs*, and also explains how *nabīs* are both similar to and different from one another. It also entails a statement of what *nabīs* are not. What appears to be separate phenomena are often parts of sets of alternatives, and the one adopted entails the one rejected. A story attributed to Mulla Nasrudin makes the point in a more efficient way: the Mulla rushed out into his garden and excitedly commanded his neighbor, "Congratulate me! I'm a father!"

"Is it a boy or a girl?" asked the neighbor.

"Yes," replied the Mulla, "but how did you know?"[2]

Much of the Qur'an records a battle of wits between Allah and those who do not accept His messages. Since much of the refusal to accept the messages is expressed in terms of skepticism about Muhammad as Allah's chosen emissary, much of Allah's effort is spent bolstering Muhammad's authenticity and, by extension, his authority. To do so, Allah must counter the audience's efforts to miscategorize Muhammad. Allah does so in a variety of ways, prodding Muhammad's audience to categorize him in a role not everyone seems to recognize or to understand in the correct way. A major part of this effort depends on Allah's control of a subtle interplay of similarity and difference, that is, of superior strategies of comparison. Allah becomes the orchestrator of comparisons that work at many levels. His labor involves not just answering what rejecters say, or telling Muhammad how to counter his rejecters. It also involves Allah as predictor: at each step of a hypothetical dialogue, sometimes from past experience, Allah predicts what the rejecters will say when told certain things; that is to say, He anticipates objections, particularly miscategorizations of Muhammad, and projects a response (Qur'an 6:157ff). In fact, one of the most prominent rhetorical devices in the Qur'an is *mathl*—likeness/similitude and, by extension, example or model. What we would call metaphor, analogy, or parable tells only a small part of the story that unfolds with masterful and multiple scenarios in the Qur'an.

To understand the making of the Qur'an, we must engage the robust yet subtle force of Allah as its maker. While we must bear in mind the social competition implied in rhetorical strategies, we must focus most on the dynamics of qur'anic strategic comparison. The goal is to see how the qur'anic style of comparison effects a shift from one set of classifications to another, much the way *muqarnas* (literally, comparison) arches, often called honeycomb arches, articulate the transition from a circular column to the square part of an arch in Islamic architecture. What we are talking about here is strategic comparison as a means of transition; indeed, as a modality of change.

Just as the *muqarnas* arch acts as a transitional zone to break down the distinction between a vertical curved area and a horizontal dome,

---

2. Idries Shah, *The Pleasantries of the Incredible Mulla Nasrudin* (London: Octagon Press, 1977): 56.

so too must strategic comparison make transitions subtly and skillfully in order to be effective. The paradigm shift must seem graceful and self-evident. On one level, the qur'anic Allah simply has to show how Muhammad is unlike some people and like others. But the situation, as becomes more and more evident in the Qur'an, is not so simple. Indeed, the effort to move the audience from one paradigm to another is presented as arduous in the extreme, requiring continual reiteration and elaboration (i.e., a lot of complicated give and take). In the process, comparisons are refined. In fact, consistent reiteration, connected with reminding people of something they should already know, is put forward as a major proof of truth to the rejecters and a major source of reinforcement and reassurance to the acceptors. Those who persist in rejecting Muhammad's message are thus characterized as stubborn deniers, those who consistently accept the message are considered faithful and steadfast, and those who oscillate between rejecting and accepting are portrayed as confused and hypocritical.

The things Muhammad is said to be absolutely unlike are numerous and various, and understood variously by different members of the qur'anic audience—thus, explanations for why he is unlike them have to vary as well. Also, he is said to be like certain past figures that were in their own time also unlike the figures Muhammad is unlike, but in slightly different ways. At the same time, those who reject Muhammad are said to be just like those who rejected the previous figures whom Muhammad resembles (or Muhammad's forerunners). The Qur'an must, out of necessity, emphatically dismiss the claims of Muhammad's rejecters in order to uphold the integrity of Muhammad and his message. That is to say, the audience may be making fine distinctions as well, but, as a rhetorical strategy, Allah must dismiss these distinctions as ridiculous in order to strengthen Muhammad's position in a competitive environment.

Those who persist in likening Muhammad to things that, according to Allah, he is unlike, are shown to want it both ways. In fact, their inconsistency in the face of qur'anic consistency is indicated as a major proof of their wrong-headedness. Wanting it both ways is itself a complicated thing. One minute they are said to say they don't take Muhammad seriously because he is like or unlike something or someone; the next minute they say if only he were like or unlike those same things, they would be more inclined to accept him. That is to say, Allah's adversaries are presented as engaged in their own, much less efficacious, game of comparison. Also, when they reject him because he is like or unlike something else, it is not clear whether they do not take that thing seriously at all, or whether they just think it is different from what he claims to be.

Those who accept him, or even reject him, because they accept Allah's likening of him to historical precedents do not all understand those precedents in the same way. In the course of testing their understanding of the precedents against Allah's, they cause Allah to make new and finer distinctions, which often minimize differences while maximizing similarities. The likenesses that Allah strikes seem unable to evoke only the similarities; differences also get invoked that have to be explained away. The similarities Allah stresses are to figures in the distant past, and thus reminding becomes part of the comparative strategy in two senses: reminding in the sense of causing to remember, and reminding in the sense of suggesting similarity. One of the most common qur'anic verbs for this is *dhakara*, which bears both senses, as can "remind" in English. Reminding people of what they should already know is connected with the larger qur'anic goal of remembering the whole history and substance of what Muhammad is said to be inheriting. *Dhakara* also has the connotation of "mentioning," and this is connected with the qur'anic claim that to mention should be to remind, especially if mentioning occurs repeatedly. The ability to be reminded through comparison then becomes a major distinction between those who are on the right track and those who are on the wrong track.

The aesthetic tone that informs qur'anic use of comparison is dialogic. It is at once conversational and contrapuntal, but not dialectic. Much like the *muqarnas* honeycomb arches, this process of conversation produces simplified, narrowed distinctions between similarities that are defining and differences that are incidental, and vice versa. Those arches in architecture have been referred to as frozen music, paralleling the form of the Qur'an in its final version. But what we need to hear first is the music as it was played: live notes, not frozen music, to reflect the *qur'ans* in process as distinct from the end product of the book, the Qur'an as a seamless, single symphony.

Sihr—usually defined as "magic" or "sorcery"—is one of the most frequent dismissive categories applied to Muhammad's recitations by his qur'anic rejecters. He is not generally accused of being a sorcerer (i.e., someone who specializes in the activity of *sihr*), although the existence of "professional" sorcerers is attributed to Mosaic Egypt. The labeling of qur'anic recitation as sorcery is presented as a dismissal of qur'anic claims that Muhammad is something other than a magician. The Qur'an does not explain whether those who dismissed Muhammad's recitations in this way did not take sorcery seriously at all, or rather thought that such a label simply undermined Muhammad as presented (i.e., that magic might be good for some purposes, but not a good justification for taking Muhammad seriously). If magic itself were in ill repute with these individuals, it obviously would not have helped Muhammad much to invoke this particular comparison. If the rejecters were serious about the label and not just thinking of something dismissive to say, it would seem to indicate that he could be labeled a practitioner of magic in a way that would make his role more rather than less appealing to certain members of the audience. What is clear is that Allah casts magic and sorcerers in a bad light.

For now, let us limit ourselves to what can be known about the meaning of this accusation without resorting to later dictionaries, commentaries, narratives, or secondary scholarship.[3] According to one qur'anic passage, Allah says magic was taught to human beings by malevolent beings, *shaytans*, who learned it from two misbehaving angels, Harut and Marut (Qur'an 2:101–2). It is something that harms, not benefits; a heavenly secret that should not have been taught to human beings. It is presented as a skill or craft with a paradox: it is a learned gift, which has an extra-human source but which one human can also teach to another (Qur'an 2:102). It is something, or the appearance of something, that human beings make or create on their own, at a time of their choosing, regardless of its origins (Qur'an 21: 28–36, 78–82).

Sorcery is most frequently associated with the qur'anic story of Moses, a figure with whom Allah classes Muhammad. It is from this story that the nature of magic as an activity becomes clearer. In this case, both Moses as a sorcerer, and other magicians summoned by Pharaoh, engage in changing one thing into another in a captivating manner: in Moses' case, staff into serpent and natural skin into white skin. In fact, the other magicians accept Moses' claim to be a "messenger of the lord of the worlds" because, in their view, his magic is better than theirs. Thus, magic at its "best" can be enticing, fascinating, entertaining, captivating, frightening, and, above all, transforming, in more than one sense of the word. In changing things, it changes minds, persuades (or deludes), turns heads as it were (it is interesting that Allah accuses His rejecters of turning away so as to avoid being captivated by the message). As a result of his initial display of magic, Moses is recognized as *saahir 'aalim*—a learned sorcerer, and only others who are also *saahir 'aalim* are summoned to assemble in his presence (Qur'an 26:34ff).

---

3. See, e.g, George Lindbeck, *Nature of Doctrine: Religion and Theology in a Post-Liberal Age* (Lexington, KY: John Knox, 1984).

Another major figure accused of sorcery is Jesus, again in connection with changing one thing into another: clay into bird, blind into seeing, leprous into healthy, dead into alive. Those who rejected Jesus are said to have dismissed these activities as magic, or as the Qur'an often phrases it, *sihr mubin*. This usage, *sihr mubin*, is an important part of the story. *Mubin* is the adjective most often linked to *sihr* as a dismissal. *Mubin* has two major meanings: patent, obvious, or manifest, and plain, clear, or articulate. The root of the word means "between," and some forms are involved when discussing contrast and contradiction. So, the clarity conveyed by *mubin* is a comparative clarity that comes from sharp distinctions—not clear as in crystal-clear or pellucid, but clear as in clear-cut. *Mubin* is one of the most common adjectives employed by Allah to express the overpoweringly obvious persuasiveness of Muhammad's special recitations, as distinct from any other form of verbal utterance. The rejecters say *sihr mubin,* usually understood by translators to mean patent or obvious magic. Allah says *ayat mubin,* meaning obviously clear verses (or signs)—a play on words which turns a negative into a positive and probably makes better use of both senses of *mubin*: (so) clear-cut, (it should be) obvious. If this war of comparisons is a rhetorical form of the co-optation Muhammad engaged in among his audiences, wordplay like this becomes an important part of the game's aesthetics.

To make a finer distinction, qur'anic *sihr* may be defined as "supranatural transformation" in order to avoid easy equations with "magic." What might it mean when applied to Muhammad's recitations? On the surface the qur'ans do not seem to parallel the material objects transformed in other acts deemed as "magic." Incidentally, we should remember that words may have been considered material objects in the milieu under discussion. Beyond that, though, Muhammad claims to have transformed the words of an ordinary mortal and a human language into something too captivating to ignore without intense dispute. The charge of *sihr*, assuming the qur'anic Allah is responding to an actual accusation, may apply not only to the appearance of extraordinary speech from an unexpected source, but also to its head-turning quality that its rejecters wished to resist. Therefore, the charge of *sihr* lies not only in the transformation of human language into eloquence, but into an eloquence that can change minds. Of course, as we will see, Allah presents eloquence as head-turning, too, but not as sorcery. His rejecters say it may be a good trick, but in the end, it's still only a trick.

Those who rejected Muhammad's recitations as magic were fearful of the effects of these words upon other audience members; like *sihr,* his recitations seemed to cast a spell. At the same time that the rejecters dismiss qur'anic verses as magic, they also demand Muhammad to perform even greater magical acts, such as change the Qur'an or produce another such book (Qur'an 10:15). In their eyes, his inability to do so, no matter how well justified by Allah's overarching paradigm, makes him a poor magician, rather than no magician at all. His audience's demands for magical acts may also be considered in the framework of the English idea of miracles, which are more closely related to figures such as Jesus, rather than with magicians. "Miracle" has positive connotations and connections to respected figures that "magic" lacks. Furthermore, when Allah repeatedly challenges rejecters to make something like the Qur'an, He is in part inviting comparison with the contest between Moses and the other magicians, which draws the distinction between divinely-inspired supranatural transformation and magic tricks.

The charge of *sihr* may also have been stimulated by Allah's stories about figures whom He insists Muhammad is like, figures like Jesus and Moses, who were also perceived this way by some of their audiences. Moses' gift from God was besting Pharaoh's magicians at their own game, so why would this not be true of Muhammad? In the cases of both Moses and Muhammad, their deeds may not have really been magic, but they sure did look like it, and not everyone could tell the difference. Both sides—Muhammad's accepters and rejecters—emphasize that appearances can be deceiving. Allah's resolution is skillful. Rather than state, as a modern anthropologist might, that some figures invite such comparisons, Allah demonstrates in numerous stories about other figures, that this is an accusation made by uncomprehending audiences of all figures like Muhammad (Qur'an 51:52). As Allah says, do you reject because you do not understand, or because you do? (Qur'an 27:84). Allah not only draws comparisons, He also suggests their unequivalence: one side must always be judged as correct and the other as flawed.

On several occasions, Muhammad's audience calls him a *sha'ir* (a poet) as a means of dismissing his claims. However, there is little elaboration in the Qur'an itself on the particulars of this role, or the role's connotations for Muhammad's audience. We know from Qur'an 69:41 that it involves a special way of speaking: *qawl*. In Qur'an 36:69, Allah denies having taught it to Muhammad, so we may infer that it is understood as a learned skill. The fact that Muhammad is dismissed as being only a poet suggests either that poets are not held in high respect by those using it as a dismissal, or that being a poet would rule out Muhammad being what Allah claims him to be. There is some Qur'anic support for both interpretations, the latter in the case of Qur'an 21:5: "Nay, but they say: 'A bunch of dreams! Nay, he has made it [up]. Nay, he is a *sha'ir*. Let him bring a sign like the messengers of old did.'"

Allah's primary reason for rejecting the category of poet is because of its association with malevolent beings. The poetry of the *sha'ir* was considered to be inspired by *jinn*, or supernatural beings, but ultimately was a learned gift "made" by mortals for other mortals. An important passage, Qur'an 26:224–6ff, highlights this point: "And the *sha'irs*, the *gha'un* [those who lead astray; perhaps *shaytans* accompany them] hast thou not seen how they wander [also delude] in every *wadi*, and how they say that which they do not?" Although Allah links evil spirits and poetry, those who call Muhammad a poet associate the term with *jinn*, beings that may or may not be malevolent, and the state of possession by *jinn*: *majnun*. This distinction is evoked in Qur'an 37:36: "Should we give up our own deities just for a poet possessed?" *Majnun* literally means taken by the/a *jinn*, and is exemplified by abnormal behavior. Thus, what we call madness and what we call inspiration are two faces of the same thing. As in many cultures, the line between the two is difficult to draw: although many translators take *majnun* to mean mental instability, madness, or derangement in our terms, in qur'anic language we cannot assume that possession by a spirit is never present in some form or another. Possession can take a variety of forms, some of which can be socially productive or insightful, and some not. Regardless, Allah clearly states that He is not associated with the *jinn* (Qur'an 37:158) except to judge them, and that, therefore, Muhammad may not be properly called *majnun*.

According to Allah, Muhammad's actions reflect his teachings, whereas the poets speak but do not take responsibility for their words or act upon what they say. Allah represents them as numerous and roving aimlessly outside of the accepted social structure. If, as Michael Zwettler argues, what early Muslims called pre-Islamic poetry really was poetry,[4] we could also infer that this type of poetic utterance was fully inflected rhyming metered verse, which employed the special non-vernacular linguistic idiom known as *'arabi*.[5] If we are willing to include this extra-qur'anic understanding in our analysis, we may then follow Zwettler's lead and explore how the qur'anic distinction between *'arabi* and *'ajami*, two different modes of speech, relates to the issues raised when Muhammad's audience confuses him with the poets.

---

4. Michael Zwettler, *The Oral Tradition of Classical Arabic Poetry*: 86–8.

5. *Ibid.*: 171–2.

Allah frequently authenticates Muhammad's recitations by designating them as *'arabi,* the non-vernacular speech form. Furthermore,
Allah states that the recitations are clear, consistent, and require no
interpretation. This implies that the other verbal forms with which
Muhammad's recitations are compared are unclear, inconsistent and/
or require interpretation. Which of these might apply to *sh'ir*? If, as
Zwettler described, the idiom *shi'r 'arabi* was highly articulate, could it
have been so articulate that it was perhaps not universally understood?[6]
If its complex poetics required interpretation for a common, vernacular
understanding, it would then be easy to disagree about its meaning.
In fact, Allah frequently says that if people disagree about something
clear, they must not have understood it. Whereas most translators take
'ajami to mean "foreign tongue" and *'arabi* to be "native tongue,"
Zwettler's interpretation is far more nuanced and less dichotomous.
'Ajami becomes a less articulate way of speaking the vernacular tongue,
while *'arabi* becomes a more articulate, learned form reserved for
special communication. In the same passage where Allah denies having taught Muhammad poetry, he clarifies that the opposite of *shi'r*
is both *dhikr* (reminder) and *qur'an mubin* (clear recitation). Allah is
saying that *shi'r* has no long-term resemblance to previous recitations,
whereas *qur'an* is a reminder of what is already known and what previous prophets have tried to convey, and that *qur'an*, unlike *shi'r,* has no
'iwaj (tortuousness, crookedness).

Here we begin to touch on another opposition, between learned
gifts and unlearned gifts. There has been much scholarly argument
over the adjective *ummi* as applied to Muhammad. *Ummī* signifies
"illiterate," "unlettered," or more broadly, "people without the book."[7]
Many interpreters have focused on the connotation of "unlettered" (i.e.,
unable to read or write, to stress the miraculousness of an illiterate
bringing forth the Qur'an). One obvious problem with this interpretation is that it is possible to be unlettered, but not uneducated, if one is
educated in an oral form. Additionally, the principal figures with whom
Muhammad is "confused"—the magician *(sahir),* soothsayer *(kahin),*
and poet *(sha'ir)*—are learned or taught, which may indicate that a
better interpretation of *ummī* is "untutored" or "uneducated," because
of the distinction it creates between Muhammad and these others. For
example, in the case of *shi'r*, a form of oral poetry, literacy does not

---

6. *Ibid.*: 163–4.
7. Sebastian Günther, "Ummī," *Encyclopaedia of the Qur'an*, ed. Jane Dammen
   McAuliffe (Washington, DC: Brill, 2010).—Ed.

bar someone from learning it. So, if Muhammad was speaking in a way that reminded his audience of *shi'r*, it would have to be demonstrated that he had not been instructed in any way, even verbally. Furthermore, in one important case, being taught is explicitly associated with being *majnun*, or inspired by *jinn*: "How is a reminder possible for them (such that their profession of faith could be true), seeing that there has come to them a Messenger making the truth clear (and embodying it in every element of his life and character), but they turn away from him and say: 'One taught by others, and possessed'" (Qur'an 44:13–14). Muhammad is frequently accused of having been taught by either *jinn* or humans, and so these accusations associate him with figures such as the magician, soothsayer, and poet, all of whom either possess learned gifts, or are, in the eyes of some, "possessed."

We may also extend Zwettler's inquiry to ask if hearing these kinds of stories spoken in *'arabi* rather than *'ajami* (a formal as opposed to a vernacular speech form) was the source of this confusion. In one passage, Allah states that the mortals who Muhammad was accused of being taught by couldn't possibly have taught him, because He knows those mortals, and they speak *'ajami*, whereas the Qur'an is in *'arabi* (Qur'an 16:103). In short, Allah asserts that the Qur'an's quality clearly makes it *'arabi*, while Muhammad's rejecters use this same quality to classify him as an ordinary poet. By the audience's logic, if Muhammad were a poet like all the other poets, that would make him an ordinary mortal, and thus unqualified to do what Allah insists only a gifted mortal can do. According to Allah, only the articulateness of *'arabi* is worthy of conveying His words—but then He has to establish *'arabi* as an appropriate speech form for His messenger and as distinct from the poets' use of *'arabi*.

Just as Allah asserts that Muhammad is not like a poet, He also emphatically denies that Muhammad is a soothsayer (*kahin*), often in the same breath. There is even less said in the Qur'an about the soothsayer than about the poet. As with the role of poet, Allah denies that Muhammad is a soothsayer by emphasizing that he is something else, particularly by focusing upon the sanity, clarity, and gravity of Muhammad's personage and his message, contrasting this with the behavior of the soothsayers. The gravity, or "heaviness," of his speech is described in the Qur'an as *"al- qawl ath-thaqil,"* or "weighty word" (Qur'an 73:5). Implied in this comparison is the argument that the words of the soothsayer are flimsy, mad, or confusing. As with those who called Muhammad a poet, those who were said to have labeled him a soothsayer had a variety of motives for this comparison. Those who were skeptical of soothsayers may have dismissed Muhammad entirely by putting him in the same category as other soothsayers. Those who took soothsayers seriously might also have rejected Muhammad's claims to be different from them. Still others might have said he was not a very convincing soothsayer, or just an ordinary one. In any case, labels such as "poet" or "soothsayer" were meant to be dismissive. No individual in any of these categories is mentioned by name in the Qur'an, only by role label. Allah tells Muhammad directly that he does not fit any of these categories, and Muhammad in turn expresses this to his audience. While this is usually interpreted as Allah reassuring Muhammad and his audience, it may also have served as a reminder to Muhammad not to be tempted into these roles.

The Arabic root of *kahin* has to do with predicting or auguring. The Qur'an says nothing directly about what a soothsayer does, except that it is like *qawl-i sha'ir*, a form of spoken word (*qawl-i kahin*; Qur'an 69:42). Another similarity between the poet and the soothsayer is that both are associated with being *majnun,* driven by *jinn* (Qur'an 52:29–30). The actions of a soothsayer and a poet are contrasted with those of a messenger, and with the sending down (*tanzil*) of messages from a higher source, as opposed to the acquisition of a learned skill. Beyond these few explicit references to soothsayers in the Qur'an, further understanding of the role of soothsayer would need to derive from speculation about whether general things Muhammad is said not to be or do contain inklings of what his opposites are or do. From extra-Qur'anic sources, we are told that soothsayers are mantic, that they engage in a kind of automatic speech in rhymed prose known as *saj'*, and that they may have a wild or eccentric appearance. Soothsayers exhibited a learned gift driven by an extra-human source, but were not dependent on that source for the details of each performance. We are told in Qur'an 6:50 that Muhammad does not know the unseen, only Allah does. Did soothsayers claim to know the unseen? Qur'an 6:125 states that not everyone who asks can receive messages like Muhammad's; Allah sends them down according to His will. Is this in contrast to verbal forms that were more widely distributed? In Qur'an 7:186ff (see also 17:85), we are told Muhammad knows only what Allah chooses to tell him. Does this contrast with styles of insight and wisdom less restricted to direct communication with the source? In Qur'an 53:3, we are told Muhammad does not speak from desire or caprice (i.e., not at will). Did soothsayers or poets have more freedom to speak according to their own will? In Qur'an 25:32 and in numerous other passages, Muhammad is faulted for delivering his messages not all at once but only piece by piece. Did others deliver everything all at once? In several instances, Allah says He has been asked why Muhammad would eat and go about his business in the marketplace in a normal manner (Qur'an 21:8, 25:7), which prompts several more questions about soothsayers— did they behave eccentrically? Were they associated with fasting? What were the general expectations of Muhammad's audience with respect to individuals who were claiming to have contact with the unseen? While these questions cannot be fully answered now, they are certainly worth raising.

Given that Allah's denials are often repeated, it would seem that the denials were unconvincing, or, in the case of total skeptics, that continuously labeling him as a soothsayer or a poet was purely a polemical gesture. Indeed, it would be surprising if controversy and confusion evaporated soon after Muhammad announced he was the exclusive channel to not just any spirit, but the superior heavenly being. In order to make a strong argument against being compared to a soothsayer or a poet, he would need to simultaneously downplay any similarities between himself and these other figures as insignificant, while also finding unequivocal differences. It is Allah's insistence on Muhammad's being a *nabī* and a *rasūl* that puts in a different light whatever similarities he might seem to have to other pre-existing roles. Allah argues that Muhammad did not belong in a category with soothsayers and poets, but rather with prophets and messengers. Interestingly, in this initial phase of legitimizing Muhammad, Allah's emphasis was not on the singularity, originality, or finality of Muhammad—such distinctions were later developments that came only once Muhammad had already been established as a legitimate prophet. At this point, when Muhammad first spoke to his audiences, Allah concentrated on drawing simple distinctions between Muhammad and figures with whom He did not wish Muhammad to be compared, and made reinforcing positive comparisons between Muhammad and *nabīs/rasūls.*

It may be useful at this point to think more generally about non-casual communication, especially that which is associated with privilege— whether this privilege is for the source, for the speaker, for the audience, or for the form and content of the communication itself. Understanding privileged communication in a general sense helps us to better understand particular qur'anic uses of comparison. Communication associated with privilege is very common, and most human beings engage in it to some extent. Some individuals engage in it frequently, especially those who occupy roles that require extensive communication, such as "parent" or "teacher." But, of necessity, most people who engage in privileging communication do not engage in it all of the time. Nor is it always easy to tell when a particular speaker chooses to engage in it. In many cases, privileged communication is hard to distinguish from everyday communication, except that it comes from a person in a privileged position, on a particular occasion, or in a particular context. Sometimes the privilege is derived from the personage of the communicator, sometimes from a profession that requires this type of communication, sometimes from a quality of the communication itself, and sometimes from a combination of these elements.

When, however, a human being is perceived to have access to what we might call an "extra-human" source, the resulting communication is usually recognized as, or claimed to be, distinguishable from everyday communication, and to be beyond the speaker's control. In some cases, the perceived uniqueness of the communication is taken to both reflect and reinforce a recognized, institutionalized role, such as that of a priest. In other cases, the unique communication allows the speaker to acquire authority and legitimacy outside of pre-existing roles. Whereas the "extra-human" communication of many figures operates within the status quo, the privileging communication of others serves as the basis for opposition to it. Since both uses of privileging communication often inhabit the same semantic field, we should not be surprised that they are often found in competition with each other, and that they can in fact turn into each other or take turns in the same individuals. We must be careful not to make categorical distinctions between them.

Consider, for instance, the apparent significance of the soothsayer and poet. Their frequent mention suggests that the power of the spoken word, and the centrality of special locutions in privileging communication, were well established in Muhammad's environs. When Muhammad began speaking in special locutions, he entered into a competitive relationship with other privileging communicators who depended on the unique nature of their speech. What was required of him to displace the authority of their speech? How was their privileged communication linked with their social function, and how did Muhammad navigate his relationship to the status quo? Unlike Weber,[8] we should not assume that it is easy for such a figure to establish himself as different from other related figures by the force of personal charisma alone. The central question instead is this: how did Muhammad, emerging in an environment with active, highly institutionalized modes of privileging

---

8. Max Weber, *The Sociology of Religion* (Boston, MA: Beacon Press, 1993): 2.

communication, manage to be different enough to make a difference? To be heard, he would have to be recognizable enough through familiar role paradigms to be acknowledged in the first place. To become distinctive, he probably could not be so different as to be dismissed, nor could he only present himself as better than those "just like" him. He would probably have to be just different enough to rework, recombine, and transcend the pre-existing roles. If indeed qur'anic style shifted, as appears likely, from apocalypticism to oppositionalism to legislation, this is also an indicator of how public perceptions of Muhammad shifted.

However, presumably some of Muhammad's audience found soothsayers and poets more inviting than others did, so attracting both audiences would require different strategies. Those who liked soothsayers and poets needed to be convinced that Muhammad not only had something better to offer, but also that the soothsayers and poets could not compete with it. Those who were skeptical of soothsayers and poets would need to be convinced that Muhammad was something else entirely. Those who were attracted to him because he reminded them of either of these figures would need to be convinced that the content of his messages superseded the messages of the soothsayers or poets. Those who already interpreted him through other paradigms, such as Christians who could have likened qur'anic messages to those of the Gospels, would need to be provided with clear ways to distinguish him from the soothsayers and poets, and also with ways to compare him favorably with previous prophets and messengers. The rejecters' comparison of Muhammad to the soothsayers or poets required Allah to draw careful distinctions, often operating on several levels at once, in order to clarify Muhammad's role and shift the audience from one paradigm of thought to another.

The Qur'an is much more preoccupied with likening Muhammad to past figures than it is with denying his affinity to other roles like soothsayers and poets. The Qur'an uses two terms, *nabī* and *rasūl*, to identify the class in which it places Muhammad (sometimes also using the adjective *mursil*, "the one sent"). Each of these terms has to do with announcing important news. In addition, *rasūl* refers both to angels used by Allah as messengers, and to messengers sent by human beings to other human beings—as in the case of sura 12 of the Qur'an, where Jacob sends a messenger to the imprisoned Joseph. The phrase *"rasūl Allah"* is used to distinguish a messenger sent by Allah from a messenger sent by a human. It is important to note that *rasūl Allah* refers only to *human* messengers sent by Allah, not to angels.

According to the Qur'an, Muhammad's predecessors include Aaron, Abraham, Ad (sent to the people of Hud), David, Elisha, Enoch (Idris), Ezekiel (Dhu al-Kifl), Isaac, Ishmael, Jacob, Jesus, Job, John, Jonah, Joseph, Lot, Moses, Noah, Salih (sent to the people of Thamud), Samuel, Shu'ayb (sent to the people of Midian), and Solomon. The Qur'an mentions Abraham and Moses most often. It also alludes to other messengers who remain unnamed. The resulting list is a large set of individuals, each possessing unique traits and historical particularities. Such diversity among its members, however, reinforces rather than undermines the coherence and integrity of the *rasūl/nabī* category. In fact, part of accepting Allah is refraining from making any distinctions (*farq*) among the various messengers (Qur'an 2:136; 3:84). The Qur'an chastises those who "deny Allah and His apostles, and [those who] wish to separate Allah from His apostles, saying: 'We believe in some but reject others'" (Qur'an 4:150).

Since Allah does not specifically mention the names of any figures Muhammad is said to be unlike, we should wonder about the rhetorical advantages of naming and describing so many members of the group to which he is said to belong. Refraining from mentioning specific names could, for example, be seen as a simple form of dismissal, while naming could also merely be a means of verifying the existence of the named individual. But if we consider the advantages vis-à-vis strategies of comparison, another answer appears: naming so many, and reiterating specific historical details associated with each, generates a larger number of possible comparisons and a richer array of similarities and differences to explore. Furthermore, in setting up a series of tableaux of Muhammad and other messengers (Muhammad and Moses, Muhammad and Jesus, etc.), the comparison creates a memorable image for the audience. Comparing Muhammad with a particular soothsayer, for instance—even negatively—would place him in a tableau with this individual, thereby creating that image in the minds of the audience members. By only naming members of the group to which Allah claims Muhammad belongs, Allah reinforces the comparisons and individuals that He wants the audience to remember, and dismisses the figures He does not want placed beside Muhammad.

The qur'anic conversation between Allah and Muhammad's audience is directed at "the unbelievers," those who attempt to detract from or discredit Muhammad's message. Here both essential differences and similarities emerge between Muhammad and the past messengers with whom he is likened. Allah repeatedly tells Muhammad that the *qur'ans* comparing him with past messengers are as much for Muhammad's encouragement as they are for the instruction of his audience. In the Qur'an, then, comparison is a two-pronged rhetorical device allowing Allah to refine the *nabī/rasūl* classification exactly as He wishes to, all while giving encouragement to Muhammad:

> All that We relate to you of the exemplary narrative of [the lives of some of the earlier] Messengers is in order that whereby We make firm your heart. In all these accounts there comes to you the truth, as well as an instruction and reminder for the believers.   (Qur'an 11:120)

In sura 12, the Qur'an relays the story of Joseph, a messenger who overcame ill treatment and exile by his own kin, finding liberation in his privileged relationship with Allah. Part of sura 18 describes Moses' encounter with a strange figure possessing special knowledge of God's mysterious ways. Known as Khidr in Islamic tradition, he leads Moses through a series of apparently malicious acts, dismissing the protests that Moses voices at every step along the way. For example, Khidr makes a hole in a ship docked at a riverbank, causing it to sink. To Moses' surprise, each act of mischief ultimately serves a benevolent purpose. By sinking the ship, for example, Khidr saves its innocent owners from a "king" who was taking ships by force. An important message of sura 18 is to trust unquestioningly in God's ways; it applies to both the messenger, Muhammad, and to his skeptical audience.

The Qur'an also vigorously rebuts inappropriate or unfair conclusions that the detractors draw from Allah's comparisons. The Qur'an also makes it clear that some in the audience have more familiarity with, or respect for, the stories that are told than others do. For example, one of the most common dismissals of Muhammad's recitations is that they "merely" retell stories of the ancients that contain no moral force for his contemporaries. In reply to such charges, Allah claims that mere human beings cannot create these stories (Qur'an 17:88). The implication here is that the Qur'anic renditions of such stories are superior ones, told in particularly articulate language that is too special to be dismissed as just some mortal's version of them. Indeed, the delivery of these "mere legends" in *'arabi* does more than make such a dismissal difficult to sustain; it has the effect of discrediting any such claims.

As we have now seen, even in the group of messengers within which Allah places Muhammad, both differences and similarities play an important role. Let us begin with the similarities—those elements that identify an individual as belonging to the class of messenger:

- Messengers are guided and instructed only by Allah. The quantity and style of guidance a given messenger receives is subject to Allah's desire and discretion.
- Messengers are chosen by Allah, usually from among their own people, without seeking to be chosen, and are commissioned to deliver particular messages.
- A messenger's mortality is unquestionable and unequivocal. The Qur'an distinguishes messengers from angels (*mala'ik*), who are neither divine nor human, but can assume the form of a human, particularly when they serve the function of messenger (in this connection, *rasūl*).
- By Allah's design, messengers polarize their audiences, eliciting rejection from some and acceptance from others. Those who oppose them may simply dismiss them verbally, but they might also physically harm or expel them.
- The messenger's main function is to deliver Allah's clear and unequivocal messages verbatim. The messages are of two main sorts, good news and warning, but both explain Allah's unmistakable signs. The same word, *aya*, is used for both types of messages.
- Like Allah, these messengers invite (*da'a*), but do not force, adherence to their messages. Their detractors will do anything to refuse the invitation to adhere. The Qur'an describes many of their behaviors in physical terms that should be taken more literally than they often are: they turn away, plug their ears, cover themselves and hide, make noise so they won't hear, and show refusal on their faces: "God has set a seal upon their hearts and on their hearing, and on their eyes is a covering. For them is a mighty punishment (in the Hereafter)" (Qur'an 2:7).
- Messengers exhibit a constellation of exemplary personal characteristics including patience, consistency, unswerving devotion, compassion, trust, and steadfast opposition to associating (*shirk*) anything with Allah.
- Obeying Allah's messengers is equivalent to obeying Allah.

Now we turn to the differences among Allah's messengers. They seem to be of two types. First, there are those differences that are intended and acknowledged by Allah; as such, they do not undermine the integrity of the class. These include things valued by Muhammad that are present in some but not all of the class. In regard to these differences, Allah explains how He has exalted some of the messengers above others in certain respects (Qur'an 2:253; 17:55), has given books to some and not to others, has made some leaders of their people and not others, and has each speak in the language of his own people. Allah highlights the diversity of his messengers in order to demonstrate that their different qualities allowed them to fulfill the particular needs of their time, place, and audience, while still retaining the essential qualities of "messenger."

Second, there are differences cited by skeptics who wish to call the entire class of messengers into question. Allah dismisses these differences as unimportant or not formative of the class:

> And thus it is that We have set against every Prophet a hostile opposition from among the satans of humankind and the jinn, whispering and suggesting to one another specious words, by way of delusion. Yet had your Lord willed (and compelled everybody to behave in the way that He wills), they would not do it. So leave them alone with what they have been fabricating.
>
> (Qur'an 6:112)

Furthermore, Allah states that "for every Prophet We have made an enemy (band) from among the disbelieving criminals committed to accumulating sins. But Your Lord is sufficient as a guide (to truth and the right course of action) and a helper (against the plots and practices of your enemies)" (Qur'an 25:31; see also Qur'an 3:184; 6:34; 25:37; 34:45; 51:52).

Besides invoking what they interpret as troublesome differences among Allah's messengers, the detractors in the Qur'an raise a variety of other doubts about Muhammad's authenticity. For example, they often ask why Allah has not sent an angel, rather than a mere human, as a messenger to them (Qur'an 23:24; 25:21). This challenge arises from a close reading of (or attentive listening to) the stories that Allah relates in the Qur'an. For example, angels serve as messengers (*rasūl* or *mursil*) to Abraham and Mary. The demands for an angelic messenger suggest that the detractors feel shortchanged by Muhammad's humanity, and that a non-human messenger might have elicited more respect from them. Allah answers this challenge by noting that He could send angels if he wanted—indeed, He has sent them before; and that if His audience were composed of angels rather than men, He would have sent angels as their messengers (Qur'an 17:95).

More frequently, however, Allah's detractors ask for a more impressive human messenger than Muhammad. This messenger would possess a number of extraordinary characteristics, including freedom from normal human needs, activities, and desires, such as hunger; extraordinary powers, such as the ability to make the heavens fall; special treasures or sources of wealth; or special social or personal standing (Qur'an 25:7–8). Such a messenger would also bring some sign (*aya*) other than his verses (*ayat*). A frustrated Allah replies, "Isn't the book enough?" The detractors then respond with another intriguing challenge: "Why can't the messenger bring the book all at once?" (Qur'an 25:32). Allah is ready with a number of reasons: He simply wishes to send it that way, it is easier to understand when sent in smaller parts, and the whole book exists in the form of a guarded tablet in heaven (Qur'an 85:22). The piecemeal nature of the revelation emphasizes God's close control of the process. None of the detractors seem to doubt that a human being can receive direct revelation from Allah; they are simply unconvinced that such revelation is occurring through Muhammad (Qur'an 36:15).

Again, these demands could arise from qur'anic stories themselves, or from details of the stories that do not appear in any *qur'an* yet do appear in other sources such as the Old Testament. Solomon had treasures (Qur'an 27:36), Job endured misery (Qur'an 21:83; 38:41), Moses and Jesus performed transformations (Qur'an 2:60; 5:110), Joseph interpreted dreams (Qur'an 12:46–7), Shu'ayb's prediction about the she-camel came true (Qur'an 11:64–7), Moses and Jesus are associated with the whole Torah and Gospels, respectively (Qur'an 2:136). Allah's skeptics expect Muhammad to exhibit more flamboyant, "prophet-like" characteristics than these previous messengers: "The rejecters said: "If only Muhammad were like Moses, we would accept; we told them Muhammad is like Moses, and still they refused" (Qur'an 36:14). Allah explains that Muhammad *is* like these other messengers if the appropriate comparisons are made (Qur'an 33:40; 36:3).

As we have seen, most of the rejecters' reservations about Muhammad arise from the fact of his mortality and normality (Qur'an 74:25). Muhammad's detractors claim that if Allah truly had an important message to deliver, He would have sent an angel or at least a much more extraordinary human being than that which Muhammad appears to be (Qur'an 41:14). It would be easier for the audience to associate Muhammad with the Qur'an's cohort of previous messengers if he were a more magnificent figure. In reply, Allah insists that all of His messengers have been mortal (Qur'an 25:20) and that Muhammad would have been severely punished if he had acted on anything other than His authority. The formulaic distinction between what Muhammad is, as *nabī* and *rasūl*, and all of the things the audience expects him to be, occurs over and over again in the Qur'an. Allah rejects the audience's expectations by emphasizing that Muhammad is only a warner and a bringer of good news:

Say: it is not within my power [to deal benefit and harm, so] unless God wills [and allows me to], I can neither bring benefit to, nor avert harm from, even myself. Had I knowledge of the Unseen, I would always have been in profit [with no loss at all], and no adversity would ever touch me. I am only a warner [against the evil consequences of misguidance] and a bearer of glad tidings [of prosperity in return for faith and righteousness] for a people who will believe and who will deepen in faith.

(Qur'an 7: 188; see also Qur'an 25:56; 27:92; 34:28; 35:23; 48:8)

Indeed, the Qur'an repeatedly emphasizes that Muhammad's only function is to recite the messages that are revealed to him. In dispelling doubts about Muhammad's role, Allah deflates his audience's expectations by reminding them of messengers' narrow function and their humble attributes.

Allah's technique of comparing Muhammad with other messengers is known as *amthal*, meaning likenesses. In fact, the Qur'an characterizes Allah as the best bringer of *amthal*, implying that the ability to make comparisons is a both a very important skill and a feature of Allah's power. In turn, *amthal* is a means of *dhikr*, or reminding: by comparing Muhammad with past messengers, Allah reminds his audience of their religious-spiritual heritage. Furthermore, such comparisons legitimize this heritage and establish Muhammad as an extension of it. In other words, Allah's comparisons place Muhammad squarely in the realm of narratives that people already (should) know. *Dhikr* thus becomes an answer to frequent charges that Muhammad is asking people to abandon the ways of their ancestors. The *amthal–dhikr* connection constitutes Muhammad as calling people to the ways of their ancestors rather than asking them to deviate from tradition. Just as Allah is the best comparison-maker, He is also the supreme reminder. Those who understand Allah's comparisons are identified as the more intelligent, knowing, and insightful members of the audience. Indeed, by these comparisons, Allah "leads many astray, and thereby He guides many" (Qur'an 2:26). The same comparison may confuse one audience member and enlighten another.

The classification of Muhammad as similar to previous *nabī/rasūl* figures has disadvantages as well as advantages. On the one hand, it identifies him as the latest link in a long and cosmically meaningful history, and thus provides powerful precedents for his own career. But left unadjusted, unshorn of all the cultural baggage that such a narrative brought with it, comparisons might be evoked and expectations stimulated that are inconsistent with the qur'anic purpose. For one thing, even in Allah's stories about these figures, they often do things that

Muhammad does not do. For another, members of the audience seem to have associated these figures with additional expectations that are not specifically encouraged by qur'anic renditions.

Why, then, does the Qur'an use two terms, *nabī* and *rasūl* (and sometimes *mursil*, "one sent"), to characterize Muhammad and his predecessors? Much has been written, by Muslim and non-Muslim commentators alike, attempting to explain the distinctions between these apparent synonyms, both of which denote someone who enunciates or delivers a message. Perhaps using both terms facilitates a translation from the biblical tradition to Muhammad's cultural context: using the terms in conjunction to create a unique identity for Muhammad and his predecessors, saying, "you know what a *nabī* is and you know what a *rasūl* is, and these people are *rasūls* like *nabīs*, or possibly *nabīs* like *rasūls*." This interpretation rests on an assumption that *nabī* is the inherited word for the figures described and that *rasūl* is being drawn from the mundane world of actual messengers (i.e., humans sent by other humans to deliver messages). The conjunction of the two terms, each correcting and controlling the other, expresses the totality of Allah's presentation of Muhammad. Problematically, the only way we can suggest what an earthly *rasūl* would have been is to extrapolate from work done on earlier periods. In doing so, we find that, by using the term *nabī,* the Qur'an necessarily links Muhammad with the cosmic history that included Abraham, Moses, and Jesus. However, it also raised expectations that were inconsistent with Muhammad's role. *Rasūl* excludes the inappropriate things about *nabī*, without losing the desired similarities. It also focuses on the loyal, consistent, clear delivery of a message created by the sender, not the messenger. This might explain why Muhammad was not to be expected to know more than he was told, or to explain or defend everything about the message he brought except on specific instructions from the sender.

How do we learn more about Muhammad's dilemma by examining other prophets? One stratagem is to take language of messengership seriously. Presumably, the Qur'an uses "messenger language" because its audience would be receptive to the idea of messengership. While we know little about the connotations that messengership carried in Muhammad's time, research done on the ancient Semitic world suggests that the messenger motif would be effective with an audience familiar with figures that they might compare to professional messengers.

Scholarship on "earthly" messengership, particularly Samuel A. Meier's work *The Messenger in the Ancient Semitic World*, is uncannily relevant to our understanding of Muhammad in the role of messenger.

Meier deliberately focuses on the duties and characteristics of messengers, while considering how prophets in the ancient Semitic world may have used the notion of the messenger role as a metaphor for their social status and message.[9] Of course, there is a vast interim between the second and first millennia BCE and the mid-first millennium CE, but the parallels between Meier's conclusions about ancient messengers and Muhammad's role as presented in the Qur'an are too suggestive to be ignored—both in terms of similarities and differences, and the way in which such a comparison expands the pool of questions.

One of the two terms that guides Meier's focus is *malak*. This is a term commonly used for an angelic messenger in the Qur'an, and it reminds us of yet another concept that would need to be included in a full survey of the map of relevant messenger roles. Of course, the Qur'an portrays one particular *malak*, Gabriel, as the messenger angel who delivers *qur'an* to the messenger man. That in turn reminds us how much the labeling of any one role depends on distinguishing it from other related roles. It makes us consider, for example, what a professional messenger was called in Muhammad's part of the world, and how much the various locutions of *r-s-l* in the Qur'an overlapped with that. For example, according to Mustansir Mir, a Qur'anic scholar, the fourth form of the root combines sending a messenger with imposing something on someone, as well as showering riches or blessings on someone—both of which are consistent with what Meier says about earthly messengers.[10]

On the surface, the major occasions that Meier lists for sending messengers—festivals, renewals of fealty, explaining or compensating for not sending a messenger earlier—seem different from Allah's reasons for sending Muhammad. However, the latter two occasions could be seen as relevant to Muhammad's case. If one takes seriously the Qur'an's claim to rediscover an older covenant (Qur'an 3:81), the real meaning behind contemporary Arabian custom, then sending Muhammad does involve a renewal of fealty. If one also takes seriously the claim that Muhammad is the culmination of a historical chain of messengers (Qur'an 33:40), then the gap between revelations is less important than the final renewal and completion of the revelatory process. Another possible difference between Meier's messengers and those of the Qur'an is that many of the former volunteer for the role, whereas the latter do not. Furthermore, whereas bargaining with a king generally

---

9. Meier, *The Messenger in the Ancient Semitic World*: 9.
10. Mustansir Mir, *Verbal Idioms of the Qur'an*: 145–7.

wasn't possible, resisting Allah's commission became an important component of Muhammad's image, just as it had been for many biblical figures. For Meier's messengers, messengership was not necessarily a career except for those who garnered a reputation for it. The Qur'an, however, does seem to conceive of it as not only a career, but also a life-altering directive.

Meier's research is particularly helpful in exploring the Qur'an's insistence on the oral and verbatim nature of Muhammad's messages. His survey of literary and non-literary texts reveals a variety of relationships between the words of the sender and those delivered by the messenger, and between oral and written media. Among other things, his findings show how much the role of messenger can differ from one mode of presentation to another—from literary to clay tablet letters, for example. His findings also direct us to look at variations that seem dependent on the status of the sender. Most importantly, perhaps, they suggest a possible contrast between the qur'anic Muhammad and the professional messengers of his day. Insistence on verbatim oral reproduction of the sender's message seems more likely to be an element of the messenger role in Meier's materials when a god or divine king is the sender. For example, in the case of the Mesopotamian incantation priest, a ritual or greeting message might start "with the messenger normally speaking as if he were the sender, that is, in the first person."[11] The Bible reports a case in which King David gives a group of ten messengers an exact message they are to deliver "as though it were David speaking in the first person."[12]

In other cases involving oral messages, the sender asks for faithful reproduction of the sender's words and meanings, but not necessarily for a verbatim reproduction. The messenger could even judge when to withhold and to reveal. In light of the Qur'anic emphasis on orality, it is particularly interesting that the Ugaritic, Akkadian, and Sumerian texts Meier analyzes show a preference for oral messengers. On the other hand, clay-tablet letters show a scribe writing a message for someone else to carry, as well as a scribe reading out the message a messenger has brought. Sometimes, oral and written versions of the message were compared with, and possibly distinguished from, each other. All of this meant that the messenger need not necessarily be literate (i.e., able to read the message he brought). It is important to remember that in everyday messengership, messages often flowed between different language

---

11. Meier, *The Messenger in the Ancient Semitic World*: 182–3.
12. *Ibid.*: 39–40.

groups and thus required translation—a function perhaps more befitting a scribe than a messenger. This fact raises a new consideration about the Qur'an. Allah's emphasis upon the clarity of the Qur'an's plain Arabic message (Qur'an 19:97) seems linked not only to the oral nature of the revelation but also to the unusual fact that it was being delivered within a single language group. But there is something else to consider. Although the Qur'an insists on the importance of Muhammad's bringing an oral message, in many respects he is more akin to the messenger who brings a written message that he cannot read, write, or change. Whereas in the cases of oral messengership that Meier describes, a messenger could decide what to reveal and what to conceal, Muhammad theoretically could not. As a result, his diplomatic skills would have been more important *after* the delivery of a message he had just carried than during. Indeed, Muhammad becomes increasingly empowered as an interpreter during the extended period of his prophecy in Medina and then (after 630 CE) in Mecca again. And his interpretive power increased still more after his death. William Graham reminds us that the distinction between Muhammad as revealer and Muhammad as interpreter became blurred after his death, when *sunna* and *hadith* arose to explain Muhammad's words and behavior.[13]

The issue of oral versus written messengership should also be considered in relation to the skills most valued in someone chosen for the task. According to Meier, someone with almost any social background could be chosen—male/female, rich/poor, stranger/relative, king/slave—precisely because certain personality traits were more important than others according to the particular situation.[14] Apparently, perfect memory and literacy were not *de rigueur*. As Meier notes, "eloquence and tact, diplomacy and faithfulness were paramount, not a good memory."[15] Other attributes were also relevant in Muhammad's case, including a reputation for speaking the truth, faithfulness, ability to speak articulately/diplomatically, good memory, and tirelessness. In Muhammad's case, the ability to reproduce messages verbatim was connected with their being received in an altered state of consciousness, not with having a good memory in the ordinary sense. Likewise, in the cases that Meier analyzes, memory and the ability to deliver messages verbatim were less important than the qualities a messenger displayed

---

13. William A. Graham, *Divine Word and Prophetic Word in Early Islam: A Reconsideration of the Sources, with Special Reference to the Divine Saying Or "Hadith Qudsi."* (Berlin, Germany: Walter de Gruyter, 1977).

14. Meier, *The Messenger in the Ancient Semitic World*, 16.

15. *Ibid.*: 167.

after delivering his message. In this comparative light, Muhammad might be seen as the apotheosis of messengership: he delivered his message verbatim without the aid of mundane memory skills, and exhibited the interpretative, diplomatic, and personal attributes valued in earthly messengers after the delivery of the message.

Why were certain traits valued more than memory skills? The messengers Meier describes were often charged not only with carrying a message but also with conveying its contents in a diplomatic manner. After a message was delivered, a messenger might be tested to see whether he was "a genuine representative of his reputed sender" and might be asked questions that the message itself had not answered.[16] According to Meier, during such interrogations the messenger's "central task lies in responding to unanticipated issues in a manner which would please the sender."[17] Also, "The messenger's responsibility ... could also include defending and explicating the message's claims and veracity before a reluctant or incredulous listener."[18] In addition, messengers had other duties, including transporting goods, carrying out transactions in the marketplace, and serving as legal witnesses (i.e., defending those whom he represents).

The lines of distinction among messengers are often thin, and the same trait or issue can appear in different ways in a number of different roles. In fact, roles seem to be differing combinations of traits chosen from a common pool. There is, for example, a thin line between being led astray by a malevolent non-human being and being just plain wrong, between being deluded or beguiled (*musahhar*) and beguiling others (*sihr*). Beneath the numerous technical terms, there seems to be a smaller set of spectra on which one privileging communication can be distinguished from another:

- volition, from eagerly seeking the role to being forced to play it;
- autonomy, from having powers that may be used at will, or depending on the source of inspiration moment by moment;
- intention of source, from malevolent to benevolent, inconsistent to consistent;
- preparation, from highly schooled/trained to completely unprepared and unlikely; and
- stance toward status quo, from oppositional to supportive.

---

16. *Ibid.*: 203.
17. *Ibid.*: 205.
18. *Ibid.*: 208.

The office of messenger carried no diplomatic immunity, as it were, and such messengers were, according to Meier, "often treated brutally in these interrogations and dialogues."[19] For that reason, among others (e.g., the messenger is tireless and never rests), the task of the ideal messenger was not portrayed as a safe or enviable one. Understandably then, while some volunteered for the task, others resisted the call to messengership. Moreover, the arrival of a messenger was not always a welcome event, as some communities viewed a messenger as "a sign of foreboding."[20] Therefore, the arrival of a messenger might be literarily portrayed as a time of apprehension, with mistaken expectations foregrounded. The Qur'an presents just such a situation. Was there a culturally patterned way of characterizing these and other aspects of the messenger role in Muhammad's time?

In the case of a professional messenger, a sender wishing to respond to his audience or clarify his earlier message could only do so by sending another message—a time-consuming process. In the case of Muhammad, however, the response could be virtually instantaneous, with Allah, the sender, speaking through Muhammad, His messenger. In other words, the sender (Allah) in the qur'anic case was in the unusual position to convey His reaction to the audience's reaction, which in the situations Meier examines, ranged from neglect to rejection. Indeed, messengers could be completely ignored by the recipient(s) of the message. As the Qur'an demonstrates, holding the office of messenger did not guarantee that one's message would be welcomed or heeded.[21] By the same token, "bowing toward the messenger is a sign of submission to the one who sent the envoy."[22] Therefore, when the Qur'an speaks of rejection of, or resistance to, Muhammad's messages, it may in fact refer to a refusal to bow to Muhammad's employer, Allah.

In the end, what seems most relevant about Meier's work is his characterization of the messenger as a social actor. Meier makes the following observations about the social role of the messenger, all of which seem relevant to Muhammad. First, messengers reaffirm social bonds in times of crisis or celebration.[23] Muhammad might be seen as performing such a function, for a sense of crisis certainly permeates the Qur'an. For Meier, the ancient messenger also extended social bonds

---

19. *Ibid.*: 207.
20. *Ibid.*: 131.
21. *Ibid.*: 146.
22. *Ibid.*: 158.
23. *Ibid.*: 36.

beyond "horizons of immediate awareness."[24] Muhammad fulfills this role in two principal ways. First, he puts his contemporaries in touch with their past by recounting stories and traditions relating to previous prophets and messengers; second, he facilitates interaction among his contemporaries where they would not normally take place. Especially important is the connection Meier sees between extending "economic transactions in an urban and cosmopolitan" setting and perpetuating "human values in what could be an increasingly impersonal world of expanding dimensions."[25] In all of this, Meier sees the messenger not as an impersonal element, but as an important social actor: "The messenger's humanity and personal involvement in his task enhanced his role as a mediator of human relationships in a society that could easily subvert such relationships."[26] This connection between Muhammad as reciter of *qur'an* and as mediator of its social impact is perhaps the most prominent insight offered by Meir's work.

In qur'anic discourse, the identity of Muhammad emerges largely from comparisons within a system of what we have called privileging communication. The comparisons occur throughout the qur'anic conversation between Allah and a fluid set of antagonists among Muhammad's audience. Whether or not Allah or his antagonists invoke similarities or differences depends on what kind of advantage they are seeking in the argument. For example, Allah claims Muhammad's similarity to previous messengers in order to establish his authenticity, while the antagonists cite differences between Muhammad and previous messengers in order to discredit him. Comparison is, on all sides, a form of reminding, but with different intent.

However, no single comparison is absolutely satisfying to either party. The antagonists' charges have a kind of scattergun quality: they raise various objections without pursuing any single one consistently. This is another way of saying that only combinations, or perhaps hybrids, of previous *nabī–rasūl* models fully explain who Muhammad is, either from Allah's point of view or from the antagonists' point of view. That is to say, the conversation is fueled by the porousness of existing boundaries between roles and styles of communication, and, in fact, by the failure of styles and roles to align neatly with each other. Is this simply a rhetorical strategy? Or does the nature of the qur'anic conversation between Allah and the unbelievers also hint at the sociometric

---

24. *Ibid.*: 36.
25. *Ibid.*: 36.
26. *Ibid.*: 36.

condition of available messengership/commissioned communicator roles in Muhammad's society?

As presented, none of the roles that the antagonists use to dismiss Muhammad are capable of producing leadership in weighty matters. The *nabī–rasūl* hybrid that has been proposed here benefits from that weakness, uncertainty, and confusion.[27] But does it also benefit from what is presented of Muhammad's, and others', provoking opposition? The qur'anic Allah makes an important distinction between being oppositional and provoking opposition. Allah has no intention for Muhammad to be oppositional, especially since His aim is to recover ancestral practice rather than overthrow it. On the other hand, Muhammad, like all of Allah's messengers, invariably provokes opposition. Yet Allah's role in orchestrating Muhammad's opposition, as well as the role that persuasion and comparison play in overcoming that opposition, remain unresolved. A central part of Muhammad's message is the promise of doom for those who refuse to accept the Qur'an. Thus if there is no opposition, the justification for the sending of the messenger dissolves.

At this point, it is worthwhile to raise some general questions about other normative texts and their relationship to the formation of new communities. Are other normative texts such prominent sites of strategic comparison as the Qur'an is? Did comparison get located in the Qur'an for reasons independent of normative texts, and did it get located somewhere else in the formation of other communities? For example, in exporting images of Jesus and the Buddha, translation from one language to another and from one iconography to another may have evoked comparisons that worked something like the process of disclosure and revelation identified by Muhammad and his listeners as *qur'an*. These other two avenues were not available to the first/early Muslims, due in part to the close association of *shirk* (polytheism) with image fixation and idol worship.[28]

As we now begin to link rhetorical strategies with social practice, some larger questions about comparison as a modality of change arise. Is it easy to invite comparison, and in fact opposition, or does it require effort? Is there a practical difference, and is it worth the effort? That is, is there something special about comparison as a negotiator of

---

27. Peter Brown, "The Rise and Function of the Holy Man in Late Antiquity," *Journal of Roman Studies* 61 (1971): 80–101.

28. Marshall G.S. Hodgson, *The Venture of Islam: Conscience and History in a World Civilization, vol. 2: The Expansion of Islam in the Middle Periods* (Chicago, IL: University of Chicago Press, 1974): 502–7.

opposition? Are strategic uses of comparison always associated with (bids for) change, and vice versa? As Jonathan Z. Smith has pointed out, the comparative enterprise does not deal with phenomena in their totality; rather, it selects certain aspects to examine closely. These comparisons are never self-evident—they are always strategic choices made to deal with specific questions. Comparison is a means of re-visioning, of deconstructing and then reconstructing phenomena to solve particular theoretical or societal problems.[29] For Muhammad, comparisons were a means of establishing his role both as familiar to his audience, through likenesses with previous prophets and messengers, and as different from contemporary roles such as the sorcerer, magician, and poet, in order to make his bid for change in society and to establish himself as a new type of spiritual leader.

It is worth noting that some of the things closely associated with the English-language category of "prophet" are absent in the foregoing analysis—most notably predictive ability and personal eccentricity. We exclude these attributes from the category of figures we would normally want to think of as prophets. According to Allah, the fact that Muhammad lacks magical power and is not mad actually proves that he is who Allah says he is. Our English term "prophet" does not encompass Muhammad's activities, and yet it is the one nearly always employed to describe Muhammad. The term's shortcomings and our insistence upon it may perhaps help to illuminate how preconceptions of categories limit our understanding of the figures we place within those categories—and why Allah goes to such great length in the Qur'an to define Muhammad against pre-existing categories in order to craft an appropriate role for him that would allow for maximum receptivity of his message.

Put simply, the foregoing analysis might cause one to chafe at the search for a universal category called prophecy/prophet/prophethood, regardless of efforts to create systems of alternatives, as scholars like Joachim Wach have done.[30] Before considering the value of "prophethood" as a category, we must understand Muhammad as an exemplar and foil, and his role as an intercommunal norm.

---

29. Jonathan Z. Smith, *Relating Religion: Essays in the Study of Religion* (Chicago, IL: University of Chicago Press, 2004).—Ed.
30. Joachim Wach, *Types of Religious Experience, Christian and Non-Christian* (Chicago, IL: University of Chicago Press, 1951).

3

BEYOND COMPARE: MUHAMMAD
AS EXEMPLAR AND FOIL

The Prophet of God is one of us,
with whom no one, Arab or non-Arab,
can be compared.
(The Caliph al-Razi: reigned 322–329 AH/930–940 CE)[1]

IMAGINING MUHAMMAD

By the early ninth century of the common era, the Muslim empire
stretched from the Atlantic Ocean to the Indus River, in present-day
Pakistan. Strategic comparisons did not become obsolete once Muslims
established their control over southwest Asia; on the contrary, they
proliferated, especially during the first few centuries of the Muslim
empire. These strategic comparisons played a major role in transforming Muslims from ruling minority into norm-setting majority, and were
used to redefine communal boundaries. In city settings where Muslims,
Jews, Christians, and sometimes Zoroastrians coexisted, each community's self-definition and self-legitimation was a process of comparing itself to the other communities as a way of shaping boundaries
and differences, in what Steve Wasserstrom has called "symbiotic
interdefinition."[2] Because all of these communities revered past figures with prophetic authority, comparisons between different messengers were particularly significant. New kinds of comparisons between
Muhammad and previous messengers helped define Muslim identities over and against the various subject communities who claimed

---

1. Roy P. Mottahedeh, *Loyalty and Leadership in an Early Islamic Society* (London:
   I.B. Tauris, 2001): 104.—Ed.
2. Steven M. Wasserstrom, *Between Muslim and Jew: The Problem of Symbiosis
   under Early Islam* (Princeton, NJ: Princeton University Press, 1995): 11.

to "own" many of the same figures. At the same time, comparisons between Muhammad and other Muslim leaders shaped the pluralization of Muslim identity itself. Ironically, it was comparison that institutionalized an image of Muhammad as "beyond compare." From Qur'anic *primus inter pares*, Muhammad slowly emerged, for the majority of the population, as the last and greatest of all messengers. Those who disagreed generally framed their disagreement in terms of that norm, especially when, as they often did, they responded with their own claims to uniqueness. For majority and minority alike, then, comparison could lead to uniqueness, and uniqueness could pre-empt further comparison.

The process of comparison involved the subject populations in many ways. Newly converted Muslims, who had been brought up with other identities or whose near ancestors had been new Muslims, invariably compared themselves with other "older" Muslims. At the same time, non-Muslims were challenged to reconsider and reformulate their understandings of their own "messengers," often with the twin objectives of advancing arguments among themselves as well as between themselves and the ruling population. So this new environment for politically staged comparison must have been even richer than that represented in Qur'anic discourse, especially given the variety of individuals and groups brought into the debate, and the number of written and oral messenger-narratives put into play.

Where the Muslim side in Qur'anic debates would have defended Muhammad's key messenger-traits, now these characteristics became so integral to his image that they found their way into the jokes Muslims told. In one story, a man is brought before the caliph claiming to be God. The caliph says to him, "How dare you say that? Why last week we had some claiming to be only a *nabī*, and we executed him." "That's a good thing, too," says the defendant, "because I certainly didn't send him!"[3]

In another, a man is brought before the caliph claiming to be a *nabī*. The caliph asks, "What wonders can you perform?" The man says, "I can see what you're thinking." "So what am I thinking?" "You're thinking I'm a liar and can't see what you're thinking."[4]

In yet a third story, the identity of Muhammad as seal of the messengers is given a literal-minded and gendered twist: a woman was brought before the caliph claiming to be a *nabī*. The caliph says to her,

---

3. Bernard Lewis, ed., *Islam: From the Prophet Muhammad to the Capture of Constantinople* (New York: Walker and Company, 1974): 278–9.
4. *Ibid.*: 284.

"Don't you know that Muhammad, peace be upon him, said there will be no *nabī*s after me." She replies, "Well he didn't say *nabīya* (female) did he?"[5]

If humor like this reflected many Muslims' confidence in Muhammad as the seal of the prophets, it also reflected their disdain for those Muslims and non-Muslims alike that still tried to transgress those limits, either by questioning the authority of Muhammad or by claiming to be a prophet. This caused conflict within and between communities, sometimes to the point of armed uprisings. Like qur'anic discourse, these intercommunal exchanges assumed conversation partners with unequal power relationships that were now reinforced by social and political structures. These new comparisons invited, even as they reflected, three variant responses: opposition, competition, and co-option. They had to be inviting enough both to validate those who resisted converting to another faith, and to discourage those who found conversion tempting. These new comparisons also entailed a new sort of linguistic translation: Muslims translated other peoples' stories into Arabic, and much of the subject population already wrote and spoke in related languages or adopted Arabic as a first or second language. Some of their sacred writings were written in related languages as well.

Of course, conceptions of gifted leadership were only a small part of a much larger process of reciprocal reshaping of allegiances and loyalties. Even the use of strategic comparison itself went beyond the issues of legitimacy and leadership and into exegesis and heresiography. We need to assess the varied differential impact of both exegesis and heresiography on several communities, no two of which reacted to the elevation of Muhammad in quite the same way.[6] As we shall see through selected examples, some religious communities redefined their primary exemplar as a past figure that, like Muhammad, had been sent by the one God with a book to a particular community. Some went on to exalt their figure well above others, including Muhammad, just as Muslims were exalting Muhammad over theirs. Others looked to past messengers for a standard that was everything they argued Muhammad was not: devoid of earthly motives, non-materialistic, non-militant, and capable of performing miracles. Still others looked to living figures, particularly

---

5. *Ibid.*: 279–80.

6. The quality and quantity of research on these larger topics has increased so much in recent years that it has been very difficult to limit this chapter so severely. The limit has an advantage, though. It forces us to compress and decide which are most relevant to our inquiry.

end-of-time heralds, whose role both invoked and exceeded what was claimed for Muhammad. By examining the place of Muhammad with respect to exegesis, heriosography, and alternate messenger figures, we will be able to foster the comparisons of comparisons.[7]

In what follows, I will look at a small sample of the varied ways in which communities reshaped their views of messenger-figures. I will consider the spectrum of possibilites, and attempt to account for them in terms of the social agendas of the various actors. Yet at the same time, I see one thread that could be used to tie them together loosely, and that is what Steven Wasserstrom has called "the tease of ultimacy."[8] I will argue that the Muslim claim to the finality of Muhammad's message, as last and complete—ultimate—is part of a general competition at the time for closure. As different as the reactions were, they could all be said to be addressing the issue of finality, some in the direction of the uniqueness of a past figure, others in the direction of anticipating a final figure in the future. In this light, the emphasis on the finality of Muhammad that engaged most Muslims could be seen also as a reaction to what was going on among others, Muslim and non-Muslim. That is to say, giving some past figure a firm place in cosmic history, but well before the eschaton, could be a way of competing with the heavy stress on apocalyptic figures we find elsewhere. There has been a tendency to distinguish prophets from messiahs, especially in modern Western comparative religion, but what I'm suggesting is that they may, when located in a historical cultural context, be alternatives to each other, or competitors for that paradoxical but familiar search for ways to close off extra-human inspiration and maintain access to it at the same time. In the case of Muhammad, there is a tendency to say that although he appears apocalyptical in Qur'anic discourse—after all, the warning and good news he brings are about what will happen on the Last Day—he still plays a major role in historical time, and that role, in the first few centuries of the new Islamic dispensation, provides an alternative to the more pressing claims of apocalypticism.[9]

---

7. Here one must note the efforts at a similar process of reflexivity in gauging the nature of religious discourse, pursued by Jonathan Z. Smith. Is comparison a magic or a science? How does one assess the origin of origins? And also, one must not neglect to observe "what a difference a difference makes."

8. I have been unable to locate the specific page number, but it is probably in Wasserstrom, *Between Muslim and Jew.*—Ed.

9. See, for example, Fred M. Donner, *Narratives of Islamic Origins: The Beginnings of Islamic Historical Writing* (Princeton, NJ: The Darwin Press, Inc., 1998): 228–9.—Ed.

Since what follows relies on conventional broad groupings—Muslim, Christian, Jew, and Zoroastrian—let me underscore their heuristic value rather than historical accuracy. The first two centuries of the Islamic era were a period in which communal loyalties were overlapping and blurred. It was often difficult to tell who belonged to which faith communities, and, furthermore, some people did not want to choose between communities, and instead had ambiguous loyalties.[10] Muslims in their need to classify communal lines for tax purposes, and subjects in their need to be so classified, often disagreed with each other about who was what. Recent scholars have provided new, more generic phrases like "piety-minded opposition," or use hybrid terms like "Jewish–Christian," but we still don't have terminology that can convey the shifting slipperiness of these particular paradigms. We must therefore resort to anachronistic convention and use Muslim, Christian, Jew, and Zoroastrian to designate these groups. However, I have pluralized each term and indicated overlaps as well. We could use lower case for all identities to remind us of the problem, but I have opted to retain upper-case spellings for ease of reference.

In discussing the ramification of Muhammad's images, we come up against a tautology about figures who come to be viewed as foundational after their deaths: the greater the variety of images they acquire over a longer time, the more foundational they become. That raises a question of why some images ramify and some don't, a question taken up more directly in a subsequent chapter where we will need to ask whether foundational figures really become powerful only through this posthumous process. For now, we will say that the ramification of Muhammad's images in an environment of intercommunal exchange and competition was important as a source of integrity and a way to sustain Muslim communal activity. As with other foundational figures, such as Jesus, Moses, and the Buddha, we have a number of excellent studies of the fleshing out of that ramification.

In the pages that follow, we will attempt to draw out the ramifications that pertain to Muhammad as *nabī/rasūl* and that reveal points of contact across communal boundaries, with a special emphasis on the implications of Muhammad's "ultimacy" as the seal of the prophets. We will examine how these ramifications varied from community to community. It is impossible that all of Muhammad's functions—exemplar, warrior, perfect man, mediator, legislator, ruler, patriarch, and friend

---

10. See, for example, Wasserstrom, *Between Muslim and Jew.*—Ed.

of God—were assumed by Muslims to be entailed in the role of *nabī/ rasūl*. For some, these functions may have been incidental to *nabī/ rasūl*, but to others, including non-Muslims, they may have been part of Muhammad's appeal. Furthermore, Muhammad's images varied among Muslims, and different Muslims concentrated on different traits of his varied profile.

MUHAMMAD AS ULTIMATE PROPHET: MUSLIM PERSPECTIVES

For the Muslim component I want to look at three different means of addressing Muhammad's ultimacy: narrative accounts of his career (*sīra* or biography), first-hand reports of his exemplary nature (Hadith), and social movements formed around other kinds of eschatological leaders. The Qur'an contains only one reference to his being *khatm al-anbiyā'* ("seal of the prophets"), and given what we know of the early Muslim empire, it wasn't at all obvious that this single reference would entail the focus on Muhammad's finality that became normative by the end of the ninth century.[11] Yohanan Friedman, in his study of the Ahmadiyya, has pointed out that "last" or "final" is only one of many possible meanings of "seal"—it could also mean a seal of approval, and *khatm* may also be translated as "ring." Up until the third century of the Islamic era, many still interpreted "seal of the prophets" as a title designating Muhammad's superiority, not his finality, and Friedman states that "the meaning of *khatam al-nabīyyin* as 'the last prophet' is by no means as certain as the exegetical tradition has made it to appear."[12] It is worth considering why and how this definition of "the seal of the prophets" emerged and what competitive or comparative functions were fulfilled by this particular interpretation.

---

11. *The Qur'an*, trans. Ahmed Ali (Princeton, NJ: Princeton University Press, 2001), 33:40. See also Uri Rubin, "Muhammad," *Encyclopaedia of the Qur'an*, vol. 2, ed. Jane Dammen McAuliffe (Leiden, The Netherlands: Brill, 2004): 440–58; and Wim Raven, "Sira and the Qur'an," *Encyclopaedia of the Qur'an*, vol. 3, ed. Jane Dammen McAuliffe (Leiden, The Netherlands: Brill, 2007): 29–51.—Ed.

12. Yohanan Friedman, *Prophecy Continuous: Aspects of Ahmadi Religious Thought and Its Medieval Background* (Berkeley and Los Angeles, CA: University of California Press, 1989): 81.

The biography of Muhammad

The integration of the line of messengers began in the first *hijri* century. Thanks to the work of Gordon Newby, we can now see how closely this development was connected with writing coherent accounts of the life of Muhammad, especially of his career as *rasūl Allāh*. This is in turn connected with the growing importance of the Hadith form (discrete transmissions of reports about Muhammad) and of the selective appropriation and transformation of what Muslims called *Isrā'īliyyāt*;[13] that is, stories attributed to Jewish and/or Christian sources that helped to extend and integrate the Qur'anic line of messengers into a cohesive whole.[14] The first Muslim author to achieve this integration—and whose work survives—was Ibn Ishaq (who died c. 767 CE). His biography is distinctive not only for its historical primacy but also for its use of sources, which included interviews of ordinary Jews and Muslims. This technique did not outlive him since the stories quickly became Islamized, and their origins were either ignored or forgotten. As Newby notes, "In the generation after Ibn Ishaq the use of extra-Islamic sources fell into disrepute."[15]

Ibn Ishaq lived in a tumultuous and diverse environment. The grandson of a Persian prisoner of war, he became Muslim as an adult. Not only did he write "in a world where Christians, Jews and Zoroastrians vastly outnumbered Muslims,"[16] but also his Muslim contemporaries disagreed with one another about the nature of religious discourse. Especially in dispute were assertions about Muhammad's authority, and a work like Ibn Ishaq's could not make factual statements that found universal acceptance. Ibn Ishaq tried to convey the full implications of Muhammad's status as the "ultimate" prophet, in both senses of the word—final and utmost. He was particularly interested in eschatological functions that linked Muhammad to prior prophets whose mission he both acknowledged and completed. Is Muhammad a second Adam or a second Moses, and what would such attribution mean from a Muslim perspective?

---

13. See G. Vajda, "Isrā'īliyyāt," *Encyclopaedia of Islam*, ed. T. Bianquis P. Bearman, C.E. Bosworth, E. van Donzel, and W.P. Heinrichs (Leiden, The Netherlands: Brill, 2007).–Ed.—Ed.

14. Gordon Darnell Newby, *The Making of the Last Prophet: A Reconstruction of the Earliest Biography of Muhammad* (Columbia, SC: University of South Carolina Press, 1989): 3.

15. *Ibid.*: 4.

16. *Ibid.*: 1.

One important issue to consider, already highlighted by Newby, is whether, how, and to what extent, Muhammad's roles as a prophet, community leader, and military commander are all entailed in the category of *nabī/rasūl*? Significantly, this development is contemporaneous with events around the reign of al-Mansur (754–775). Ibn Ishaq responded to the challenge of identity presented by the paradox of a new rule by a minority community surrounded by older religious groups. He weaved their histories to construct a meta-narrative that privileged Muhammad as an embodiment of the central moment in world history. As Newby notes: "By including all the world's history the work demonstrated that time's course led to Islam, which embraced the prophets and holy men of Judaism and Christianity, and finally produced the regime of the Abbasids, whose empire embraced Muslims, Christians, and Jews."[17]

There is a telling irony in the legacy of Ibn Ishaq. By formulating a unique—and uniquely powerful—history of Muhammad in the context of competing religious narratives, he helped end an "era of open scholarly inquiry into Jewish and Christian knowledge ... By concentrating on Muhammad and raising Muhammad above the other prophets, Ibn Ishaq helped make Islamic scholarship independent of Jewish and Christian sources." His successor and epitomizer, Ibn Hisham (died 833), lived at a time when Islam had triumphed over its Abrahamic rivals, and so omitted much of the material that made Ibn Ishaq's narrative so compelling. This included all the stories relating to the time before Muhammad. In Ibn Hisham's rendition, Muhammad stood on his own literally and figuratively: he had no antecedents, no precursors, and therefore no rivals. Ibn Ishaq, on the other hand, needed to explain what happened before Muhammad in order to "place Muhammad in the context of the long and continuous history of the salvation of the world."[18] For Ibn Ishaq, writing in a culturally diverse setting with many competing religious discourses, "Muhammad was the fulfillment of prophecy; Isaiah had foretold his coming. His life was the replica of the prophets and the patriarchs, just as Islam was the restoration of the true monotheistic worship of God."[19] Significantly, the pursuit of *Isrā'īliyyāt* was much wider than Ibn Ishaq. It was certainly a popular intellectual engagement of the men and women in the first generation after Muhammad. To the extent that comparisons and conversations

---

17. *Ibid.*: 7.
18. *Ibid.*: 8–9.
19. *Ibid.*: 8–9.

that led to depicting Muhammad as the ultimate *nabī/rasūl* succeeded, they no longer became necessary. Through comparisons with other prophets, Muhammad was deemed superior and thus beyond compare. A process of comparison that establishes differentiation and uniqueness only pertains in a context where this differentiation within and between communities is deemed to be vital.[20]

While the interest in prophethood at the time included study of the history of other prophets with whom Muhammad had to be compared, it also went hand in hand with the process of defining what it meant to be "Muslim," an ascendant minority in the world of Jews and Christians. As Fred Donner notes, "the development of an interest in the past and a desire to record it as history was integrally connected with the early Believers' developing conception of themselves as Muslims."[21] Newby suggests that Ibn Hisham's departure from Ibn Ishaq's use of the *Isrā'īliyyāt* may have been connected to the slow rate of conversion: it is possible that he did not want to rely "on the texts and scholarship of those in the religious majority."[22] At the same time, Ibn Ishaq's

---

20. Uri Rubin provides an interesting angle on this issue—the Umayyads' use of the stories of the prophets, especially the concept of hereditary authority in the line of prophets, to formulate an authoritative vision of their own claim to power. Uri Rubin, "Prophets and Caliphs: The Biblical Foundations of the Umayyad Authority," *Method and Theory in the Study of Islamic Origins*, ed. Herbert Berg (Leiden, The Netherlands: Brill, 2003): 73–100.—Ed.

21. Donner, *Narratives of Islamic Origins:* 282. Donner's work parallels that of Newby: both try to discern the writings of the early Muslim authors in consequent materials. Newby reads al-Tabari and others to see traces of Ibn Ishaq. Donner reads the same material by looking at themes that later writers were forced to deal with precisely because they were so dominant in the earlier discourses. For Donner, the earlier writings imposed a certain framework of thinking, especially in relation to such themes as prophethood, community, governance and conflict—see *ibid.*: 84, 279. Also, see Fred M. Donner, "From Believers to Muslims: Confessional Self-Identity in the Early Islamic Community," *Patterns of Communal Identity*, ed. Lawrence I. Conrad, Studies in Late Antiquity and Early Islam, vol. IV (Princeton, NJ: Darwin Press, 2003).—Ed.

22. Newby, *The Making of the Last Prophet:* 12. Reuven Firestone suggests an alternative impetus for the cessation of the use of the *Isrā'īliyyāt.* He looks specifically at the competing and co-existing versions of the Ishmael–Isaac story: the Syria-based narrative according to which Isaac was destined to become Abraham's sacrifice, and the Mecca-based version claiming such an honor for Ishmael. By the ninth and tenth centuries, the Mecca–Ishmael view won over, overshadowing that of his brother, which depended on the *Isrā'īliyyāt* . Firestone suggests that the motivation of prestige was at the heart of this transformation. The shift away from the Isaac-centered narrative, and the *Isrā'īliyyāt* in general,

work enabled Ibn Hisham's departure from these sources. Both reflect a view where Muhammad is elevated to "a privileged position as personal exemplar for the pious Muslim."[23] For Ibn Hisham, however, Muhammad is beyond compare: not only does he not need any comparison, but even a gesture toward comparison is otiose.

Ibn Ishaq's comparisons of Muhammad to prior prophetic figures and Ibn Hisham's elaboration on "beyond compare" were a type of comparison tied closely to a particular social reality. It occurred in a context where groups, whether jurists (like the Malikites) or rationalists (like the Mu'tazilites), had ceased to focus exclusively on Hadith about Muhammad. Put another way, it was the collective profile (Sunna) of Muhammad that made him distinctive from other messengers, who were now as much compared to him as he earlier had been compared to them. While Muhammad himself and his subsequent followers had initially compared him to other prophets as a means of establishing his legitimacy, by now he was an established enough prophetic figure that it was a comparison to him that conferred legitimacy.

Before the Sunna became codified, "the lives of the prophets before Muhammad, the subject of the excised *Kitāb al-Mubtada'*, were enjoyed as tales told by popular preachers or used piecemeal by scholars to comment on the Qur'an."[24] It is important to remember the pleasure as well as the utility of such narratives. These were enjoyable as well as edifying comparisons, and the ability to entertain them was enhanced by large numbers of new Muslims and subject Jews and Christians. In his restoration of *Kitāb al-Mubtada'*, Newby identifies four types through which Muhammad is compared, connected, and distinguished from his predecessors: Prophet, Community Leader, Ideal

---

occurred because "according to an Islamic world view by the ninth and tenth century, CE, the Syria–Isaac exegesis had two major weaknesses. First it was a nearly perfect parallel to the biblical version. This trait would have provided it with great authority in the first century of Islam when the new Arab Muslims were searching for information that would shed light on the difficult passages of the Qur'an. But as Islam preferred to rely on its own authoritative sources at the intellectual height of the Abbasid Caliphate, and as the genealogical connection with Abraham, Ishmael, and the northern Arab became more firmly established, the Isaac legend was deemed increasingly suspect until it was eventually rejected." See Reuven Firestone, *Journey in Holy Lands: The Evolution of the Abraham-Ishmael Legends in Islamic Exegesis* (Albany, NY: SUNY Press, 1990), 150–51.—Ed.

23. Newby, *The Making of the Last Prophet*: 12.
24. *Ibid.*: 14.

Man, and Spiritual Guide.[25] For Ibn Ishaq, such relationships work both ways: Muhammad's life affects previous figures and vice versa. This meta-history starts with Adam and creation, and includes all of the prophets in the Qur'an and many others. In this large picture of prophetic world history, Mecca emerges as the new Jerusalem, Ka'ba as the new temple, and Muhammad as the new Jacob, who actually goes to heaven. Muhammad here, while not determined by previous models, shares some specific aspects in common with all of them—Abraham and Muhammad even look alike, according to Ibn Ishaq. Through such details, one might even see the audience for Ibn Ishaq's narrative, which would include Muslims, Jews, and Christians. Its edifying aims could—and did—go beyond telling about Muhammad; they also included a lesson on the relationship between the various prophets and, hence, the communities that claim allegiance to them.

Looking closer at Ibn Ishaq's story of Muhammad, we can differentiate the following stages, or elements of instructive life experiences:

1. An auspicious birth and youth,
2. A young adulthood spent in close association with conventional spiritual practices and norms and also in experimentation with unconventional ones,
3. A sudden, strongly resisted, frightening "invitation" to serve as a messenger, at the age of 40 and while in a place made special by frequent retreat,
4. Initial preaching among his own people, met by suspicion, resentment, and outright hostility, producing a small but devoted core of followers,
5. Emigration to a more receptive environment and a difficult, gradual development of a larger following,
6. Expansion and incorporation of former enemies into a new socio-political unit, and continuing leadership of same.

Key here is the emphasis on certain experiences that all prophets share: they are all rejected at first, they all suffer, and, eventually, their communities triumph. Ibn Ishaq relates this cosmic history in the context of his own time, marked by much rejection, opposition, and armed revolt. Through the lens of meta-history, Muhammad is foreshadowed by others; he was predicted by Isaiah and descended from Ishmael, and is now God's chosen prophet. Like Moses, he is a lawgiver and military leader.

---

25. *Ibid.*: 17.

Unlike Moses, but like Ezra, he enters heaven alive. And yet, unlike Ezra, he returns to tell the tale. Muhammad, in this story, performs miracles that remind one of Jesus feeding multitudes. Most important is the commonality that prophets share: they are all alike because they partake of the same office. Their differences become incidental, perhaps even more so than in the Qur'an. The apparent lesson to the audience is that followers of prophets should then participate in the same community.

Ibn Ishaq's influence on those who would later retell these stories is quite salient, if we are to look at the choices he emphasized and his imitators followed. For example, where the Qur'an de-emphasizes the significance of Solomon's magical abilities (with the emphasis on God's grace; Qur'an, 27:16), Ibn Ishaq and those after him emphasize this particular entertaining point, which comes across as even more important as a point of comparison with other prophets, including Muhammad. Yet Ibn Ishaq does follow the view of history presented in the Qur'an: Muhammad as part of the divine scheme, integrated with previous messengers. The difference is a matter of emphasis. As Newby notes, whereas "the Qur'an promotes such a view of [Muhammad], the *Sīrah* merely makes it explicit, expands it, and offers more proof than the sparse references in Scripture."[26]

Newby makes some interesting observations about the relationship between the *Sīra* and Qur'an, believing that "insofar as the *Sīrah* supplies material that locates the occasion of the revelation of a Qur'anic passage within the history of Muhammad's career or supplies auxiliary material for understanding the meaning of a particular passage, Ibn Ishaq helped form a view of the Quran that became part of the community's understanding of the canon."[27] While it is important to note that, except for Dhu'l Nun, every *nabī/rasūl* in the Qur'an is treated by Ibn Ishaq, it is equally important to note that he also includes a number of figures that do not appear at all in the Qur'an, or appear there in some role other than *nabī/rasūl*. It will be instructive to consider several examples of the other figures treated by Ibn Ishaq as either prophets/ messengers or as examples of prophetic qualities and prophetic history. We can divide these examples in three categories:

1. those mentioned in the Qur'an by name;
2. those not mentioned by name, but portrayed by Ibn Ishaq as being alluded to in the Qur'an; and
3. completely extra-Qur'anic.

---

26. *Ibid.*: 25.
27. *Ibid.*: 3.

In all cases, the process of the *Sīrah* complementing the Qur'an is explicit, providing a further elaboration and development on the Qur'anic concepts of prophethood, through comparison to what is familiar to Ibn Ishaq's—rather than the Qur'anic—audience. Because Ibn Ishaq adds extra-Qur'anic details in all the stories, the Qur'anic emphases are never left intact; instead, they are re-emphasized, reshaped, or de-emphasized.

Among the personalities of the first category, those named in the Qur'an, we find the Queen of Sheba, Ezra and the Companions of the Cave:

- *The Queen of Sheba*. The female ruler of Sheba (Saba') is a significant figure in the extended Qur'anic account of Solomon, who is a *nabī* in the Qur'an (34:15–21). This story, however, is not about her, but about the land of Sheba and the penalties it suffered for ignoring prophets (*ānbiyā'*). It includes also a tolerant account of the activities of another category—seer (*kāhin*)/seeress (*kāhina*)—whose functions include augury and prediction. The Aws and Khazraj, two Medinan tribes who helped Muhammad, are shown to have originated from the aftermath of her reign.[28]

- *Ezra*. Like the Queen of Sheba, Ezra (al-'Uzayr), is mentioned in Qur'an (9:30), but only in reference to the Jews falsely thinking of him as son of God. In Ibn Ishaq's rendition, this mistake occurs after Ezra's death and is corrected by the sending of another prophet. Ezra himself is a returned prisoner from Babylon. He is weeping over the punishment of his people when an angel teaches him how to prepare for his *nubūwa*, which is described as a teaching of laws, duties, and ordinances from the Torah replicated in Ezra's breast, an obvious parallel to the procedure Muhammad underwent in preparation for his prophetic mission. And, like Muhammad, Ezra had followers who loved his teachings "like they never loved anything else."[29]

- *The Companions of the Cave* are more prominent in the Qur'an than in Ibn Ishaq's version. They are the subject of an entire Qur'anic chapter (18:9–26), not as *nabī/rasūl* but as figures similar to the Seven Sleepers of Ephesus, who are made by Allah to fall asleep and

---

28. *Ibid.*: 172.
29. *Ibid.*: 191. The importance of Ezra is compounded with reference to Christ, and the double denial of divine sonship to *both* prophets. This issue is taken up by S.M. Wasserstrom, *Between Muslim and Jew*: 183–4.

then to dispute when they awake. In Ibn Ishaq's version, a new twist appears: they are followers of the Gospel who are suffering because they have fallen away from Allah's path. Like other characters in the *Sīrah*, their being awakened after falling sleep evokes Allah's ability to revive the dead, a point often stressed in the Qur'an.[30]

The second category, personalities not mentioned by name but, according to Ibn Ishaq, alluded to in the Qur'an either by other names or through some actions, include Samuel b. Bali, Khidr, Alexander, Ezekiel, Isaiah, and Habib:

- *Samuel.* Like Tabari, Ibn Ishaq claims that there is an allusion to Samuel in Qur'an 2:246 as a *nabī* to the Children of Israel after Moses, although Samuel is not mentioned by name. In Ibn Ishaq's story, Samuel's being a *nabī* is tied especially to his ability to locate lost animals.[31] Allah denies in the Qur'an that Muhammad can see the unseen, but the denials are linked, obviously, to the presence of a significant expectation that he should be able to do so.
- *Khidr.* Khidr is not mentioned by name in the Qur'an (18:60–82)[32] but became a very important figure later, especially to the Sufis.[33] Ibn Ishaq identifies him with Jeremiah, and, consistent with the overall purpose of the *Sīra*, gives him a number of traits in common with Muhammad—he was "formed in his mother's belly, purified before he was born, and made a prophet while still a child....weak and sinful without God's intervention ... [his] humanity overcome only through divine guidance."[34]

---

30. Newby, *The Making of the Last Prophet:* 213–23. Also note the extraordinary set of connections made between these figures and other instances of apocalyptic imagery in Norman O. Brown, *Apocalypse and/or Metamorphosis* (Berkeley, CA: University of California Press, 1991): 69–94.—Ed.
31. Newby, *The Making of the Last Prophet:* 154.
32. See a review of exegetical treatments of Khidr in Brannon Wheeler, *Prophets in the Qur'an: An Introduction to the Qur'an and Muslim Exegesis* (New York: Continuum, 2002): 223–37; and also Brannon Wheeler, *Moses in the Qur'an and Islamic Exegesis* (Leiden, The Netherlands: Brill, 2002).—Ed.
33. On the significance of Khidr for Sufis, see Hugh Talat Halman "Al-Khidr," *Encyclopedia of Islam and the Muslim World*, vol. 1, ed. Richard C. Martin (NY: Macmillan Reference, 2001): 390–91.—Ed.
34. Newby, *The Making of the Last Prophet:* 182.

- *Alexander* is often identified with Qur'anic Dhu'l-Qarnayn, whom Moses accompanied on his search for wisdom (Qur'an 18:6–102).[35] According to Newby, Ibn Ishaq presents him to us as "a messenger who went to the limits of the earth to bring the whole of the world to the proper worship of God. By means of an eloquent prayer, we are shown that even the great Alexander relied on God for his powers and strengths. And God promised to open his breast [i.e., make it wide enough to encompass understanding] to give him the powers of a divinely commissioned messenger."[36] The ideal pious ruler, Alexander, shapes the ideal pious community. According to Newby, this community is depicted as "a Muslim utopia. Everyone acts according to proper ethical and religious ideas, and, as a consequence, lives in peace, harmony, and without disease."[37] Furthermore, Alexander is given an eschatological role: he walls up Gog and Magog, who will appear only at the end of time led by the anti-messiah, Dajjal.

- *Ezekiel* is identified by some commentators,[38] but not by Ibn Ishaq, as the Qur'anic figure Dhu'l-Kifl, whom the Qur'an includes in a list of "patient" ones, along with Isma'il and Idris, each of whom the Qur'an (21:85) explicitly calls *nabī*. Ibn Ishaq's identification of Ezekiel is more oblique: he is "the one who prayed for the people whom God mentioned to Muhammad" (Qur'an 2:243). For Newby, the point of this story "is that God has the power to bring to life those who had died."[39]

---

35. Also, see Wheeler, *Moses in the Qur'an and Islamic Exegesis*; and Brannon Wheeler, "Moses," *The Blackwell Companion to the Qur'an*, ed. Andrew Rippin (Malden, MA: Blackwell Publishing Ltd., 2006).

36. Newby, *The Making of the Last Prophet*: 193. But he is also linked to Khidr as a mysterious emissary of the One God. Firdawsī's (died 411 AH/1020 CE) *Shāhnāme* names al-Khair as Alexander's guide in his quest for the fountain (or spring) of life in the Land of Darkness. In fact, Alexander's relationship to al-Khaḍir (also rendered Khiḍr) is strikingly similar to that of Moses to his unnamed guide in sūra 18. Alexander did not reach the fountain, because he became distracted, just as Moses failed in his quest because he asked too many questions. See John Renard, "Alexander," *Encyclopaedia of the Qur'ān*, general ed. Jane Dammen McAuliffe (Leiden, The Netherlands: Brill, 2010), Brill Online, www.brillonline.nl/subscriber/entry?entry=q3_SIM-00016, accessed 23 August 2010.—Ed.

37. Newby, *The Making of the Last Prophet*: 194.

38. See, for example, 'Abd Allah b. 'Umar Al-Baydawi, *Anwar Al-Tanzil Wa-Asrar Al-Ta'wil*, 2 vols. (Beirut: Dar al-Kutub al-'Ilmiyya, 1988).—Ed.

39. Newby, *The Making of the Last Prophet*: 145.

- *Isaiah.* While Isaiah is not mentioned in the Qur'an, the foretelling of Muhammad is.[40] And in Ibn Ishaq's story, it is Isaiah who foretold that event, as well as the coming of Jesus. Ibn Ishaq explicitly classifies Isaiah as a *nabī*.[41]
- *Habib.* Ibn Ishaq identifies Habib as the person who assisted the three messengers of God in Qur'an 36:13–32. A pious sickly martyr, he comes to the defense of three messengers, who are rejected by the ruler of his city.[42]

In the third category we find Samson, George, and the young men of Israel—Daniel, Hananiah, Azariah and Mishael. Completely extra-Quranic personalities, they are nonetheless included as further illustrations of the prophetic meta-history:

- *Samson.* Newby notes that the key feature of Ibn Ishaq's story of Samson is repentance and reliance on God: "Through repentance and calling on the strength of God, Samson is able to triumph over evil and destroy the enemy."[43] It is a highly entertaining story about a male Muslim consecrated to God by his mother but almost fatally tempted by another woman. It also shows God's ability to put a fragmented body (Samson's) back together, as the Qur'an insists He will do at the end of time. Another important detail is the Qur'anic theme of God's working miracles on behalf of a messenger, when God brings forth water from the jawbone of a camel. With God's help, Samson punishes his enemies.
- *George.* The story of the martyr St. George Megalomartyros, who opposed the Roman emperor Diocletian (245–313 CE), is yet another entertaining tale with plenty of gore. In Ibn Ishaq's telling, George is a messenger sharing many traits with other messengers. He is Aaron to the emperor, even though the emperor is himself a tyrant, another Pharaoh. Like Moses to Pharaoh, George bests the ruler's magicians at their own game, and is resurrected many times in the course of his trials.
- *Daniel, Hananiah, Azariah, and Mishael*—all are the young men of Israel spared by Nebuchadnezzar's destruction. Ibn Ishaq calls them

---

40. Ibn Ishaq starts with Qur'an 17:4–8, while other possible references to the foretelling can be found in Qur'an 2:89, 4:47, etc.—Ed.
41. Newby, *The Making of the Last Prophet*: 174–82.
42. *Ibid.*: 227–9.
43. *Ibid.*: 229.

the offspring of the prophets. Under threat of gruesome death, they are forced by Nebuchadnezzar to recount to him a vision he has seen but forgotten. Like many pious personalities of the Qur'an, they trust in their deliverance by God and they turn to Him for information about the vision. In the vision, a thunderbolt shatters a statue, and in their interpretation, a prophet is sent to shatter the kingship and take command himself.[44]

There are many ways to explain these extra-Qur'anic narratives employed by Ibn Ishaq. He was a royal tutor and used some stories to give advice to the prince in his charge. He wanted an audience, and so he included things that were especially entertaining. Some stories were just too good to omit, not only because they were entertaining, but also because they were already popular among audiences he was seeking. Others reflect personal preferences, like Ibn Ishaq's alleged preference for Medina over Mecca, which possibly influenced his rendition of the story of Sheba with the added detail about the Aws and Khazraj.

But it is also the case that these dozen figures illuminate some aspects of Ibn Ishaq's treatment of Muhammad that Qur'anic stories don't support, at least to the "uninformed" reader/listener. One aspect is God's ability to wake the dead/asleep (the Seven Sleepers), revive the dead (Samson), or take someone into heaven alive (Ezra), as well as His wonder-working on behalf of messengers, which is central to Ibn Ishaq's retelling of the story of Solomon. Second, Ibn Ishaq emphasizes the miraculous attributes of messengers: wondrous births and pre-births, as in the case of Khidr, or the ability to see the unseen, as in the case of Samuel. A third aspect is Ibn Ishaq's sense of eschatology, as in Isaiah's foretelling of Jesus and Muhammad. A fourth is variants on the relationship between God's revelation and temporal authority, as in, for example, the story of Alexander. In other ways too, these twelve figures take Qur'anic stories further, particularly on the theme of rewards for suffering on behalf of one's faith and ultimately triumphing. The rejection of prophets becomes a very important theme, not just in these extra-Qur'anic stories, but also throughout the *Sīrah*. It is important to note that Ibn Ishaq wrote at a time when there was considerable resistance to caliphal rule, and extensive polemic in other communities against Muhammad and his community's beliefs and practices.

In the end, for Ibn Ishaq, all messengers are comparable with others, comparable meaning not only that they all share the same office, but

---

44. *Ibid.*: 193–200.

that all before Muhammad prefigure him. Since there will be no books or messengers after him, he is in effect given an eschatological role, embodying a key transitional point in cosmic history. He ushers out an age in which messengers are present in the world in person, and he ushers in a new and final historical age in which the presence of the message becomes the major fact before the eschaton. During Ibn Ishaq's day, the notion of another eschatological role for Muhammad was also developing, not of primary end-of-time redeemer (usually called *mahdī*), but of guide for his community on the Day of Judgment. For Sunnis, the open-ended closure of which I have spoken came in many forms, one of which was the development of Hadith as a source of personal piety and ethico-legal guidance.

Muhammad's own words as exemplary profile

In Ibn Ishaq's day, Hadith about Muhammad were becoming a genre unto themselves. These reports of the life and sayings of Muhammad were a major vehicle for establishing his identity as ethical and legal exemplar (i.e., his identity as a standard of proper Muslim conduct, perhaps even proper human conduct).[45] However, the use of Hadith and the understanding of Sunna were not limited to these purposes.

---

45. Especially controversial is the subject of the role the Hadith accounts in the development of early and consequent Muslim self-understandings and self-regulations, which has been disputed since the very beginning of modern Islamic studies. Herbert Berg provides a lengthy review and analysis of extant literature, and also offers his own method of deciphering provenance of a body of the Hadith: Herbert Berg, ed., *Development of Exegesis in Early Islam: The Authenticity of Muslim Literature from the Formative Period* (Richmond, UK: Curzon Press, 2000). Chase Robinson, like Berg, argues that the quest for the authenticity of the Sunna has often been "at the expense of its significance and cultural meanings": Chase Robinson, "Reconstructing Early Islam: Truth and Consequences," *Method and Theory in the Study of Islamic Origins*, ed. Herbert Berg (Leiden, The Netherlands: Brill, 2003): 118. Daniel Brown provides an important contribution to the study of cultural meanings of the Sunna: Daniel Brown, *Rethinking Tradition in Modern Islamic Thought* (Cambridge: Cambridge University Press, 1996). He outlines, for example, early views on Sunna as "sound conduct," not necessarily a canonized record of Muhammad's actions and word (9). Also of special pertinence is Scott C. Lucas's analysis of the role of Hadith scholars in formulating Sunni orthodox interpretations of Muhammad: Scott C. Lucas, *Constructive Critics, Hadith Literature, and the Articulation of Sunni Islam: The Legacy of the Generation of Ibn Sa'd, Ibn Ma'in, and Ibn Hanbal* (Leiden, The Netherlands: Brill, 2004).—Ed.

They were also quoted, collected, and used to comment on the Qur'an (*tafsīr*), and furthermore, employed to narrate Muhammad's career as *nabī/rasūl* (*sīra*), describe military campaigns (*maghāzī*), and recount the history of the community (*Ṭabaqāt, tārīkh*). The multifaceted elaboration of Sunna provided ways for Muslims to compare themselves to Muhammad as Muslims without comparing themselves to him as *nabī/ rasūl*.[46] We will also want to see whether this detailed elaboration of Muhammad as multifaceted model made Islamic identities more or less inviting than other competing identities at the time.

We will want to ask whether the extent of the halo effect—the spread of Muhammad's aura from the *nabī/rasūl* role to other aspects of his person—was unusual in early Islamic intercommunal interaction, or at least whether other communities could have perceived it as unusual. We need more research on what kinds of personal exemplars were available to other communities and also within the Muslim community. I argue that Muhammad was unusual in how much attention was focused on him, even among Muslim alternatives, as a single person and as object of attraction. It's also interesting that his record could provide such a broad standard of comparison for ordinary human behavior and at the same time be acquiring more and more wondrous non-ordinary qualities without becoming divinized. As we analyze that, of course, we need to think of Muhammad as situated on a larger map of exemplification.

In general, in the areas occupied by Muslims during the initial expansion of Islam, the power of a bearer of privileging communication could certainly be limited to that person's extraordinary speech and statements, and might not extend to his or her whole person. Many such figures appear to have been authoritative on the basis of a relatively small part of their entire persons. Even in the Qur'an, the fact that one had chosen to deliver divine messages did not mean that everything about his or her person should be taken as exemplary. Even if it did, there were also other authorities, such as tribal elders, who could, and did, set exemplary precedent through their persons. We know for certain that an individual could be recognized as a bearer of special messages but might not be recognized as an exemplary human being,

---

46. For more on this, see Jonathan A.C. Brown, "Criticism of the Proto-Hadith Canon: Al-Daraqutni's Adjustment of Al-Bukhari and Muslim's Sahihs," *Oxford Journal of Islamic Studies* 15.1 (2004): 1–37. Brown suggests that the the Sahih Hadith collections of Muhammad b. Ismail al-Bukhari (d. 256 AH/870 CE) and Muslim b. al-Hajjaj (d. 261 AH/875 CE) became a synecdoche standing for the prophet as exemplar, at onæ elevating him and avoiding the content of his Sunna.

or as a model for other human beings to emulate. Moses, for example, could serve as a model person, called by God and faithful to His will, but his personal behavior did not become the major source of precedent for the details of Talmudic law, nor has a record of it comparable to Hadith been compiled. In fact, it is a character failing that becomes one of his distinguishing features and keeps him out of the promised land. Jesus is more obviously a personal exemplar, but he is divine model as well as human model. "Imitation of Christ" certainly meant conforming to his life in the broad sense, but not necessarily to the fine details of his mundane behaviors. As Fred Denny has observed:

> Both [Jesus and Muhammad] ... were so close to the source of their inspiration and so thoroughly dominated by it that in their words and gestures people have discovered clues and demonstrations of divine activity in the historical process. Jesus shows how God behaves among his creatures. Muhammad's life is exemplary in showing people how they should behave in the presence of God. The Muslims move heavenward through Muhammad, whereas the Christians receive their Lord in his earthward condescension, which later moves toward an ascension.[47]

As Muslims acquired a reworked understanding of these earlier figures, they assigned them an exemplary role similar to Muhammad's. For example, in a famous letter addressed to the Caliph Umar II (reigned 717–720 CE), Hasan al-Basri justified his exhortation to poverty by invoking the character of four major messengers of God: Muhammad, Moses, Jesus, and David.[48] In fact, this extension of personal moral exemplification to figures not treated in that way by other religious communities provides further evidence for the distinctly Islamic nature of this distinctive linkage between messengership and exemplification. At the same time that accounts of Muhammad's career began to appear, the Hadith were being consolidated as a literary form for conveying Muhammad's Sunna. Interested primarily in declaring Muhammad the best interpreter of the Qur'an, one important party among the *'ulamā* (learned men) argued that Muhammad's Sunna was the only one that

---

47. Frederick Mathewson Denny, *An Introduction to Islam*, second edition (New York: Macmillan Publishing Company, 1994): 158.

48. See Suleiman Ali Mourad, *Early Islam between Myth and History: Al-Hasan Al-Basrī (D. 110H/728 CE) and the Formation of His Legacy in Classical Islamic Scholarship* (Leiden, The Netherlands and Boston, MA: Brill, 2006): 121–39.—Ed.

mattered, and that only these written texts, the Hadith, as transmitted by Muhammad's own associates, could reliably document it. It was these individuals who were the victors in an intra-Muslim conflict for control of both the form and the content of the collective memory of Muhammad and the history of the community—which translated into control of the institutions and standards of the social order. Some of their opponents placed no particular emphasis on Sunna; others argued for the Sunna of the early community and its successors more broadly; and still others for the "living Sunna" (i.e. the agreed-upon practices, assumed to be continuous with Muhammad's time, of pious Muslims).[49] However, for the Hadith-minded or Hadith folk, Muhammad was obviously the best interpreter of revelation and the model for imitation, not least in his everyday fastidiousness.[50] Accompanying the victory of the Hadith-minded was the emergence of the doctrine of *'isma*:

> That every act he [Muhammad] made after the beginning of the Revelation was preserved by God from error; had it not been so, then the Revelation itself would be cast into doubt, a thing God could never have permitted. Therefore, Muhammad's slightest act was rightly guided and of moral value. For traditional Muslims, everything the Prophet did is a part of his Sunna: his treatment of children, the way he broke his fast, how he cleaned his teeth and wore his beard, are all worthy of study and emulation.[51]

The doctrine of protectedness from error was also extended to other messengers before Muhammad, but as the Muslim community expanded and came to exercise its hegemony, Muhammad was raised above all others as the most perfect exemplar.[52]

By the end of the ninth century, the singularity of Muhammad's Sunna and his ability to interpret the Qur'an had also been extended to his authority as legislator, largely through the efforts of Muhammad b.

---

49. Daniel Brown gives a summary of various understandings of "Sunna" before al-Shafi'i. See Daniel Brown, *Rethinking Tradition in Modern Islamic Thought*: 8–17.—Ed.

50. On distinguishing the Hadith folk from their eighth- and ninth-century contemporaries, see Christopher Melchert, "The Piety of the Hadith Folk," *International Journal of Middle East Studies* 34 (2002): 425–39.—Ed.

51. John Alden Williams, *Islam* (New York: G. Braziller, 1961): 84–5.

52. The issue of *isma* evolved into the doctrine of prophetic infallibility, even though it does not sit well with orthodoxy, especially because of its comparability to the Shi'ite notion of the charismatic flawlessness. See Brown, *Rethinking Tradition in Modern Islamic Thought*: 60–63.

Idris al-Shafi'i (died 820).[53] As a student of *fiqh* (legal understanding), al-Shafi'i traveled widely in Muslim-governed lands to study in the major centers of Muslim learning. His experience of considerable diversity in legal practice and method moved him to argue for a uniformity of source criticism. After insisting on the Qur'an as the primary source of law, he made Muhammad's Sunna the next source, followed by communal consensus (*ijmā'*) and analogical reasoning (*qiyās*). By the time of al-Shafi'i, the power of the caliphs' administrative law was threatening to displace the emergent sacred law, and al-Shafi'i's system of legal reasoning provided a more powerful competitor than other available versions, since it replaced "a multiplicity of starting points with that of a tradition which stemmed from a single origin, the [divinely-inspired] actions of Muhammad."[54] Despite later modifications, his "fundamental thesis—that the terms of the divine will were more precisely indicated than had hitherto been recognized, that the supreme manifestation of God's will lay in the Sunna, or practice of Muhammad, and that the function of human reason in law was subsidiary and complementary—was never after him seriously challenged."[55]

The scope and detail of Shari'ah is stunning. While Halakhic law is its closest parallel, Shari'ah defines duties even more precisely than does the Jewish Talmud or later European jurists. Indeed, an early modern European jurist would be struck not just by the interpretive detail, but also by the mixing of what appears to be the unimportant and

---

53. Much contemporary scholarship has been devoted to the role and influence of Shafi'i, see for instance Joseph E. Lowry, *The Legal-Theoretical Content of the Risāla of Muhammad B. Idrīs Al-Shāfi'ī*, PhD thesis, University of Pennsylvania, 1999. See also Bernard G. Weiss, ed., *Studies in Islamic Legal Theory* (Leiden, The Netherlands: Brill, 2002). Of note is Weiss's other volume, which explores Shafi'i's influence on the inheritors of his methodology: Bernard G. Weiss, *Search for God's Law Islamic Jurisprudence in the Writings of Sayf Al-Dīn Al-Āmidī* (Salt Lake City, UT: University of Utah Press, 1992). In light of what follows in this chapter, particularly interesting is Wael Hallaq's suggestion that although Shafi'i's legal thought came to re-shape the field, it was virtually ignored for several decades after his death. See Wael B. Hallaq, "Was Al-Shafi'i the Master Architect of the Islamic Jurisprudence?," *International Journal of Middle East Studies* 4 (1993). Also, see Asma Afsaruddin, *The First Muslims: History and Memory* (Oxford: OneWorld Publications, 2007). She notes that "recognition of the profundity of al-Shafi'i's legal formulations did not happen right away, but rather occurred toward the end of the ninth century, when the genuine synthesis between rationalism and mystical traditionalism took place" (139).—Ed.

54. Noel J. Coulson, *A History of Islamic Law* (Edinburgh: Edinburgh University Press, 1964): 57.

55. *Ibid.*: 61.

important, mundane and sublime: from the most earth-bound bodily functions (eating, elimination, hygiene, clothing and ornamentation, copulation, and awakening), through societal necessities and niceties (taxation, contracts, marriage, inheritance, and salutations), to the most transcendent aspirations and obligations (compassion, generosity, prayer, pilgrimage, and fasting). As G.E. Von Grunebaum explained, "The distinction between important actions and unimportant detail of daily routine loses much of its meaning when every step is thought of as prescribed by divine ordinance."[56] The act of emulating Muhammad extends beyond the individual Muslim; it is also a means of reinforcing a sense of community. According to S.H. Nasr, the fact that all Muslims use Muhammad as an exemplar provides a foundation of community among Muslims.

> For nearly fourteen hundred years Muslims have tried to awaken in the morning as the Prophet awakened, to eat as he ate, to wash as he washed himself, even to cut their nails as he did. There has been no greater force for the unification of the Muslim peoples than the presence of this common model for the minutest acts of daily life.[57]

Fine distinctions aside, the scope, range, and detail of Halakha and Shari'ah are recurrently similar. Halakha, or more properly Talmud or Oral Torah, stands in a similar relationship to Written Torah as Shari'ah does to Qur'an. However, unlike Halakha, Shari'ah uses a single human exemplar as legislator, model, and legal precedent. Moses' legislation is, of course, precedent-setting for the Talmud, but not his personal speech and acts. Furthermore, although both Halakha and Shari'ah aim to cultivate a certain kind of person, Shari'ah, as the legal system of a politically hegemonic community, also tries to shape the larger society in which such an individual would flourish. Whereas the anthropology of Halakha imagines human beings living in detailed accord with God's will without the ability to shape the larger society, Shari'ah reflects an Islamic anthropology that envisages pious humans as situated in the ideal society, and helped by this community to overcome their inborn limitations. According to this anthropology, which recognizes what is as well as what can be, all human beings are "muslim," forgetful, ethical, and gendered.

---

56. Gustave E. Von Grunebaum, *Medieval Islam: A Study in Cultural Orientation* (Chicago: University of Chicago Press, 1953): 108.
57. Seyyed Hossein Nasr, *Ideals and Realities of Islam* (Chicago, IL: ABC International Group, 2000): 82.

The human as muslim

What is known of the history of Muhammad's career suggests that "islam" and "muslim" began as generic concepts that were later, of necessity, "capitalized," in all senses of the word. Since most pre-modern Muslims were not readers, and since none of the written forms of their languages used case markers, most if not all words carried the possibility of being generic and/or proper, depending on context. In the Qur'an, a muslim is someone who is also *mu'min*, which means, roughly, "faithful to God and His messengers." A muslim is also some-one who does islam, which is presented as the relationship established by any human being who recognizes God's oneness, worships Him exclusively, and avoids *shirk* (the assigning to God of any partners). Since one messenger of God before Muhammad, Abraham, is explic-itly called "muslim" in the Qur'an (2:131), the term cannot have been entirely restricted to the particular historical community that later capi-talized it.

Even after "islam" and "muslim" came to be thought of as proper nouns, probably before Muhammad's death, they continued to refer to the natural and original spiritual state of human beings. Islam is described as "natural" because human beings are automatically inclined to it before they are made into something else by historically specific communities, and "original" because the first human being, Adam, was in that relationship with God, as was Abraham, who was the ancestor of Arabs and Israelites and the founder of the Ka'ba in Mecca. The religion of islam has been offered to all humanity since the beginning of time, but is temporarily represented only by the community of Muhammad, which successfully achieved it. In other words, "Islam" and "Muslim" are only proper nouns in the meantime, until they become universal again and refer to all humanity. Islam was the religion of all humans before the emergence of historically specific communities (i.e., Jews and Christians), and can become so again when the sustained Muslim domination of various subject populations has made it possible for non-Muslims to come to islam again.[58]

When one looks at the kind of human being Shari'ah seeks to shape, one is, in the short run, looking at guidelines for Muslims, with a capital

---

58. On the issue of the emergence of "muslim" as a community marker, especially imagined within a larger schematization of prophetic history, see Fred Donner, *Narratives of Islamic Origins:* 275ff., and now also Fred Donner, *Muhammad and the Believers: At the Origins of Islam* (Cambridge, MA: Harvard University Press, 2010): 71–2.—Ed.

"M," but in the long run at potential guidelines for all other human beings who are invited to become "muslims." Moreover, since Shari'ah accords a higher status to Muslims and takes precedence over the codes of the subject communities, Shari'ah is by definition the code capable of becoming universal. Similarly, although Muhammad is presented as the model for the ideal Muslim, he is by extension the ideal human being—the culmination of a long, continuous, and unitary series of God's messengers to humanity.

The human as forgetful

Muhammad represents a human being who, through God's guidance, overcame his human limitations and helped other human beings to do the same. The Qur'an presents the human being as inherently likely to fall away from God's guidance without the help of human messengers to remind humanity of His will. Like Jews and Christians, Muslims have used the Garden of Eden story to substantiate their anthropology. However, to Muslims the story does not describe a fall from a relationship with God that can be recovered only through a new covenant with a particular people, nor does it describe the inception of sin that can be overcome only through a cosmic event. Rather, it describes human beings as human—that is, as created beings dependent on a creator, and therefore possessed of mental limitations that only the creator can help them overcome. Although the Qur'an itself does not tell the story of the Garden of Eden, it makes the same point in its own way through its repeated identification of the Garden of Eden with the Garden of Paradise, which is promised as a reward for those who remember to follow God's guidance (Qur'an 7:19–25).[59] Since it is their natural forgetfulness that allows humans to make mistakes, the remedy for the human condition is mindfulness and guidance. The more specific the guidance, the more likely correct behavior will ensue.

One could even say that being reminded (*dhikr*) is one of the key motifs of all of Islamic culture. Muslims are reminded by Qur'anic quotations on the walls of mosques, by frequent quoting of Hadith or Qur'an, and by having a clear and detailed path, Shari'ah, to follow. Shari'ah, like many sacred institutions, is conceived of as a way to help human beings overcome, though not erase, an inborn limitation. This

---

59. Also, see Brannon Wheeler, *Mecca and Eden: Ritual, Relics, and Territory in Islam* (Chicago, IL: University of Chicago Press, 2006).—Ed.

reminding is considered all the more necessary because one of the most important things that humans tend to forget is being born muslim and what that entails.

The human as ethical (or at least capable of ethical judgment)

Despite the image of Islamic law as coercive and filled with severe penalties, the penalty structure of Islam accounts for only a small proportion of the whole, and is not the primary reason why it has become such a pervasive influence in Muslim communities. Most matters dealt with in Shari'ah are not in the category of acts that have a clear earthly penalty or clear remedy of any sort, and much of what is recommended or required in Shari'ah is good or bad irrespective of earthly penalties or remedies. The tendency of many modern Muslim governments to focus on the penalty-structure, the most visible aspect of the system, has diverted attention away from the predominant emphasis in Shari'ah on the striving for moral perfection and the cultivation of ethical judgment, and its preference for exhortative rather than punitive control.[60]

I am using both "moral" and "ethical" in their dictionary senses:

> Moral: 1. Of or relating to principles of right and wrong in behavior: ethical. 2. Expressing or teaching a conception of right behavior. 3. Conforming to a standard of right behavior. 4. Sanctioned by or operative on one's conscience or ethical judgment. 5. Capable of right and wrong action.[61]

> Ethical: 1. Of or relating to ethics. 2. Involving or expressing moral approval or disapproval. 3. Conforming to accepted standards of conduct.[62]

I stress these dictionary definitions because the ways "moral" and "ethical" are commonly used in spoken English exclude many of the areas of

---

60. Nigeria and Pakistan are the most evident examples. For a contemporary Muslim voice opposing this punitive reading of the Shari'a, see Muhammad Khalid Masud, Brinkley Morris Messick, and David Powers, eds, *Islamic Legal Interpretation: Muftis and Their Fatwas*, Harvard Studies in Islamic law (Cambridge, MA: Harvard University Press, 1996).—Ed.

61. *Merriam-Webster's Collegiate Dictionary* (through Encyclopaedia Britannica online), http://search.eb.com/dictionary?va=moral&x=25&y=19, accessed 16 August 2010.

62. *Merriam-Webster's Collegiate Dictionary* (through Encyclopaedia Britannica online), http://search.eb.com/dictionary?va=ethical&x=0&y=0, accessed 16 August 2010.

practice, conduct, and behavior addressed by Shari'ah. They also ignore the sense in which the human is presented as capable of thinking about morals (cultivating "ethical judgment") and of embodying, enacting, and experiencing moral values (striving for moral perfection).

To grasp the layers of interpretation in pre-modern Muslim thought, one must distinguish between moral and ethical, or between practice and reflection on the practice of norms. Shari'ah has both moral and ethical dimensions, which are closely related to its dependence on the Sunna, which in turn presents Muhammad and those who appear in the Hadith with him enacting exemplary moral behavior at the same time as they reveal ethical concerns by frequently reflecting on the moral rectitude of their actions. As observed by Tarif Khalidi, "The Hadith is full of real persons struggling with concrete problems."[63] Khalidi also notes that the majority of Hadith relate to Muhammad's Medinan period and that "Hadith, therefore, has tended to leave its imprint on Islam by concentrating on a period of the Prophet's life when he was legislating for his community, with an emphasis on man's deeds. The good deed is at the heart of Islamic life in Hadith."[64] Or, as Marshall Hodgson puts it, "the dominant tone of Muhammad's piety was to suffuse everyday life with a powerful sense of transcendently divine requirements."[65] In Hadith, Muhammad is often presented as demonstrating his preferences, not asserting or theorizing them, as in the following example:

> Uqba ibn Amir said, "Someone sent the Prophet a silk gown and he wore it during the prayers, but on withdrawing he pulled it off violently with a gesture of disgust and said, 'This is unfitting for Godfearing men.'"[66]

The preference for morality that is demonstrated on specific occasions also left considerable room for scholars to interpret the implications and applications of these enactments of values. The example of the silk gown can be used to consider how the Sunna was used to derive the moral and legal prescriptions of Shari'ah. To paraphrase Hodgson's delineation of the same process, Muhammad avoided wearing silk (Sunna); there is a report to that effect (Hadith) transmitted through a chain of reporters (*sanad*); the *mujtahid* (one who applies his reasoning) studies this

---

63. Tarif Khalidi, *Classical Arab Islam: The Culture and Heritage of the Golden Age* (Princeton, NJ: The Darwin Press, 1984): 35.

64. *Ibid.*: 43.

65. Marshall G.S. Hodgson, *The Venture of Islam*: 185.

66. H.A.R. Gibb, *Mohammedanism* (New York: Oxford University Press, 1962): 51.

report (*ijtihād*) and decides that its use is recommended not only for Muhammad but for the ordinary male believer (*fiqh*); it is therefore to be included in Shari'ah, and a mufti (consultant) may deliver a *fatwa* (opinion) to an inquirer, telling him he should do it, but as it is merely recommended, the judge (*qadi*) will assess no penalty if he does not.[67]

Shari'ah is not a legal system in the Western sense of the term. Rather, it is a system of law and morality, prescriptions and norms, which are not fully merged with one another. From this perspective, works of Shari'ah are ethical as well as legal treatises, if one thinks of "ethical" in the sense of "treating of morals, morality, or ethics" or "of or relating to moral action, motive or character." As Noel Coulson explains:

> The ideal code of behavior which is the Shariah has in fact a much wider scope and purpose than a simple legal system in the Western sense of the term. Jurisprudence (*fiqh*) not only regulates in meticulous detail the ritual practices of the faith and matters which could be classified as medical hygiene or social etiquette—legal treatises, indeed, invariably deal with these topics first; it is also a composite science of law and morality, whose exponents (*fuqahā'*, sing. *faqīh*) are the guardians of the Islamic conscience.[68]

Just as dependence on Sunna promotes the ethical emphasis of Shari'ah, so do the contents of its other major source, the Qur'an. The Qur'an is predominantly ethical, not legal; law in the narrow sense is very scarce in the Qur'an. There are only about six hundred verses of the Qur'an (less than ten per cent) that even pertain to rule-governed activities, and most of those have to do with a range of matters both narrower than Shari'ah and broader than our conception of law (e.g., prayer, fasting, pilgrimage, inheritance, sexuality, marriage, and divorce). Only about eighty verses contain specific prescriptions. Naturally, because of such inevitable ellipticism, Shari'ah scholars, like the rabbis, fleshed out the sacred text considerably. For example, the Qur'an forbids both wine drinking and usury, but assigns a penalty to the former and not to the latter. Shari'ah places wine drinking in the category of criminal offense and specifies the penalty of flogging, but puts usury in the category of civil acts, where it becomes merely an instance of invalid contract with no penalty except the lapsing of the contract.[69]

---

67. See Hodgson's schematic model, involving Muhammad's use of a toothpick, in Hodgson, *The Venture of Islam:* 338.—Ed.
68. Coulson, *A History of Islamic Law:* 83.
69. *Ibid.:* 11–12.

Furthermore, there are some topics in Shari'ah literature that are not treated in the Qur'an. Perhaps the most interesting example is contraception (natural, mechanical, and herbal). Somewhat like Maimonides, Muslim legal scholars took an interest in medical matters. But unlike their pre-modern Jewish and Christian counterparts, pre-modern Muslim legal scholars, unconstrained by any scriptural prohibitions, took a generally positive attitude toward contraception, recognizing the right of both males and females to satisfy their sexual appetites lawfully. The theological justification hinged on a Hadith: "There is not a soul who is [destined] to be born for the day of resurrection, but that it will be born [in this world]."[70] From this Hadith, and an assumption that God's power should not be shared or diminished in any way, it was reasoned that, since contraception is not totally reliable, God could interfere any time He wished. While Shari'ah does strive to discipline the body, it also affirms desire by placing it within a rule-governed context.

In addition to the general absence of penalties and remedies, the way Shari'ah classifies acts requires frequent judgment and exercise of conscience. Most acts fall between obligatory and prohibited, and even where punishments and rewards are specified, they are most often postponed to the Hereafter. Al-Shafi'i and his successors devised the following categorization of human actions:[71]

- *wājib* (obligatory), commission rewarded, omission punished;
- *mandūb* (recommended but not obligatory), commission rewarded, but omission not punished;
- *mubāh* (indifferent or permissible), no consequences for reward or punishment;
- *makrūh* (disapproved but not forbidden), omission rewarded, but commission not punished; and
- *harām* (prohibited), commission punished, but omission not rewarded.

The voluntary nature of the system, its amorphousness and vastness, and its attempt to be comprehensive of all quotidian behavior, was an asset to its being "enforced" in another sense, through ease of invocation. Since it came to be woven almost unconsciously into the

---

70. John Alden Williams, *Islam*: 115. Also, see Williams's translation of Bukhari, *Sahih*, VII, 137.

71. Coulson, *A History of Islamic Law*: 84. Also, see Hallaq, "Was Al-Shafi'i the Master Architect of the Islamic Jurisprudence?," 40–41.—Ed.

fabric of many of these societies, people could think they were following it without seeking documentation. Since a high correlation could
be assumed between what Shari'ah and Sunna required and what good
Muslims did in their daily life, much of what good Muslims did day
to day could be assumed to be in Shari'ah or Sunna without the need
to check. Sometimes, unfortunately, such invocation could be used to
justify social practices less desirable than its highest ideals. For, as with
any large and often orally transmitted corpus, highly selective invocation can be used to support almost any desired end.

The human as gendered

Since Shari'ah frequently establishes different norms and makes separate provisions for men and women, it obviously views the human as a
creature with gender. Furthermore, it presents its quintessential human
exemplar as clearly male, not a surprising phenomenon in any society
which has taken males to be the unmarked case. Yet the actual picture
of gender in Shari'ah, Sunna, and Hadith is more complicated, and
much less studied, than one would think. Muhammad is not explicitly
presented as a model for males only, but his being a model for females
is also not stressed, or even explicitly raised. The issue of gender is not
foregrounded, or at least normative practices are not organized around
it. There are ways in which women cannot emulate Muhammad, yet
there are also ways in which Muhammad has served as an exemplar
for women. This is in part due to the fact that, as in most patri-oriented
societies, a male exemplar can simply "be said" to transcend gender,
whereas a female exemplar is for females only. Yet at the same time
that there are ways in which Muhammad has served as an exemplar
for women, there are also ways in which Muhammad serves as a guide
when he cannot serve as a model.

Although we can assume that large numbers of women have followed Muhammad's guidance (i.e., his legislation or prescriptions), we
have no reliable information, almost no information at all, on whether
or how much women have in the past tried to emulate him. All we can
do, and encourage others to do, is to begin by surveying and delineat-
ing, in a sober fashion, the various ways in which women have been
involved in Sunna, Hadith, and Shari'ah. There are at least six ways,
many of them overlapping and expanding, that stand out.

First, simply because Muhammad was male, there are some behaviors and traits that men can emulate and women cannot, either because

they pertain to roles and attributes objectively male (e.g., trimming the beard, being named Muhammad) or generally considered masculine by the societies in which his emulation originated (e.g., going to war). But these same traits, if generalized to a higher level of abstraction or taken as metaphors, could be emulated by women. Furthermore, there are some things that might or might not be unisex depending on the context. Guidelines for greeting those encountered in the street could be used by both genders in theory, but in practice women in some places have little occasion to be on the street or by custom tend to greet each other more subtly than men do, and of course, are not required to greet men at all, which many view as a comfort. There is no way to know when possible exclusions functioned as actual exclusions from male society, but it is clear that women as women received guidance from Muhammad by his telling them what to do, rather than by his showing them, whereas Muhammad in the Sunna can demonstrate how to be male as well as how to be human.

Second, in Kelibia, Tunisia, the use of kohl on the eyes is a case where we can see how fluid the gendered use of Sunna can sometimes be. In the Sunna, Muhammad recommends the use of kohl for health reasons. In Kelibia, although kohl is used medicinally on infants of both sexes and sometimes by adult men for the same purpose, it is generally used as adornment only by women. Although women are by custom prohibited from wearing make-up at funerals, some women argue that kohl can be worn at funerals because according to Muhammad's Sunna, it is a health aid and not an adornment, that is, a substance for humans, not just for women. Men, who generally do not wear kohl, sometimes do wear it at celebrations of the birthday (*mawlid*) of Muhammad, because he was given to using it, and on this occasion he is being remembered as a messenger of God, not as a male. So the use of an item well documented in the Sunna varies by gender and occasion depending on what is being foregrounded.

Third, there are other personal behaviors, as well as non-gender-specific qualities, that women can emulate, such as compassion, generosity, and pious self-discipline (even if their forms of piety may, in some instances, differ from men's—going on pilgrimage to sites associated especially with women, for example, or praying at home rather than in the mosque). In a popular reader on Islam, out of a dozen Hadith chosen to illustrate Muhammad as exemplar, all are either not presented in a gender-specific way, could easily be generalized to women, or involve women in some way. These Hadith treat kindness to animals, kindness to humans (transmitted through Aisha), moderation in religious observance (as conveyed by Muhammad's wives), accept-ability of contraception (in this case *coitus interruptus*), enjoying fresh dates and cucumbers, the need to accept death and to show compassion and mercy to the bereaved (occasioned by an incident involving one of Muhammad's daughters), avoidance of judging others, avoidance of oppression, rewards for lawful satisfaction of appetites (including conjugal relations), and the need for un-self-interested love of fellow human beings.[72] Whether women actually chose to emulate the things they could, such as Muhammad's tastes in food or style of teeth-clean-ing, is of course impossible to know on a statistically significant level, just as it is impossible to know which aspects of the Sunna have been stressed in which times and places.[73]

Fourth, through Sunna, and by extension Shari'ah, Muhammad has legislated or recommended for women in many different scenarios, sometimes to their advantage over men and sometimes not, depending on one's point of view. A case of the former: because Muhammad found silk and gold unbefitting a pious male, Muslim men who emulate him do not wear them, but he did not disallow them for women. The ability to wear gold has played an important part in the economics of being female, giving women a significant degree of financial protection and independence.

Fifth, sometimes Muhammad, through his Sunna, encouraged posi-tive views of women, as in the Hadith, "Learn half of your religion from *al-humayra*" (the "little ruddy one"), the Prophet's nickname for A'isha.[74] In certain cases, both sexes have enjoyed the same advice, for example, because the Prophet enjoyed perfume, it is permitted for all. But in the case of a similar exhortation to modesty directed to both

---

72. See Arthur Jeffery, ed., *A Reader on Islam: Passages from Standard Arabic Writings Illustrative of the Beliefs and Practices of Muslims* (The Hague, The Netherlands: Mouton & Co., 1962).

73. Note, for example, the anti-female or misogynist character of some Hadith highlighted in Fatima Mernissi, *The Veil and the Male Elite: A Feminist Interpretation of Women's Rights in Islam*, trans. Mary Jo Lakeland (New York: Basic Books,, 1991). Contrast this with the positive evaluation of 'A'isha as Hadith expert in D.A. Spellberg, *Politics, Gender, and the Islamic Past: The Legacy of A'isha Bint Abi Bakr* (New York: Columbia University Press, 1986).—Ed.

74. See Spellberg, *Politics, Gender, and the Islamic Past:* 55. Spellberg quotes Muhammad ibn Bahadur al-Zarkashi, *Al-Ijaba Li-Irad Ma Istadrakathu 'A'isha 'Ala Al-Sahaba* (Cairo, Egypt: Matba'at al-'Asima, 1965). Also see Nadia Abbot, *'A'isha: The Beloved of Mohammed* (Chicago, IL: University of Chicago Press, 1942).—Ed.

men and women, the specific forms of modest dress that emerged for women, not required in the Hadith, Sunna, or Shari'ah, proved considerably more restrictive than acceptably modest dress for men, and also got bound up with an austere sense of women's honor. Women, especially those related to Muhammad or his Companions, often figure in the Hadith stories, and played an important role in transmitting Hadith. Women also could and did invoke the Sunna for their own purposes, either themselves or through a male surrogate. For instance, since the cases that most often come before the *qadi* are likely to relate to family law, women may have often appeared in Shari'ah courts, accompanied by a man, who, as Richard Antoun's fieldwork shows, "speaks for, or more accurately, attempts to speak for them."[75]

And finally, the Sunna makes a more nuanced place for women than does the Qur'an, which acknowledges their equality before God but subordinates them to males both in this life and the next. In this connection, one would want to consider the female relatives of Muhammad who become special role models for women, especially Khadija, A'isha, and Fatima. Furthermore, beyond the Sunna are a series of other female role models, some of whom are treated as models for males, too, such as Rabia, the mystic, and Usamah b. Munqidh's mother.[76]

The Prophet, his family, and the Imams

Overlapping with the development of Hadith was a series of social movements that looked to additional kinds of final figures, and as a result redefined Muhammad's eschatological role. In many of these cases, "finality" meant the end of historical time, rather than the inauguration of a final historical age. I will focus on the Imami Shi'is and their use of comparison with Muhammad and other messengers. At the same time, I will introduce the notion of the subtle difference between similar and same, or what it took to be just different enough to be very similar without inviting exclusion from Muslim identity.

---

75. Richard T. Antoun, *Muslim Preacher in the Modern World: A Jordanian Case Study in Comparative Perspective* (Princeton, NJ: Princeton University Press, 1989).

76. Among the numerous recent works on Islam and gender in the formative years of Islamicate civilization, see Kecia Ali, *Sexual Ethics and Islam: Feminist Reflections on Qur'an, Hadith and Jurisprudence* (Oxford: OneWorld, 2006) and Omid Safi, *Memories of Muhammad* (San Francisco, CA: Harper, 2010).—Ed.

I want to focus specifically on the development of the concept of the imamate at the hands of Imām Ja'far al-Sādiq's (died 765).[77] It is interesting to note that Ja'far was roughly contemporaneous with Ibn Ishaq. Both tried to push the limits without crossing the line of what could be acceptable to their communities. At the time that both men lived, there were many figures emerging among Muslims and non-Muslims who claimed elevated status for themselves. Some were self-categorized as *nabī/rasūl* like Muhammad, bringing a new book and thus not accepting Ibn Ishaq's interpretation of the seal of prophets. Some claimed to be end-of-time redeemers, or to be the last harbingers of such figures. Some claimed to be divine or partly divine. Much of this activity was aimed, by the figures themselves or by their followers, at the authority of the caliphs, and much of it manifested itself in armed rebellions against them. After all, the Abbasids themselves had started out as just such a movement, and had in fact usurped the caliphate.

To use a baseball metaphor, the Shi'i segment that became most secure and most numerous located itself in left field, but not outside the park. One might say it was the most successful alternative to an Ibn Ishaq-like "seal of the prophets" interpretation of Muhammad. This stance involved a careful comparative positioning. It posited as extreme those people and things that threatened political accommodation with the authorities, at the same time that it openly maintained differences that were just barely acceptable by the majority, and hid those that weren't. The doctrine I want to focus on is the view of the Imamate as the continuation of the Prophet, and where, in this way, "the Imams together form the foundation of *al-takif al-sam'i* [duties known by revelation or something dependent on it]."[78] The Prophet and the Imams, in this view, are the *hujaj* (proofs) of the revelation, and "through these *hujaj* ... God makes His will known to mankind and exposes them to the attainment of *al-thawab* [reward]."[79]

Shi'is understood Muhammad's temporal functions to be fused with his prophetic functions to such an extent that their leader, the Imam of the Age, could, and did, interpret the Qur'anic messages as an echo of the Prophet. Their leader, though not in the same category as Muhammad, also combined those two functions, which was insured by sharing blood with Muhammad. However, according to the teaching

77. See Abdulaziz Abdulhussein Sachedina, *Islamic Messianism: The Idea of the Mahdi in Twelver Shi'ism* (Albany, NY: State University of New York Press, 1981).

78. *Ibid.*: 119.

79. *Ibid.*: 119.

of Ja'far, they will not be fully combined until the messianic Imam returns. Meanwhile the Imam of the Age reigns but does not rule, again making him different from Muhammad. The Imams are not the same as prophets, but, through this maneuver, they have equal status. The former continue the latter's work: they do not bring a new Qur'an, but function rather as the speaking Qur'an, keeping alive Muhammad's ability to interpret the Qur'an without distorting it. As Sachedina puts it, "the Prophet and the Imam both stand as the *hujja* of God on an equal footing, or rather, the later *hujja* (i.e., the Imam) is even more important because the true interpretation of the revelation depends entirely on him, since it would otherwise fall into the hands of those who are incompetent in performing this crucial duty."[80]

Thus, many Sunnis and Shi'is alike did not approach the Qur'an as the only proof of God. It was also of paramount importance that correct use of it was located in a person, the second proof. For Sunnis, this was the person of Muhammad, as exemplified in Sunna conveyed in Hadith. For Shi'is, this proof existed in a human custodian from the lineage of the descendants of the Prophet; the Imam alone could make inaccessible inner meanings knowable. While the Prophet elucidates the divine revelations via Hadith, the Imam must keep explaining correctly what the Prophet brought, or else prophetic guidance is lost.

Theologically, then, Imams and Prophets were two different things, the one completing the other. An Imam could not be considered a *nabī/ rasūl* after Muhammad, which maintained the seal of the prophets. In addition, there are two other kinds of comparisons that help keep the taboo intact. First, the Imams inherit things from Muhammad, especially weapons, which are a special mark, reminiscent of the ark (*al-tabut*) of the Israelites, that designate its possessors as inheritors of everything prophetic. Reflecting a meta-historical historiography of the world reminiscent of that of Ibn Ishaq, the legacy of Muhammad granted to the Imams included "the knowledge of all the ancient prophets and their legatees."[81] This led to the second kind of comparison, which extends the boundaries without breaking the taboo: Imams are analogous in many ways to prophets before Muhammad. In the Shi'i meta-historiography pioneered by Ja'far, frequent comparisons are made between the birth of Imam Mahdi and that of Moses. A special marker of their unique role is the similarity between their mothers, neither of whom had, by God's design, "any visible signs of conception up

---

80. *Ibid.*: 67–8.
81. *Ibid.*: 21.

to the time the child was born"[82] lest they be killed by their respective
rulers. In addition, comparisons are also made between the Mahdi and
Jesus in terms of their ability to speak as children with the authority of
grown men.

Such comparisons could evoke complex relationships without challenging the taboo of projecting prophetic authority after the death of
Muhammad. Comparisons, once again, are crucial yet elusive: they
construct analogies, but always within implicit boundaries. Ja'far, for
example, analogized the gap between Jesus and Muhammad to the
anticipated gap between the Imams and the *mahdī*, the end-of-time
figure. It was presumed that if the earth had been without a *nabī/rasūl*
for a length of time, thus would it remain without prophet or Imam
"until God would send the Qā'im [legatee] from among the descendants of Muhammad when required, to restore the true faith as he had
done before."[83] Unlike the Sunnis, Shi'is privilege legatees as nodes of
prophetic authority that operate in the absence of prophets. Just as all
prophets before Muhammad had legatees who inherited their knowledge without reproducing it, so Muhammad had legatees in the Imams.
In effect, the kind of work authors like Ibn Ishaq were doing, or at least
the image of messengers they reflected, anticipated and facilitated the
comparisons the Shi'is made for their practical meta-historiography.

MUHAMMAD AS AUGUR OF APOCALYPSE: CHRISTIAN PERSPECTIVES

During the first several hundred years of Muslim rule in southwest Asia
and northern Africa, "Christian" very gradually changed from majority
identity in the conquered lands to the identity of only a small minority.
As Montgomery Watt has put it with apparent regret: "The disappear-
ance ... of most of the Christian culture of the region ... was a gentle
death, a phasing out. Yet the result of the process was an important
'event' in world-history, which deserves more attention from historians
... than it has hitherto received."[84]

Yet as Watt also points out, "Christian" was not a single identity in the
first Islamic lands in the early Islamic centuries, nor could "Christian,"

---

82. *Ibid.*: 72.
83. *Ibid.*: 48.
84. William Montgomery Watt, *The Majesty That Was Islam: The Islamic World,
66–1100* (London: Sidgwick & Jackson, 1974): 257.

at least on the ground, be so neatly distinguished from other overlapping affiliations, like Gnostic, Mandean, and Manichean.[85] And there certainly was no unified "Christian" response to Muhammad and the rule of his community. In fact, those claiming to represent official Christian leadership had to compete with these overlapping alternative affiliations, and the appearance of Muhammad's community as a new alternative may have stirred the pot. Furthermore, relations were complicated between Greek Christians not brought under the control of Muslims and non-Greek Christians who were. When the Muslim Arabs took control of southwest Asia, Christians had for two hundred years been involved in a departure from Greek Christian culture in favor of a variety of local alternatives; Coptic, Melkite, Jacobite, and Nestorian most notable among them. Yet Greek and non-Greek communities continued to influence each other, the former with its perception of Muslims as a far-away enemy, the latter with the reality of day-to-day contact with Muslims and periodic formal discussion.[86] Beyond the world of duly ordained, church-sanctioned leadership were a variety of other social leadership roles associated with what we have called privileging communication, and these must be considered as well.

One well-studied reflection of "official" Christianity is to be found in the formal Syriac and Arab Christian polemic against Islam that emerged in the first Abbasid century, 750–850 CE. However, as we consider it, we will always have to remind ourselves that "official" texts did not necessarily reflect majority opinion in the group represented, and that responses to Islam might also be addressing problems closer to home. We also have to remind ourselves that anyone speaking to any community other than Muslims would, during the first few centuries of Islam, be speaking to a smaller and smaller audience, so with the passages of time, the social and political stakes would be increasing. In early Arab-Christian polemic, strategic comparisons played an important part. The comparisons involved three faith communities: *al-Nasrānīya* (Christian), *al-Yahūdīya* (Jewish,) and *al-Islāmīya* (Muslim). These were no idle comparisons, not just because polemic often aimed to counter "invitations" to move from one religious allegiance to another, but because this was a time when the invitation rate was unusually high.

---

85. William Montgomery Watt, *Muslim–Christian Encounters: Perceptions and Misperceptions* (London: Routledge, 1991): 1–8.
86. On the Muslim side of the engagement, see Nadya Maria El Cheikh, *Byzantium Viewed by the Arabs* (Cambridge, MA: Harvard University Press, 2004).—Ed.

The politically staged comparison of Arab–Christian polemicists relied on a set of intricately interconnected distinctions. They made these distinctions in the course of defending their fundamental premise that "miraculous signs, worked by the prophets in the name of God, or by Jesus in his own name, are the only sufficiently reasonable warranty for accepting Christianity, or, indeed, any scripture, anyone claiming divine inspiration, or any body of religious doctrine."[87] For this premise to render Christian allegiance uniquely true, the polemicists—who often functioned as apologists—would have to overcome at least two problems. First, by their own admission, signs were no longer being produced on behalf of the Christian faith. Second, Jews and Muslims both claimed that signs had also been produced on their behalf as well.

They addressed the first problem, the cessation of Christian miracles, primarily by making a distinction between recognizing truth-claims when they first appear and validating them subsequently. Divine signs are necessary to endorse the establishment of a divine message, but after the establishment, correct human inference from those signs takes over. So a true faith would have needed divine signs in order to be established in the world, but could now be verified only by the best human reasoning available. And part of that human reason is to be devoted to demonstrating that "miraculous signs were present at the appearance of a given religion, even if they are no longer present in its condition of establishment."[88]

In stressing divine endorsement of human reasoning, the apologists were, according to Griffith, turning "back to their Greek philosophical sources for the raw materials with which they could build a new defense of Christianity."[89] In building that defense, they were assuming that "human reason can discover the existence of the creator God, and then conclude that mankind is the highest expression of created values. The perfections present in human beings, the argument assumes, must be in some way reflective of the qualities of the God who created them."[90] One could, then, discern "the true religion, and the true messenger of God, by determining which one of the many claimants to this role most

---

87. Sidney H. Griffith, "The Prophet Muhammad: His Scripture and His Message According to the Christian Apologies in Arabic and Syriac from the First Abbasid Century," *Vie Du Prophet Mahomet: Collque De Strasbur* (Paris: Presses Universitaires de France, 1983): 141–2.
88. Sidney H. Griffith, "Comparative Religion in the Apologetics of the First Christian Arabic Theologians," *Proceedings of the PMR Conference* 4 (1974): 68.
89. *Ibid.*: 67.
90. *Ibid.*: 66.

credibly describes God and his requirements for his creatures—according to the measure of the highest human perfections of which we are aware."[91] To be true, then, a religious tradition had to be "naturally intelligible" in their sense of the term (i.e., capable of proving itself through the rigorous use of the mind long after its divine signs had disappeared).

One Christian author, 'Ammar al-Basri, claimed that God prefers inference to signs after the establishment of a faith community. He arrived at this conclusion in a historical context that imposed the following constraints: because Christians depended on the miracles of Jesus, 'Ammar could not ignore the importance of such signs entirely, but he did not want to define them in such a way as to legitimate Judaism or Islam. However, he could not argue exclusively from signs because in his view none was being produced in his time, and because an argument exclusively from miracles would play into Muslim charges that Christians uncritically accepted their doctrines. On the other hand, he rejected arguments made exclusively from intellectual analysis, first because they left the dull-witted at a disadvantage and, second, because they allowed too much room for the free play of personal preference and opinion. However, in insisting on the ongoing centrality of miracles that were no longer present, he had to explain, in a way that did not entail God's disfavor, why miracles were no longer occurring. This he did by positing the opposite, that the absence of ongoing signs indicated God's favor, more specifically His kindness and compassion, since, according to 'Ammar, God's continuing to send signs would amount to forcing adherence that should be freely given. In this way, he explained that God now preferred intellectual activity to direct signs, and thus linked the miraculous and the rational. At the same time, he preserved a central place for God's past messengers, "who give a warranty for the truth of what they say in the divine signs that are worked at their hands."[92] He also countered Muslim charges of blind obedience. Finally, he sought to make his own brand of learned disputation as popularly inviting as possible.

The second problem—that of the claims to signs by Jews and Muslims—required a different approach. This was addressed, first, by distinguishing between worthy and unworthy motives for adhering to a faith community, and second, by distinguishing between legitimate and illegitimate messengers. The distinction between worthy and unworthy

---

91. *Ibid.*: 66.
92. *Ibid.*: 71.

motives for adhering to a faith extended the apologists' criterion of
natural intelligibility. For them, adherence to a naturally intelligible tradition cannot have any motive that is unconnected with the original evidentiary signs. As Griffith notes, they followed the logic of determining
"that there are no unworthy, imperfect traits in any specific faith-system
which may be alleged as factors to motivate a person to profess that
particular religion independently of divine endorsement."[93] Such other
reasons for adhering to a tradition constituted unworthy motives for the
establishment and persistence of a particular faith community. Their
total absence from Christian allegiance reinforces its unique claims,
just as their presence in Jewish and Muslim faith undermines their
claims, though in slightly different ways. Such traits include the sword,
material inducements, ethnic solidarity, personal preference, tribal col-
lusion, licentious laws, and a charge of *sihr* (supernatural transformation or change).

'Ammar grants that Judaism had signs in its origins and throughout
its history up to the time of the appearance of Christianity. He then
argues that God would not have taken His signs away from the Jews if
their faith could continue to be proved intellectually. He argues further
that one can find many motives, apart from signs, for Judaism's establishment in the world and for people's continuing adherence to it. That
is to say, divine endorsement has to be perceptible without reference
to any "other" motives. In the case of Islam, he argues both for a total
absence of signs and for the presence of an array of unworthy motives.
In this case, the absence of signs is connected with an evaluation of
Muhammad as illegitimate messenger of God, and with a distinction
between legitimate and illegitimate messengers.

Messengers of God do not seem to have been so prominent a focus
of comparison in early Arab–Christian polemic as in Qur'anic discourse. A distinction between legitimate and illegitimate messengers
was, however, an essential part of the apologists' efforts to rule out
Islam. Although some non-Muslims in this time period did accept
Muhammad as a legitimate messenger, the apologists discussed by
Griffith did not. They also did not rule him out in what might appear
to be the most obvious means to us (i.e., by using Jesus' unique fusion
of divine and human as their standard, or in ways used by Western
Christians, e.g., characterizing Muhammad as demon-possessed, agent
of the anti-Christ, or morally depraved).[94] Rather, their main standard

---

93. *Ibid.*: 66.
94. Griffith, "The Prophet Muhammad": 131.

of legitimacy was shared by Jesus and many previous messengers. According to them, legitimate messengers perform evidentiary miracles sent as signs directly from God. Jesus, of course, could also perform them in his own name. These legitimate messengers also exhibit appropriate conduct for a messenger of God. Muhammad, according to the Arab–Christian apologists, did neither.

What did the apologists mean by signs, and why, in their view, did Muhammad lack them? The apologists used the same word for divine signs (*āyāt*) that the Qur'an used, and seemed to give a similar definition: they are "such that no human being could produce the like of them" (Qur'an 17:88). Seeing them directly compels acceptance of any message based on them. After their appearance, when they can no longer be seen directly, "a reasonable demonstration *(bi dalālati 'aqlin)*, the like of which cannot be feigned," that they once occurred also compels acceptance. The emphasis is more on the signs than on the messengers who carry them, and therefore separates following the message from following the messenger. According to 'Ammar, "it is God who produces these confirmatory signs at the hands of someone who calls [or invites] people to accept *(ad-dā'ī)* the religion that God wants to bring to their attention by means of the signs."[95] One other effect of focusing on the "inviting" signs rather than on the "inviter" is to take attention away from any other roles the messenger might play. This puts the focus on doctrines rather than on the person of the messenger, and on following doctrines rather than following the messenger.

Of course, the distinction being drawn between real divine signs and fake ones depends on how you determine that "no human being could produce the like of them." These deeds cannot look just like every other human's, yet they cannot be completely non-human either, because that would undermine the notion of a wonder or a miracle or a gift. Thus those who evaluate the signs have to decide, given communal and individual standards, what it takes to be non-ordinary enough, that is, to do something no human (of that time and place) could be imagined to be able to do on his or her own. What constitutes proof that something funny is really going on, not to mention going on in a recognizable way? Sometimes such distinctions are very fine, and we might speculate that the finer the distinctions, the more sharply honed the competition.

In this case, two things happened. The apologists claimed "that the Qur'ān [itself] rejects the idea that Muhammad's preaching should be

---

95. Griffith, "Comparative Religion in the Apologetics of the First Christian Arabic Theologians": 68.

endorsed by miraculous signs."[96] In so doing, they discounted all extra-Qur'anic stories about miracles Muhammad performed, and also the emergent Muslim doctrine of the wondrous inimitability of the Qur'an (*I'jāz al-Qur'ān*). That meant ignoring any Qur'anic bases for that doctrine, e.g., God's saying when asked for miracles for Muhammad, "Isn't the book enough?" or God's classing the verses of His speech with the signs He has put in the world that are more than endorsements of Muhammad's legitimacy.[97] It is important to note that language competency might have distinguished Christian polemicists from others. Formal Christian polemic either used Syriac, which was closely related to Arabic, or Arabic itself. Contemporary Syriac poetry and prose, e.g., polemic, had affinities with qur'anic idiom. Such Christians may have been, then, among all groups, the ones best situated to focus on Muslim claims about the linguistic merits of the Qur'an, and to compare it with the *shi'r* of the time, just as the Qur'an had been compared with the *shi'r* of its day.

The historical setting had altered the kinds of comparisons that could and/or had to be entertained, and more specifically, what counted as something no human could be imagined to do. Here an aesthetic issue is involved. For most Muslims, the sound and beauty of the Qur'an continued to distinguish it from its closest rival, Arabic *shi'r*. For non-Muslims, Qur'anic locution was not so different from the best of Arabic *shi'r*, and *shi'r* was no longer necessarily thought to involve extra-human inspiration as the Qur'anic context assumes. One apologist, al-Kindī, actually attacked the Qur'an's "Arabic style, and argued that not only is it not an evidence of divine revelation, but it is not worthy of the best Arab poets."[98] In another twist, old arguments take a new form. 'Ammar makes a distinction between "the miracles and wonders of Christianity" and what he calls *hayālāt al-sihr*, the tricks of *sihr* (what we earlier called supernatural transformation).[99] The distinction?

---

96. *Ibid.*: 76.

97. On the concept of *I'jāz al-Qur'ān*, see Richard C. Martin, "Inimitability," *Encyclopaedia of the Qur'an*, ed. Jane Dammen McAuliffe (Leiden, The Netherlands: Brill, 2007) and G.E. von Grunebaum, "I'djāz," *Encyclopaedia of Islam*, second edition, ed. P. Bearman, T. Bianquis, C.E. Bosworth, E. van Donzel, and W.P. Heinrichs, Brill, 2010, *Brill Online*, DUKE UNIVERSITY, www.brillonline.nl/subscriber/entry?entry=islam_SIM-3484, accessed 23 August 2010.—Ed.

98. Griffith, "The Prophet Muhammad": 144.

99. Griffith, "Comparative Religion in the Apologetics of the First Christian Arabic Theologians": 73.

"The miracles and wonders of Christianity are not elusive. Rather, what is promised is achieved."[100] This reminds us that visible material object transformation is much easier to document than the head-turning eloquence of speech. Now the Qur'an is once again called *sihr*, by implication at least, in a new context.

Things that Muhammad did outside the qur'anic framework that Muslims took as too wondrous for a mere unaided human could be subordinated to his not-so-wondrous experiences. For example, al-Kindī contrasts "Muhammad's militarily unsuccessful early campaigns against the Meccan caravans, with the successful battles of biblical characters such as Joshu bar Nun."[101] Or they could be explained by reference to all-too-human motives, which brings up the issue of determining what conduct is unbecoming to a messenger of God. Just as messengers had to be confirmed directly by signs to be legitimate, they also had to exhibit proper conduct. Unsurprisingly, Christian apologists defined right conduct differently than did *sīra* and Hadith. The halo effect imagined by Muslim authors did not exist for Christian apologists. That is to say, whereas Muslim authors assumed Muhammad's full range of conduct could be understood as exemplary because messengers are to be obeyed, Christian apologists demanded a less human standard.

Here the apologists took the biographical details offered by Muslim authors and turned them to their own purpose. Their rewrite goes as follows. Muhammad gained wealth through his marriage to the wealthy widow Khadija, and that led him to aspire to leadership among his people. Unable to accomplish this any other way, he laid claim to messengership, and with the help of a renegade misled Christian monk named Bahira whose teachings were further distorted by a Jewish scribe, he attracted a following of undesirables and took over a town occupied primarily by Jews too weak to resist. His first mosque was an appropriated drying floor. He was interested in only blood, money, and women. That is to say, all of his motives were entirely this-worldly and absent of any direct divine endorsement, and his conduct was "unworthy of a genuine prophet."[102] A parallel development to this, interestingly enough, was the Muslim doctrine of *'isma* (protectedness from sin) of all messengers, in spite of their mortality.[103]

---

100. *Ibid.*: 78.
101. Griffith, "The Prophet Muhammad": 134.
102. *Ibid.*: 134.
103. On the concept of *'isma*, see Paul E. Walker, "Impeccability," *Encyclopaedia of the Qur'an*, ed. Jane Dammen McAuliffe (Leiden, The Netherlands: Brill, 2007)

What this does, in effect, is separate messengership from leadership. In so doing, the worldly activities of Old Testament figures accepted by the Christian apologists must be de-emphasized, or at least assumed to have had nothing to do with why people followed them; what mattered were the special signs they exhibited. This situation leads Griffith to say that the most striking difference between Muslim and Christian points of view was the "Muslim insistence that our only true knowledge of God comes from his own revealing speech in the scriptures."[104] Christians, on the other hand, insisted that limited, but true, knowledge also comes from the human capacity to reason. Since Muhammad carried the speech, which persists as a sign to Muslims, his conduct becomes normative. But for Christians, since signs are no longer present, only reasoning and correct inference from the signs will do.

These Christian apologists had, then, managed to draw Qur'anic discourse, now "frozen" into "The" Qur'an, into their own standards of logical argumentation. They used the polemical language of their counter parts, and, in effect, managed to undo the qur'anic fusion of aesthetic and logical persuasion. For the Christian polemicists, logical argumentation meant something other than head-turning eloquence. Furthermore, they believed that qur'anic eloquence had plenty of competition from the many Arabic *shā'ir*s who now vied for popularity in every locale and at every court.

Griffith sees a number of ways in which Christian polemic was shaped by the Islamic setting, and vice versa. Certainly, the Muslim polemicists of the ninth and tenth centuries were well aware of their Christian counterparts. To a large extent, the development of the Muslim science of theological persuasion, *'ilm al-kalām*, took place in a context where polemicists had to defend and refine their positions in response to the challenges by Muslim rationalists as well as their Christian counterparts.[105] The shared context was not only reflected in an exchange of modified, but similar accusation, such as the Qur'an as *shi'r*, but also in their mutual resort to Neoplatonic anthropology.

---

and W. Madelung, "'Ijma," *Encyclopaedia of Islam*, ed. T. Bianquis P. Bearman, C.E. Bosworth, E. van Donzel, and W.P. Heinrichs (Leiden, The Netherlands: Brill, 2007).—Ed.

104. Griffith, "Comparative Religion in the Apologetics of the First Christian Arabic Theologians": 80–81.

105. See also Josef van Ess, *The Flowering of Muslim Theology*, trans. Jane Marie Todd (Cambridge, MA: Harvard University Press, 2006). According to van Ess, the crucial question for Muslim, Christian, and Jewish theologians is where to set the limits on reason's invocation of faith.—Ed.

There are other issues that Griffith does not address. Why was there not a widespread comparison between Muhammad and Jesus? Why a stress on the signs themselves rather than the people bringing them? Why such a depersonalization? Of course, maligning Muhammad and the Qur'an was dangerous. But beyond that, countering Muhammad's inviting appeal by concentrating on the superior messengership of another figure played into the strengths of the Muslim side, where personal appeal was key, whether through the elaboration of Sunna or movements of healing and miracle-working. By concentrating on signs, Christian writers stressed that the authority in question is not vested in humans who are more than human; indeed, it is not in persons at all, but in processes of reasoning that have replaced the direct appearance of God's signs.

MUHAMMAD AS COUNTERFEIT MOSES: JEWISH PERSPECTIVES

We have already noted how misleading broad identity labels can be in this era. The Jewish label is certainly problematic in this time period. Muslims and Jews disagreed on who was a Jew, and, furthermore, there were those who made a distinction between *Banū Isrā'īl* and *Yahūd*. As Michael Morony and Steven Wasserstrom have established, the transition to rule by Muslims both reinforced and challenged formal Jewish institutions.[106] The Exilarchs (administrators) and Gaons (educational heads) became more functional, but at the same time, caliphal authorities played one group against the other, and the de-stabilizing elements of the transition opened the way for new factions appealing to newly disaffected groups. In this way, ongoing conversations were translated into new languages, figuratively and literally, and new conversation partners were engaged. What transpired between religious communities was a trans-denominational struggle in which some charged others with going too far (*ghuluww*) or not going far enough.

Wasserstrom paints a revealing picture of Jews under early Muslim rule. It was a time when the "upper" professions (long-distance traders, physicians, astrologers, town planners, poets, etc.) fared well in the midst of urban economic boom. Yet, the "lower" professions fared very poorly. These cloth-makers, blacksmiths, butchers, conjurors,

---

106. See Michael Morony, *Iraq after the Muslim Conquest* (Princeton, NJ: Princeton University Press, 1984) and Wasserstrom, *Between Muslim and Jew*.

shoemakers, pail makers, well-diggers, excrement-buriers, and tanners comprised the majority of the Jewish population. Further complicating the matter was that some Jews became successful by becoming Muslims and translating Jewish material into Islamic form. These societal and economic cleavages fueled many social movements and contributed to profound reshaping of ongoing end-of-time expectations.

Politically, the mid-eighth century was a time of widespread questions about who the proper leaders of the community should be. The brewing crisis came to a head, like so many things, during the reign of the second Abbasid caliph, al-Mansur (reigned 754–775), at precisely the same moment when the early Arab–Christian polemic began. Al-Mansur manipulated Jewish laity, administrators, and scholarly elite. He helped put down rebellions, but also played formal leaders against each other, such as the Exilarchs (administrators who claimed descent from King David) and the Gaons (heads of Jewish academies in Palestine and Babylonia who claimed to be the supreme court of world Jewry.) Exilarchs were cozy with caliphs; Gaons were not. Al-Mansur meddled in internal struggles in each camp, choosing the Persian line of Exilarchs over the Palestinian line of Gaons. And, after the Gaons rejected Anan, who became the founder of the Karaites, al-Mansur reportedly helped him to survive and found his own group. Al-Mansur also pitted Gaons of his choosing against other rebels, most notably the 'Isawiyya, who are the subject of Wasserstrom's study. The power of the Muslim caliph "ironically turned out to be something of a boon to the Jews."[107] Institutions of Jewish authority were stabilized with challenges either defeated or routinized into safe form.

In Wasserstrom's view, Abu 'Isa al-Isfahani (died c. 750) "was by far the most significant prophet-figure of early Islam" who "played on Jewish messianic expectations in an almost-successful attempt to create a new political Judaism along the lines of Shi'ism."[108] His strategy was different from anything we have seen so far: he insisted that Jesus and Muhammad were legitimate representatives of God, "but only to their own communities."[109] What is key here, and what Wasserstrom's work on Abu 'Isa demonstrated, is how accommodation and rebellion were different stages within the same movement, and how they were shaped by the new environment of the Islamic milieu. The marker of

---

107. Wasserstrom, *Between Muslim and Jew:* 18.
108. *Ibid.*: 71.
109. *Ibid.*: 72.

this change is an emphasis on *nabī/rasūl* as a precursor of the end-of-time figure (*mahdī* in Arabic.)

This emphasis represents an alternative view of the *'abd/nabī/rasūl* as a figure who is not a Jewish end-of-time figure himself (*mashiach*), but who is the last Moses-like messenger before the end-of-time figure. For most Muslims, Muhammad would not return before the end of time, nor would the end-of-time figure, the *mahdī*, for those who anticipated that figure. Moses was like Muhammad in that respect. Many Jews, however, expected a returned Moses, or cast Elijah in that role. For Abu 'Isa, five messengers served as harbingers of the end-of-time figure, he as the fifth and final, after which some accounts speak of a final inviter (*dā'ī*). Is it possible that Abu 'Isa's prophetology echoes the Qur'anic conception of God's making some *rasūl*s excel over others? Whereas Muhammad had warned of the events of the end of time, but was more and more presented as an end-of-time messenger figure within eschatological time, for Abu 'Isa, the messenger figure was justified by the appearance of another character, who would redeem the earth exactly *at* the end of time. Put as simply as possible, many Muslims separated the *nabī/rasūl* figure from end-of-time, while some Muslims continued to identify Muhammad, without supplanting him, with an end-of-time figure; many Jews blurred the lines, and Abu 'Isa drew a straight line between them. He started declaring himself as a precursor of the end-of-time, but in the ensuing armed uprising, he took on end-of-time functions himself, without apparently claiming to be the figure he preceded.

What is particularly interesting about Abu 'Isa is his move from being the best of the five harbingers of the awaited *masīh* to taking up arms to initiate the end/apocalypse in the form of a liberated Jewish community.[110] He was Jewish and Muslim at same time. It appears that he followed Jewish ritual, while accepting the messengership of Muhammad, and meanwhile was trying to locate himself on the line between *ghulaww* and non-*ghulaww*.[111] He also may have expressed Jewish disappointment that Muhammad was not the eschatological prophet some expected. Following Muhammad's model, however, Abu

---

110. *Ibid.*: 72.
111. Wasserstrom finds evidence in Muslim and Jewish sources that lead him to note that the "'Isawiyya were playing both sides against the middle. They could be recognized as Jews by (Rabbanite and Karaite) Jews because they seemed Judaically orthoprax, and could be recognized as believers by (Kharijite and Shi'ite) Muslims because they seemed Islamically orthodox." Wasserstrom, *Between Muslim and Jew*: 79.—Ed.

'Isa stressed the fact that he brought sacred books despite being illiterate, and it is also reported that he wrote by inspiration without knowing how to write. Further, like Muhammad, he had an ascension experience. Throughout, he appears sort of like Muhammad and sort of not, carefully balancing similarity and difference. His oppositional, hard-to-classify role demands a hybridizing aesthetic mosaic, or palimpsest, that works with pieces of many others, but is never exactly like any of them.

Abu 'Isa and the movement he produced was perhaps an extreme, but not the only, example of the reshaping of Jewish understandings of prophethood in the context of the gradual Islamicization of societies they inhabited. Wasserstrom proposes that the 'Isawiyya were not "merely an ephemeral aberration."[112] The trend toward Jewish images of messengers' images extended to upper classes as well. The Gaonate in al-Mansur's time was an important site of such reconsideration. Certainly, it is impossible to say how much it represents Jews at the time, or whether it represented the majority of Jews. But one element does stand out: the reshaping of Moses' biography away from his image as miracle-worker in order to emphasize his role as ruler. Here the emergence of the Muhammadan model as messenger-ruler opens the way for foregrounding an element which was already present in the Moses tradition but had not been emphasized until now.

Daniel Silver's research of Moses is particularly helpful in analyzing this transformation. As he wrote:

> Among the educated elites, for whom the value of the Torah was that it was Torah, not that Moses, its messenger, was a semi-divine man or a wonder-worker; *aggadah* is no longer accepted uncritically and *Moshe Rabbenu* [the wonder-worker] is transformed into Israel's great caliph-prophet, the Jewish answer to Mohammed.[113]

Surely, prior to Islamic times, there were occasional references to Moses as king, but none that were seriously pursued or elaborated upon. As Silver wrote, "in Islamic times Moses' coronation is taken seriously[114] ... The idea that a leader like Moses proved his virtue by political success was, as we saw, a key concept in Hellenistic [Jewish] thought. It is a new theme in rabbinic literature and has no secure base

---

112. *Ibid.*: 89.
113. Jeremy Silver, *Images of Moses*: 239.
114. *Ibid.*: 240.

in Torah."[115] Such a counter-textual emphasis is important. The new image of Moses is developed in contrast to the Torah's insistence "on Moses' indifference to royal office and its trappings and ... that he made no attempt to establish a dynasty."[116]

But viewing Moses as a political leader only brought him up to the level of Muhammad; some scholars went further by stressing a role he had and Muhammad lacked: scribe. In response to Muslim claims that the Torah had not been maintained verbatim because "Israelite society had not had the benefit of the professional memorizers who played so important a role in the Arab milieu," some Jewish scholars reclaimed a less-used title of Moses as Israel's greatest scribe, *Safrah Rabbah b'Yisroel*.[117] Moving away from Moses as oral and writing teacher, "Moses' work as God's secretary is [now] emphasized."[118] "Maimonides is careful to say that 'Moses was like a scribe writing down from dictation.'"[119] This new stress is but one example of Jewish efforts not only to have Moses equal Muhammad, but also to surpass him.

Jewish and Muslim scholars generated questions about the messenger that not only reflect the inter-communal exchange and the qualifications made therein, but, in addition, are useful distinctions for comparativists today. They also continue the kinds of distinctions that emerged from our analysis of messengership in the Qur'an:

> Could a person prepare himself to be a prophet and, if so, how? Did a prophet have to be a pious and learned man, or was prophecy an unexpected gift? What part of the mind was involved in the prophetic experience? Were there objective criteria by which a prophet's message might be judged? Must miracles accompany prophecy as proof that the words came from God?[120]

Consider a figure who represents for Jews what Griffith's early Arab polemicists represent for Christians, for instance, Sa'adyā Ben Yōsēf al-Fayyūmī, more commonly known as Sa'adyah Gaon (882–942), whose most famous work is "the first systematic exposition and defense

---

115. *Ibid.*: 241.
116. *Ibid.*: 241.
117. *Ibid.*: 243.
118. *Ibid.*: 243.
119. *Ibid.*: 243.
120. *Ibid.*: 243–4.

of the tenets of Judaism."[121] Born in Upper Egypt, he became head (*gaon*) of the academy at Sura in Iraq and, among other things, translated the *Tanakh* into Arabic. He was as much involved in inter-Jewish polemic (e.g., against his Palestinian counterparts) as against "heretical" groups like the Karaites. Like the Arab Christian polemicists addressed earlier, he adopted the methods of *kalām*, wanting his beliefs to be convincing to any reasonable man. Like them, he was in touch with the neo-Platonist strands of his own tradition, and tied together reason and miracles, wanting people of all educational levels to have equal access to the tradition. Sa'adyah believed revelation to be publicly witnessed miracles that could be attributed only to God and that were announced before their occurrence.[122] While Sa'adyah thought that "human speculation can arrive at the truth of everything disclosed in prophecy, revelation is still necessary to teach the truth to those incapable of speculation and to guide the fallible inquiries of those who are capable, since only God's knowledge is complete. Because verification of revealed truths confirms faith, Sa'adyah [considered] such verification a religious obligation."[123]

However, unlike the Christian polemicists, Sa'adyah placed an emphasis on an invidious comparison between Moses and Muhammad, using materials common to both Jewish and Muslim sources, scriptural and later. First he emphasized Moses' uniqueness as a prophet.[124] Sa'adiyah stressed that whereas Muhammad received the Qur'an in portions through the divine messenger Gabriel, Moses was the only prophet to speak to God without an intermediary. Whereas Muslims emphasized Muhammad's illiteracy as proof of his special gift from God, Jews used Moses' immediate writing down of the whole Torah as proof of its correctness. Yet Sa'adyah's stress on reasoning about revealed truths served not only to fend off invitations to Islam, but also to argue against other Jewish groups, like the Karaites, who were missionizing actively in his day and against whom he wrote a polemic.

Much later, Maimonides made four distinctions between Moses and other messengers: Moses was addressed without intermediaries, Moses was addressed in the daytime standing on his feet, Moses had no fear during prophetic meetings, and Moses could speak with God whenever

---

121. Barry Kogan, "Sa'adyah Gaon," *Encyclopedia of Religion*, vol. 12, ed. Lindsay Jones, second edition (Detroit, MI: Macmillan Reference USA, 2005): 7953.
122. *Ibid.*: 7952.
123. *Ibid.*: 7952.
124. Silver, *Images of Moses*: 244.

he wanted—"No Gabriel. No night visions. No interruption of the revelation. Moses had spoken with God openly and easily, fully awake, as one person might with another. Prophecy came to him not infrequently but daily and without any sensory distortion."[125]

Later philosophical arguments also hinged on whether a prophet prepared himself, or whether God limited "his choice to the spiritually enlightened."[126] Muslims stressed that prophecy was an unexpected gift, as did a few Jews, emphasizing God's complete control. Other Jews began to argue that "prophecy comes only to a superior person who has perfected his character, disciplined his imaginative facilities, and fully developed his rational mind" so that he is ready to be chosen by God.[127] "Prophecy is seen as the culmination of schooling, and moral discipline, combined with natural endowment, an attainment rather than a bolt out of the blue."[128] While some Jews continued to see Moses as a man not above sin, others, like Maimonides, followed Muslim notions of the sinlessness of the prophets.

These strategic comparisons also led to rituals that centered on the life of Moses, just as Muslims had rituals centered on the life of Muhammad. Whereas Muhammad's birthday became a popular celebration, Moses' death day did, particularly at a shrine built "on the spot of Moses' ambassadorial residence during his mission to Pharaoh."[129] An important site of pilgrimage, it contained an extraterrestrial stone, as did the Muslim Ka'ba in Mecca. However, the distinction between birth and death isn't absolute, since both traditions held that "The life of a righteous man was believed to be symmetrical and harmonious in every way, so his *yahrzeit* was also his birthday. Muslim tradition taught that Mohammed had died on his birthday."[130]

Just as popular poems emerged to mark Muhammad's birthday, Jewish hymns emerged to mark Moses' death day. The earliest hymn focuses partly on Moses' commissioning of Joshua as his successor, thus effectively transferring power to him, a theme that became an important part of Jewish polemic against Muslims. This detail helped argue with Muslims, but it also helped fend off intra-Jewish challenges to authority. According to Silver, there was a development even more

---

125. *Ibid.*: 244–5.
126. *Ibid.*: 245.
127. *Ibid.*: 246.
128. *Ibid.*: 246.
129. *Ibid.*: 248.
130. *Ibid.*: 249.

popular than that: the breaking of 1,000 years of taboo about naming children after Moses.

> The eighth century CE marks the end of the Moses hiatus. Jewish boys bearing the lawgiver's name are suddenly everywhere. This change coincides with the swift and dramatic conquest by the armies of Islam of most of the world in which Jews lived and is, in fact, a consequence of the Arab victories. The Quran refers often to Musa (Moses), who is listed along with Adam, Abraham, and Jesus, among others, as one of God's chosen messengers, a link in the line of caliph-apostles of whom Mohammed claims to be the last and culminating figure. There were many young Musas in the Muslim world … An old taboo had worn thin and, seeing Muslims at ease with the name, Jews broke with centuries of inhibition and reclaimed the name for their own.[131]

Role-shifting of other kinds was going on as well; naturally, Muslims and Jews took somewhat different courses. In both traditions, central messengers become model mystics. In spite of tensions between *'ulamā* and Sufis, some *'ulamā* were Sufis, and there was no absolute split between Muhammad as legislator/exemplar and Muhammad as an intimate of God. Within the Jewish tradition, the rabbi and holy man split, according to Silver. Moses' familiar title *"ish-elohim"* was given new meaning: not just God's man, but husband of Shekinah (the divine presence).

> During the Islamic period, Jews, like their neighbors, buried incantation bowls under the thresholds of their homes, paid holy men to conjure up angelic intercessors and to write amulets which could shield the anxious and ill from evil spirits. But during the ninth and tenth centuries … the rabbis as a class seem to have distanced themselves from the *ba'alei ha'shem*, the users of The Name.[132]

Here the Kabbalists made a distinction between messenger and intimate of God that Muslims made. They did not claim to expect to duplicate Moses' intimacy with God. He was the father of esoteric wisdom and first in prophetic rank.

> No mortal can expect to go where Moses had gone or know what Moses had known. The Kabbalists looked on themselves as mystics rather than prophets and sharply distinguished the two phenomena. The prophet receives the Word of God. The initiative is God's and the received words are specific

---

131. *Ibid.*: 122.
132. *Ibid.*: 265.

and miracles (supernatural signs).[138] This text emphasizes wonders associated with Zoroaster's birth and life (a wonder-literature was also developing around Muhammad). In Darrow's view, the recounting of wonders, which include things like Zoroaster's conversion of King Vishtasp, is not intended to place Zoroaster in the ranks of miracle-workers, but rather they are recounted because these "wonders are vital to confirm the truth of his message."[139] In some Muslim traditions, Muhammad's wonders serve the same purpose. In others, they bring him closer to miracle traditions of other messengers. But for Muslims, the most important miracle is the Qur'an. Muhammad is not a miracle-worker in that connection, but his one miracle is a supernatural sign that confirms the *dīn* he brought.

According to Darrow, *Selections of Zatspram* is mostly a virtue book, but also emphasizes salvation history.[140] It uses Zoroaster's early trials to illustrate his virtues of uprightness, patience, and compassion, as well as his concern for animals and the modesty of women.[141] The absorption of this key messenger figure into a personal exemplar-virtue tradition reminds one of the development of Muhammad as personal exemplar.

The last text Darrow analyzes, *Zardusht Nameh*, comes from the thirteenth century, long after the time period upon which I have focused. However, its evidence for Islamic impact is too strong and helpful to ignore. The author, Zardusht Bahram ibn Pazhdu, said he was inspired by a dream in which an angel asked him to make the story of Zoroaster more available. The issue of accessibility and availability of such stories alone is important in comparison with Muhammad's traditions, regardless of the content, since one thing the development of Hadith accomplished, if nothing else, was to make Muhammad's story widely available in written and/or oral forms. Whereas earlier texts had begun with Zoroaster's prenatal composition, this one begins with his mother's dream vision, a key element in *sīra* literature about Muhammad as well. Stories of his encounter with Ahura Mazda and his first conversion of a ruler, Vishtasp, are fuller.[142] Another difference from Muhammad is that converting a ruler—rather than becoming ruler—was more consistent with the realities of the Zoroastrian community. It gives Zoroaster an

---

138. *Ibid.*: 118.
139. *Ibid.*: 119.
140. *Ibid.*: 128.
141. *Ibid.*: 128–9.
142. *Ibid.*: 132.

indirect or vicarious temporal authority in the face of rulers whose authority came in their successorship to Muhammad. This poem contains a lengthy exposition of doctrine, which is uncommon in stories about Muhammad. It is paired with an apocalyptic vision of the coming eschaton, which does occur in the Qur'an, but not in the literature focusing on Muhammad.[143]

This latter eschatological element is important, because as a major distinction between Zoroaster and Muhammad, it became a key component to Zoroastrian assessments of Zoroaster's distinctiveness and superiority. The apocalyptic vision of Zoroaster had characterized earlier texts, but, according to Darrow, in the *Zardusht Nameh*, it is presented to underline the uniqueness of Zoroaster as the only prophet who left a clear vision of the future to his community.[144] This meant that Zoroastrians were putting Zoroaster above not only Muhammad but also all other related figures revered by Jews and Christians.

There are other elements of the *Zardusht Nameh* that parallel developments among Muslims. Like the Muhammad of later sources, Zoroaster promises to intercede for his community on Judgment Day, and he is egalitarian. Perhaps most interesting, thinking back to our account of accusations of *sihr* in the Qur'an, there is the strong and vivid presence of the world of magic and sorcery in which Zoroaster moves and which he, like Muhammad, rebels against. The rebellion against evil magic and sorcery that Zoroaster represents is "striking;" it reflects the motif of Zoroaster as "the propagator of the religion."[145] This distinction between sorcery and rationally conveyed wisdom apparently goes back to the middle Persian texts, in which Zoroaster bests the king's sages in debate and begins to win over the king. The sages, through deceit, manage to get Zoroaster accused of sorcery and thrown in prison where he suffers greatly."[146] So, like Muhammad, he tries to talk the language of persuasion and is accused of turning heads through trickery.

In Darrow's view, these developments contain a striking focus on the centrality of Zoroaster "as the bringer of the revealed book."[147] The recreation of Zoroastrianism as a book religion is clearly a product of

---

143. *Ibid.*: 134–5.

144. *Ibid.*: 134.

145. *Ibid.*: 441–2.

146. *Ibid.*: 395–9. In a telling detail, Zoroaster announces himself to king Vishtasp "in a strikingly Islamic phrase, 'I am the prophet (brought) near to you by God.'" See *Ibid.*: 396.—Ed.

147. *Ibid.*: ii.

the Islamic context and was a necessary response to it.[148] A full examination of this text would, of course, depend on putting it in its own historical context, but for now it shows the long-term result of these early interactions. It did not remain impossible forever for Zoroastrians to claim that Muhammad was inspired by Zoroaster, and to incorporate Zoroaster into the Qur'anic and post-Qur'anic chain of messengers. We can find examples of those claims in recent anthropological accounts. But that was not the first comparison entertained. Nor was it anything like the *'Isawiyya*—i.e., saying that Zoroaster is a messenger to his community and Muhammad to his. That may have something to do with Hartman's contention that the praise of Zoroaster and his miracles and the placing of him above all messengers occurred in an atmosphere of secret hostility.[149]

Even though one cannot readily identify Zoroaster with the other Biblical and Qur'anic prophets earlier described, it is clear that he resonates with some of the same traits, and others attribute to him tropes, that locate his profile within the arc of Irano-Semitic prophets, including and especially the Prophet Muhammad. The major question, still to be addressed, is: how does privileging communication work across cultures and periods remote from the ancient Middle East and early Islamic empires?

---

148. *Ibid.*: 464.
149. Sven S. Hartman, "Secrets for Muslims in Parsi Scriptures," *Islam and Its Cultural Divergence: Studies in Honor of Gustave E. Von Grunebaum*, ed. Girdhari L. Tiku (Urbana, IL: University of Illinois Press, 1971): 71.

4

AN EXPERIMENT IN COMPARISON: MUHAMMAD AND ALINESITOUÉ

With Robert M. Baum

In order to test the "extra language" of privileging communication, we[1] have chosen two ostensibly unlikely "conversation partners," Muhammad and Alinesitoué. The former is a well-known male whose impact is felt worldwide; the latter, an obscure female whose influence persists mainly among her own people. Although they were separated by thirteen (solar) centuries and five thousand miles, they both made use of privileging communication from an extra-human source to oppose the status quo. And they both emerged in environments in which privileging communication from extra-human sources was a well-established and variegated phenomenon.[2]

---

1. This chapter is adapted from Marilyn R. Waldman and Robert M. Baum, "Innovation as Renovation: The 'Prophet' as an Agent of Change," in *Innovation in Religious Traditions: Essays in the Interpretation of Religious Change*, ed. Michael A. Williams, Collett Cox and Martin S. Jaffee (The Hague, The Netherlands: Walter de Gruyter, 1992): 241–85. Reprinted by kind permission of the publisher and Robert M. Baum.

2. It is not easy to distinguish between the way such figures operated and the ways they are remembered and presented as having operated. Furthermore, even if we assume that the way they were perceived was itself an important element in the way they were able to operate, it is clearer whose perceptions are represented in Alinesitoué's case than in Muhammad's. Most contemporary accounts of Alinesitoué were written or recorded by French administrators and scholars. More recently, oral reports have been gathered from relatives or followers who knew (of) her. The only contemporary source for Muhammad is the Qur'an itself. There are eighth-century Arab Christian texts in Arabic, and ninth-century Muslim accounts written in Arabic and based on earlier sources, some of which date from Muhammad's time. Much of the information we have on pre-Islamic Arabia also comes from later Muslim sources.

ALINESITOUÉ: "EMITAI SENT HER"

Alinesitoué Diatta, a Diola woman, was born in Kabrousse, a township that straddled the border between French Senegal and Portuguese Guinea, and which had been an important slave-trading community in the eighteenth and nineteenth centuries.[3] She reached adulthood at the beginning of World War II, during a deepening crisis generated by the Vichy colonial regime, ecological dislocation, and a reinvigorated Catholic missionary presence. The war had already begun to weaken France's position as a colonial power and to disrupt long-standing trade patterns. As a consequence, French administrators in Senegal involved themselves more actively in the affairs of the Casamance region, increasing military conscription and seizures of Diola cattle and rice, despite a prolonged period of drought and poor harvests.

By the time of Alinesitoué's birth, Roman Catholic missionaries had been active in the region for almost forty years, but had won relatively few converts, except among the northern Diola, where there was also a substantial Muslim community. Like Alinesitoué, most southern Diola continued in the much older *awasena* "way" or "path."[4] For several decades, the French had identified the shrine elders of the *awasena* way as the leaders of opposition to French colonial rule, and had begun to use the power of the colonial state to undermine their authority. Sometimes the French had actually arrested shrine elders and, in several instances, executed them.[5] In the 1920s, local French administrators had for the

---

3. The Diola, who historically have been sedentary wet-rice cultivators, live on the coastal plain between the Gambia and Sao Domingo rivers of Senegal and Guinea-Bissau. They number about 600,000. See Robert M. Baum, "Diola Religion," in *Encyclopedia of Religion*, vol. 4, second edition, ed. Mircea Eliade (Detroit, MI: Macmillan Reference USA, 2005), and Baum, *Shrines of the Slave Trade*. The materials on Alinesitoué are drawn from a work in progress by Baum, "Messengers of God: Alinesitoue and the History of a Diola Prophetic Tradition in West Africa," and "Alinesitoue: A Diola Woman Prophet in West Africa," in *Unspoken Worlds: Women's Religious Lives*, third edition, ed. Nancy A. Falk and Rita M. Gross, editors (Belmont, CA: Wadsworth, 2001): 170–95. The oral histories on which this study are largely based were gathered in the course of conducting field research in Senegal in 1974–5, 1976, 1977–9, and 1987.

4. Robert M. Baum, "The Emergence of a Diola Christianity," *Africa* 60 (Fall 1990): 370–98. Peter A. Mark, *A Cultural, Economic, and Religious History of the Basse Casamance Since 1500* (Stuttgart, Germany: Franz Steiner Verlag, 1985); 93–109.

5. Shrine elders are persons who are entrusted with esoteric knowledge associated with particular cults, and with some cult responsibilities; but only certain shrine

first time begun to encourage Catholic missionary activity in the region. In 1939, a separate diocese was created for the Casamance region, which included Kabrousse, thereby inaugurating a new intensification of Christian proselytization. Taken together, the drought, the fiscal exactions of the French administration, and heightened missionary activity were having serious effects on the *awasena* way, whose rituals depended on ecological and demographic stability, a stable food supply, and a unified community for the performance of important rituals.

As the drought made rice farming a more and more uncertain source of sustenance, many young Diola began engaging in migrant labor, though few traveled as far as Dakar in search of work. Alinesitoué arrived about 1939, seeking employment as a maid or palm wine vendor. Shortly after her arrival, she was afflicted with a serious illness that produced temporary paralysis and a lingering lameness. After a partial recovery, while walking in the Sandaga market, she received a vision of Emitai, the supreme being whom the Diola saw as the source of all life-producing power and whose name (literally, "of the sky") was closely linked to rain (*emitai ehlahl*) and the agricultural year (*emit*).[6] Thought too important to be troubled with issues of minor import, Emitai could be appealed to in times of trouble or when all else failed (Emitai was also the name used for God by Diola Christians). Compelled by her vision of Emitai, Alinesitoué walked to the shore and dug a hole in the sand. When water appeared, she knew she had been chosen to bring rain; and it was revealed to her that she would be given a spirit shrine for that purpose.[7]

Overwhelmed by her experience, Alinesitoué failed to act until further visions made her fear for her life if she continued to resist. She returned to her home township of Kabrousse, but still did not reveal her visions to anyone else. Instead she appeared to her family to be

---

elders can perform the rituals themselves. For a discussion of French trials of *awasena* leaders, see Robert M. Baum, "Crimes of the Dream World: French Trials of Diola Witches in Colonial Senegal," *International Journal of African Historical Studies* 37(2) (2004): 201–28.

6. For a discussion of Diola images of Emitai, see Baum, *Shrines of the Slave Trade*. For a discussion of Alinesitoué's initial vision, see Jean Girard, *Genèse du Pouvoir Charismatique en Basse Casamance (Sénégal)* (Dakar, Senegal: Institut Fondamental D'Afrique Noire, 1969): 251.—Ed.

7. Interview with Paponah Diatta, Mlomp-Etebemaye, 21 March 1978. Jean Girard, *Genèse du Pouvoir Charismatique en Basse Casamance (Sénégal)*: 251.

disturbed, if not mad.[8] On one occasion, it began to rain after she prayed to Emitai, but still she kept her mission to herself. Finally, in early 1942, Alinesitoué revealed to the elders of her quarter that Emitai had told her to establish the shrine of "Kasila" and to teach its "charity." She also said that Emitai spoke to her directly in dreams and visions, and indirectly through the personal shrine, "Houssahara," that she also received. Both shrines became vitally involved in the procurement of rain.[9]

The use of multiple shrines dedicated to specific purposes and clienteles and overseen by overlapping groups of elders was already well-established in the *awasena* path.[10] In fact, Alinesitoué's Houssahara shrine was much like some of these shrines in that it depended on the spiritual powers of a shrine elder. These powers included the ability to see and communicate with the spirit (*ammahl*) who was associated with the shrine and who had chosen a particular human being as its channel. Such individuals were said to have "eyes" which allowed them to see into the world of the spirit. An ability to communicate with the *ammahl* was associated with the powers of a "wide head" (*houkaw houwung*). Since these powers of the eyes and head were seen as gifts of Emitai, neither could be taught. Although they were not limited to ritual specialists, they were particularly important at shrines where officiating elders were expected to communicate with spiritual beings as well as perform specific ritual tasks. Thus through her actions at the Houssahara shrine, in which she demonstrated her personal powers of the eyes and head, Alinesitoué was exercising a kind of authority already associated with certain types of Diola shrines.

However, Alinesitoué was also different from most shrine elders in fundamental ways. She was one of very few individuals considered able to bring rain directly through her shrine, thereby providing dramatic evidence of her ability to improve Diola living conditions. Furthermore,

---

8. Among the Diola, there were two major ways to explain such disoriented behavior, as the result of spiritual gifts or as the result of madness for which a cure could be sought at particular healing shrines. There was also a tradition of trying to conceal one's spiritual gifts, and of seeing recovery from a severe affliction as a sign of spiritual favor.

9. Interviews with Paponah Diatta, Mlomp-Etebemaye, 21 March 1978; Sambouway Assin, Kagnout-Bruhinban, 8 January 1979; Goolai Diatta, Kabrousse-Mossor, 29 April 1978; Alouise Diedhiou, Kabrousse-Mossor, 29 April 1978. See Jean Girard, *Genèse du Pouvoir Charismatique en Basse Casamance (Sénégal)*: 240.

10. Some of these shrines were organized along gender lines with exclusively male or female leadership and participants, but a significant number of shrines were for mixed audiences, and included women in leadership roles.

although she used her shrine to bring rain, she was thought to be able to bring rain directly through Emitai and without recourse to the shrine. Though sometimes called an "elder," she was often referred to with the special epithets, "Emitai spoke to her" or "Emitai sent her," both of which stressed her close and ongoing relationship with the most powerful being in an *awasena* system of thought.[11] While there were long-standing oral traditions about people who had visions of Emitai, these were usually described as infrequent occurrences, which were often interrupted by other people. Alinesitoué's communications were ongoing and involved Emitai's coming to her through dreams and auditory experiences as well as her journeying to Emitai.[12]

Alinesitoué was also an unconventional candidate for spiritual gifts. Barely in her twenties, she was younger than most individuals who were accepted in any kind of leadership role in Diola communities. In a society where the ability to do hard physical labor was valued, she was lame and slow in her work. Furthermore, she had strayed beyond the conventional roles of women in mid-century Kabrousse. Before many of the young women of Kabrousse, though not of other Diola communities, she had ventured on her own to seek work in the distant city of Dakar. While there, she had borne a child out of wedlock, a circumstance that was quite rare until relatively recently. As an unmarried woman returning to Kabrousse, she was excluded from the most important women's shrine. Like the male elders of certain rain shrines, she was expected not to marry or engage in sexual relations.[13] Although women were elders of several important Diola shrines, Alinesitoué transcended the limitations of such roles by assuming leadership for the entire community, by exhibiting male attributes associated with bravery, strength, and courage, and by making use of such symbols of male authority as the spear.

---

11. The French referred to her as "prophétesse," "prêtrise," or the more unflattering "fetichiste." Of course, when "prophétesse" was used, it was used on the assumption that she was a "false prophetess."

12. These dreams were described in terms of the human soul's departure from the body and its ascent to Emitai's celestial abode. For a description of Diola traditions about revelations from Emitai, see Baum, *Shrines of the Slave Trade*, chapters 2–4.

13. Until the late nineteenth century, certain male elders of rain shrines were expected to sacrifice their fertility for the fertility of the community. When Alinesitoué married after she began to teach, she thus violated something expected of male elders of rain shrines. After she was arrested and convicted, some Diola said that Emitai would have protected her had she remained celibate. This fact suggests that she or others may earlier have felt that Emitai had asked her to be celibate.

Just as she was somewhat different from other ritual specialists, her shrine of "Kasila" was different from other shrines: it was public and egalitarian. In all activities associated with Kasila, no distinctions were made between old and young, rich and poor, male and female. While the wealthier cattle-owners were expected to contribute black bulls, symbolizing rain clouds, for the ritual, this contribution did not give them special access to ritual knowledge or responsibilities. Anyone who traveled to Kabrousse could learn the shrine's detailed rites from Alinesitoué, and ritual specialists were selected by divination from a pool that included men, women, and children, rich and poor. Horns filled with soil from Alinesitoué's Kasila shrine were carried back to Diola communities and shrines were installed within full public view. In sharp contrast to usual Diola practice, there was no secret knowledge surrounding the shrine installations or the ritual performance. Once the shrine was installed in a township, it was imperative that everyone in the community participate in the shrine's prayers, songs and dances, black bull sacrifice, communal meals, and six-day abstention from work. At the rites, cult leaders stressed the power of Emitai to bestow rain and invoked that power to sustain the entire community and to ensure a good harvest.

Because of their emphasis on the importance of a more supreme being, however differently understood, and because of the public and inclusive nature of their central rite, Alinesitoué's teachings were similar to and competitive with Christianity. However, her shrine of Kasila was different from and competitive with Christianity, at least Christianity as promoted by French missionaries. No foreign products could be used in connection with Kasila, especially the French-introduced strains of rice that produced a higher yield but were less drought-resistant than Diola rice. All other foreign products could be otherwise used or grown, except for the new cash crop of peanuts, which were prohibited outright in view of their negative ecological and social consequences.[14]

Furthermore, whereas the Catholic Church restricted its priesthood to celibate males who underwent a long period of highly structured training, the rites of Kasila could be performed by anyone who had

---

14. In those Diola areas where peanuts were grown, men abandoned rice farming to concentrate on peanuts as a cash crop. In areas where peanuts were not grown, men and women played complementary roles in the farming of rice. The loss of male rice-farming labor led to a deterioration of the elaborate system of dikes utilized by the Diola to control water levels in the rice paddies. For a discussion of Diola rice-farming and peanut-growing techniques, see Baum, *Shrines of the Slave Trade*: chapter 2.

learned them properly, man, woman, or child; and the right to officiate did not require years of apprenticeship outside the Diola community or vows of celibacy. Unlike the revelations from "Emitai" that were written in a foreign language, contained in ancient books, and invoked by Catholic missionaries, Alinesitoué's revelations were ongoing, derived from Emitai's direct intervention on behalf of the Diola communities of her day, and mediated by someone who came from their own community, spoke in their own language, and shared their trials and tribulations. Furthermore, Emitai promised that by following Alinesitoué, the Diola would restore not only their collective identity in the face of the crisis of colonial rule, and their links to the land and Emitai in a time of ecological uncertainty, but also the community solidarity necessary for economic and spiritual survival.

That restoration depended not only on the rites of Kasila but also on rehabilitation of a "neglected" Diola custom, Huyaye, a day of rest for the rice paddies every sixth day. Alinesitoué presented Huyaye as an old custom that had ceased to be observed in some Diola villages and was being observed only poorly in many others.[15] She taught people to observe this day by scheduling major rituals and abstaining from rice cultivation, arguing that Huyaye's neglect had been a cause of drought and loss of autonomy. In turn, this way of reaffirming a "Diola" path presented a challenge to Catholic Diola, who neither participated in Kasila nor observed Huyaye, and who, by preferring the Christian Sabbath, reinforced the association between French-sponsored Christianity and threats to the restoration of proper relations between the Diola and Emitai.[16]

Soon large delegations of supplicants began arriving in Kabrousse from Diola villages throughout the Casamance, learning and observing the rites of Kasila directly from Alinesitoué, and remaining for several days afterwards.[17] As she began to attract large numbers of

---

15. Interviews with Goolai Diatta, Kabrousse-Mossor, 29 April 1978; Paponah Diatta, Mlomp-Etebemaye, 1 July 1976.

16. By refusing to observe Huyaye, Diola Christians failed to give the land a rest; by refusing Kasila, they withheld their spiritual strength from the rest of the community's quest for rain, fertility, and group solidarity.

17. Delegations came from virtually every sub-quarter of every Diola township among the southern Diola, from many northern Diola communities, and from closely related peoples in Portuguese Guinea and in Casamance. Interviews with Papanoah Diatta, Mlomp-Etebemaye, 21 March 1978; Henri Diedhiou, Kadjinol-Kafone, 5 July 1976; Wuuli Assin, Samatit, 20 June 1978. See also Colonel Sajous, "Commandant du Cercle de Ziguinchor a Monsieur le Gouverneur du Senegal," 17 September 1942, Archives Nationales du Senegal, 13G13, Versement 17.

followers whose loyalty she could command, and as they began to resist French exactions in her name, Alinesitoué quickly aroused the anxiety and hostility of colonial officials.[18] The Church and some Christian Diola viewed her as a threat, too, just as some *awasena* blamed the Christians for betraying her. The Diola Christians' anxiety about her leadership stemmed partly from the way in which she forced them, much as the missionaries had attempted to do, to choose sides. Alinesitoué would not allow Christian Diola to violate Huyaye and then come to her shrines, and she encouraged other shrine elders to exclude those who followed the particularistic French "way" or "path" (i.e., Christianity).[19]

Having declared her mission early in 1942, within a year Alinesitoué was arrested and tried for encouraging disobedience toward French administrators. According to the arresting officer, Colonel Sajous, her defense was a simple statement that she had a mission among her people: "she satisfied herself by affirming that she was an envoy of God, who had appeared to her several times! And that all she did was 'transmit the directives that He had dictated.'"[20] Despite her claims that she had not tried to inspire resistance to the French, she was convicted and sentenced to ten years' imprisonment, from which she never returned. Her ultimate fate remained a closely guarded secret until 1983 when the Senegalese government sent an expedition to Timbuctou and found her grave site, although interest in her has survived the seventy years since her trial, and even grown in recent years. The cult that Emitai taught her, Kasila, has also survived, although its egalitarianism has been modified so that now only men can perform its rituals. Despite this retreat from her teaching, she did open the *awasena* way to the young, to the less wealthy, and to women. Since her death, dozens of women and a handful of men have made similar claims that Emitai spoke to them, leading them to introduce new shrines, or new forms of Kasila, and to speak to the problems confronted by the Diola in postcolonial Senegal.

---

18. This resistance included attacks on French patrols in two nearby Diola communities and increasing hostility to all forms of French authority in the southern Diola areas.
19. Interviews with Sirkimagne Diedhiou, Kadjinol-Kafone, 3/15/78; Georgette Basin, Kadjinol-Kafone, 2/28/78; Antoine Djemelene Sambou, 6/5/76; Paponah Diatta, Mlomp-Etebemaye, 7/1/76.
20. Girard, *Genèse du Pouvoir Charismatique en Basse Casamance (Sénégal)*: 225.

MUHAMMAD, *RASŪL ALLAH*

Muhammad b. 'Abd Allah, an Arabic-speaking man, was born in 570 in Mecca, a demographically complex market and shrine town in the Hijaz region of western Arabia. He was a member of a lesser branch of the Quraysh, the collective name for a cluster of the town's most influential families. Recognized for his character but not for his wealth and status, he worked on his own as a trader until he joined the commercial endeavors of Khadija, an older woman he had married.

By the time Muhammad emerged as a potential leader, the Quraysh had consolidated their influence in Mecca, having settled it some two hundred years earlier. They had also begun to extend their influence over other groups, especially those migratory groups who were involved in Arabia's long-distance trade and who traveled to Mecca periodically to visit its market and its shrine, the Ka'ba. Although the Quraysh had tried to extend their influence to neighboring peoples, they had not managed to stabilize or centralize an extensive network of relationships. Such stabilization would have required them to eliminate endemic caravan-raiding and inter-group hostility, as well as a number of social and economic problems in Mecca itself, and to provide a symbolic rationale for a wider sense of identity, loyalty, and solidarity.[21]

At some point after he married, Muhammad began to engage in solitary meditation in the hills around Mecca, a practice apparently shared by a variety of others. Returning from a retreat in a cave on Mount Hira' in 610, he reported to his wife an experience in which he had been ordered by a voice to recite certain words about and from an unseen being. According to Ibn Ishaq, his eighth-century biographer, Muhammad had refused three times and had finally consented only on fear of death. Even then, he had considered suicide, fearing he was like one of two other types of figures who claimed to communicate from unseen beings on a regular basis and in a relatively uneventful manner.[22] One was called *kahin* (cognate of Hebrew, *kohen*), usually translated

---

21. See Mahmood Ibrahim, *Merchant Capital and Islam* (Austin, TX: University of Texas Press, 1990) for an account of how Muhammad's movement provided symbolic resources for the social and economic program of the Meccan leaders. The degree to which Mecca was in felt crisis is the object of lively scholarly debate. See, for example, Patricia Crone, *Meccan Trade and the Rise of Islam* (Princeton, NJ: Princeton University Press, 1987).

22. See Alfred Guillaume, *The Life of Muhammad: A Translation of Ishāq's Sīrat Rasūl Allāh* (Karachi, Pakistan: Oxford University Press, 1978): 106.

as soothsayer, diviner, or seer because its Arabic root has to do with predicting.

One of the most distinctive acts of the *kahin* involved the production of obscure or even incomprehensible ecstatic utterances, often about the future, in a special form of rhymed prose called *saj'*. These utterances were thought to come from or be inspired by a spirit—*jinn* or *shaytan*— and were produced while the *kahin* was in an altered physical state and in an altered state of consciousness. *Kahins* were often consulted before important occasions, and some of them also served in the capacity of an arbitrator (*hakam*) from outside called in to settle disputes. Thus, some may have functioned as *shaykhs* (kin group leaders); and some may even gained influence beyond their kin-group.[23]

The other figure was the *sha'ir*, the "versifier," usually translated as "poet" in English. The *sha'ir* was, like the *kahin*, generally considered possessed by an extra-human being. Yet the *sha'ir* was educated in a number of meters and formats used to communicate about topics related to the history and customary practice (*sunnah*) of his group or for the purpose of praise or blame, but not, as far as we know, in an altered physical state. The significance of these two roles suggests that the power of the spoken word, and the centrality of special locutions in privileging communication, were well-established.[24]

Convinced by his wife and a few close associates to suppress his anxieties and to think of his recitations as radically different from those of the *kahin* and *sha'ir*, Muhammad began to make public his urgent warnings of an imminent judgment day, periodically entering a special physical state in order to receive additional messages known

---

23. See August Fischer, "Kahin," *Shorter Encyclopedia of Islam*, ed. Hamilton A.R. Gibb and Johannes H. Kramers (Ithaca, NY: Cornell University Press, 1953) and Toufic Fahd, "Kahin," *The Encyclopaedia of Islam*, second edition, vol. 4, ed. Emeri van Donzel et al (Leiden, The Netherlands: Brill, 1978): 420–22. It is interesting that the spirit who spoke through them was sometimes called their ra'i ("see-er"), cognate of *ro'eh*, one of the synonyms for the mantic biblical *nebi*.

24. The fact that the Qur'an insistently distinguishes its "clear Arabic" from the language of the *sha'ir* highlights the importance of linguistic considerations. The fullest account of the linguistic dimensions of this problem appears in Zwettler, *The Oral Tradition of Classical Arabic Poetry*: 156–60 and passim. See also page 201 of the same work for the possibility that some *sha'irs* were also called *kahin*. The Qur'an, of course, assigns a negative, demonic valence to the sources of the *kahin*'s and sha'ir's inspiration.

individually and collectively as *qur'an*, "recitation(s)."[25] However, because subsequent qur'anic messages contained an unequivocal denial of Muhammad's being either *kahin* or *sha'ir*, it is possible that even after *he* dismissed this possibility, others did not.[26] Indeed, it would be surprising for such "confusion" to have yielded quickly to his claim that his source was a/the superior being and not just any spirit, and that he was its exclusive channel. The *saj'*-like form of his early utterances and the altered physical state necessary for their reception could well have continued to remind his hearers of the *kahin*, just as some of his content and its comprehensibility, especially in later recitations, could have continued to remind them of the *sha'ir*.

Referring to his extra-human source as "Allah" (i.e., the Godhead) helped to stress its superior power, as did the use of numerous attributes and circumlocutions that stressed Allah's majesty and power. However, among individuals who "confused" him with the *kahins* and *sha'irs*, those who were skeptical of those two roles would need to be convinced that Muhammad was something else. Those attracted to him because he reminded them of either or both of these figures would need to be convinced that the content of his messages superseded the content of theirs and gradually be shifted to another paradigm. Those who already had other paradigms within which to "hear" him, such as the Christians who are said to have likened qur'anic messages to gospel, would need to be provided with clearer ways to distinguish him from the *kahin* or *sha'ir* and also with ways to compare him favorably with previous communicators of revelation.

---

25. Estimates of the amount of time between his first experience and his first public recitation differ, some putting it at three years. See W. Montgomery Watt, *Muhammad's Mecca: History in the Qur'an* (Edinburgh: Edinburgh University Press, 1988): 54–60, for a summary. Although Muhammad continued to receive qur'ans until his death, their content and style changed significantly, as did his degree of readiness or desire to receive them.

26. For example, Qur'an 21:5; 36:69; 37:36; 52:29; 69:42; 81:22. The Qur'an denies the charge of "*sha'ir*" more extensively and more vehemently than that of "*kahin*." Perhaps *sha'irs* were more serious rivals. Or perhaps, as the Qur'an developed, its linguistic idiom was closer to theirs (see Zwettler, *The Oral Tradition of Classical Arab Poetry*: 160). Since *sha'irs* could make fewer claims to authority than kahins, perhaps calling Muhammad a *sha'ir* was a more serious challenge to his leadership claims. The Qur'an also denies that Muhammad was possessed or mad—*majnun*—in a more general sense of the term. Majnun literally means "possessed by a jinn," and individuals who were *majnun* often exhibited irregular physical states and behaviors. As Muhammad's career progressed, the physical manifestations of his receiving *qur'an* are said to have moderated.

Furthermore, there were many who simply found his activity unacceptably disruptive of everyday life. Located at a commercial crossroads and possessed of a diversified and variable population, Mecca depended on the suppression of intergroup conflict and raiding in order to maximize prosperity. Given this situation, and all of the other factors already discussed, it is not surprising that as Muhammad persisted in making his special utterances public, often near the *Ka'ba* itself, utterances that criticized customary practices and warned of impending doom, he generated more opposition than support.[27] In 622, his situation in Mecca was becoming untenable and he emigrated to the oasis town of Yathrib (Medina), invited there in the role of *hakam* (arbitrator), to settle disputes among the town's various kin-groups and constituencies.

After the emigration, or *hijra*, to Medina, opposition diversified and intensified, both from the community he had left behind and among the groups he had come to Medina to reconcile. Within eight years, he built a new community upon his initially fragile base in Medina and became strong enough to incorporate Mecca into it. His success depended partly on his ability to generate and overcome opposition and hostility, and to draw a new line between inclusion and exclusion. The fluidity and complexity of Medinese and Arabian "demography," with its overlapping class, occupational, communal, and kin lines, may well have enlarged the space within which he could maneuver. In fact, his activities may well have divided a fluid system into more rigid and clear-cut groupings than he found upon his emergence as a public figure.

One's view of that process is related to one's reading of qur'anic utterances as a whole and to their labels for groups or positions opposed by Muhammad. If qur'anic utterances are read not just as the fixed text, *the* Qur'an, which they came to comprise after Muhammad's death, but

---

27. Despite the strongly apocalyptic character of Muhammad's early recitations, few scholars have taken seriously the possibility that due to active messianic expectations, some of his audience could have viewed him as an awaited end-of-time figure. An exception is Paul Casanova, *Mohammed et le fin du monde* (Paris: Gauthier, 1911–1924). See also Douglas S. Crow, "Islamic Messianism," *Encyclopedia of Religion*, vol. 4, ed. Mircea Eliade (New York: Macmillan, 1987): 477–81. Crow urged serious consideration of the Casanova thesis in "The Sword of the Prophet: Aspects of Early Shi'i Messianism," University Seminar in Arabic Studies, Columbia University, 25 March 1982. If true, it would complicate the issue of reception-paradigms even further. It should also be noted that Muslims developed a tradition, based on Qur'an 17:1, of attributing to Muhammad the ability to journey to God as well as to receive God's word as it was sent down. The Qur'an, unlike the Torah, does not contain descriptions of a "prophet's" conversations with God.

as key instruments in an ongoing and evolving process of preaching, one is more likely to read various qur'anic terms of opprobrium not as references to fixed and incorrigible *groups*, but as appeals to a mixed and shifting audience formulated in the terms that were most persuasive at the moment.

For example, "al-Yahud" and "Banu Isra'il" have often been taken to refer to "Jews" as a distinguishable group, just as "an-Nasara" has been taken to refer to Christians. However, if recent studies are correct, lines of affiliation in seventh-century western Arabia were more complex and overlapping than this. For example, although some kin-groups may have been mostly or entirely "Jewish" or "Christian," others may have been mixed, and "Jews" and "Christians" may have been distinguishable from other group-members only in limited or inconsequential ways. Other labels, such as *"munafiqun"* (those who talk loyally and act disloyally), *"kafirun"* (ingrates), *"kadhibun"* (those who call the messenger a liar), and *"sufaha"* (weak-minded), have been assumed to be applied to people possessing more generic weaknesses among those who were not Jews or Christians. In addition, certain "errors," such as thinking God has a son, are assumed to "belong" to the Christians.

However, it is equally possible that "errors" could have been distributed across groups, and that one could exhibit a failing of "Jews" or certain Jews without being one, just as on any particular occasion the *munafiqun* could include members of various "groups." It is even possible to conceive, if we avoid the retrojection so common in Islamic studies, a point at which a member of the "Banu Isra'il" could follow Muhammad without giving up that affiliation, as long as his or her loyalties were correctly expressed, or a point at which "Banu Isra'il" and "Yahud" were not coterminous.

This kind of reading would imagine Muhammad's career as an interactive process of gradual disclosure of what it would mean to "follow" him, "interactive" in the sense that his explanations would have to adjust to the audience's demonstrated ability or inability to conform to his demands in changing contexts and circumstances. It would also assume that many lines of affiliation changed as a major new polarization took hold between those who followed Muhammad and those who did not. It would further argue that, for example, an identifiable "Jewish" constituency was the result rather than the cause of Muhammad's activities.

The process of redefining inclusion and exclusion, and degrees of exclusion, depended first on the identification of those faithful to God, "mu'min" with those who are faithful to God *and* follow Muhammad, "muslim." It further depended on the use of a generic term, "kafir," to categorize all those not faithful to the unique being. The process of reorganization also required the distancing of the followers of Muhammad from those who claimed to be faithful to God but whose practices were in error, for example, the "Jews" after Muhammad shifted his direction of prayer from Jerusalem to Mecca.

Qur'anic terminology for Muhammad's role is a window into this process of transformation. Two words are used for those who communicate from Allah—*nabī* and *rasūl* (often in the phrase "*rasūl Allah*"). Many Muslim exegetes through the centuries, and many modern non-Muslim scholars, have commented on the relationship between the two. Most have tried to stabilize it, even though in fact the relationship between the two has varied and changed over time. "*Nabī*" is an Arabic cognate for a Hebrew word for a spokesperson for God. Although we have no way of knowing for sure how it was used in Arabia, we can probably assume that it would have evoked in some of Muhammad's hearers the names of a number of previous figures. The root of "*rasūl*" means "to send." "*Rasūl*" is an Arabic cognate of a Syriac word that may have been used by Christians to apply to the apostles and other important figures, but again we have no way of knowing to what extent. Qur'anic usage applies one of these terms, or both of them, to many different figures prior to Muhammad, including Nuh (Noah), Ibrahim (Abraham), Musa (Moses), 'Isa (Jesus), Hud, Salih, and Yunus (b. Mattai; the only literary biblical prophet mentioned in the Qur'an).

In qur'anic usage, "*nabī*" has the general meaning of a chosen spokesperson for God but seems particularly connected with descendants of Ibrahim. "*Nabī*" is used for Muhammad only in qur'ans revealed after the *hijra,* and may thus be connected with his growing sense of the descent of Arabs, as well as the Israelites, from Ibrahim. More important in the present context is the way in which "*rasūl Allah*" analogizes Muhammad's role to previous important figures, many of whom are presented as indigenous to Arabia. "*Rasūl*" is used for someone sent by Allah at a particular point in time to a particular "people" to effect a historically significant mission through privileging communication clearly stated in their own language. Those who accept are obligated to obey not only the messages but also the messenger. Thus it has been hypothesized that during Muhammad's lifetime there may have been considerable slippage between the authority of his "special" qur'anic utterances and the guidance he issued in "everyday" language.[28]

---

28. See Graham, *Divine Word and Prophetic Word in Early Islam.*

Furthermore, since Muhammad, like any *rasūl*, "belongs" equally to all who obey him, all who obey him form a single group regardless of other lines of affiliation. In Muhammad's case, the pool of possible followers would include all who could (learn to) understand qur'anic Arabic. In fact, the nature of qur'anic locution, and qur'anic Arabic, played an increasingly important part in the emergence of the new role and its gradual separation from other similar roles. The Qur'an frequently calls attention to its inimitability and clarity and to its having expressly been designed to be comprehensible and appropriate to the audience to whom it is being addressed.

The qur'anic way of conceptualizing *rasūl*, as well as *nabī*, also gave meaning to the opposition Muhammad continued to encounter. For the existence of opposition, also attributed to other *rusul* before Muhammad, became part of the proof of his legitimacy. Occupants of the role with which he increasingly associated himself were seen naturally to meet intransigence because of their effort to correct ingrained error. Furthermore, unlike the *nabī*, who can even be killed, the *rasūl* is assured of survival and ultimate success.[29] Muhammad's success seems tied to the fact that he was in a position to structure the terms of the conflict, to interpret ongoing occurrences within the framework he had established, and to benefit from the especially strong loyalty of those who have become convinced of something they at first had violently opposed. Of course, once successful, he also benefited from the way in which the continuing presence of the unpersuaded constituted an ongoing reminder of the critical need for the guidance the *rasūl* brings from God. Conversely, the *rasūl*'s mission to bring together a community out of related groups in concert both mirrored Muhammad's effectiveness as *hakam* and the *kahin*'s trans-tribal prestige.[30]

The emergence of the role of *rasūl Allah* also generated further conflict. For opposition came not only from kin and their leaders in Mecca or from individuals and groups in Medina, but from others who claimed to receive communications from a superior being. Four are mentioned by name in the Muslim sources, three male and one female. The best

---

29. Since the Qur'an holds that 'Isa (Jesus) did not die on the cross (see, for example, Qur'an 4:157), Jesus can be counted *rasūl* as well as *nabī*.

30. See Fred M. Donner, *The Early Islamic Conquests* (Princeton, NJ: Princeton University Press, 1981) for an account of Muhammad's unusual gift for conducting negotiations and forming alliances, which appears to have been based on an exceptional knowledge of the social map of western Arabia. It should also be noted that Muhammad's economic success mirrored the successful *shaykh*'s superintendence of his group's material well-being.

known, and the one most threatening to Muhammad himself, was a member of the Banu Hanifa, Maslama b. Habib of Yamama, referred to in Muslim sources by the contemptuous diminutive "Musaylima." Like Muhammad, Maslama referred to himself as *rasūl Allah* and to his source as "al-Rahman," one of Allah's major attributes in the Qur'an. Like Muhammad, Maslama attempted to unify his own kin; unlike Muhammad, he seems not to have managed to attract support beyond that group.[31]

Although Muhammad did not recognize Maslama, Maslama allegedly recognized Muhammad. If the Muslim sources can be trusted on this point, perhaps it was possible for at least some claimants to the role, as well some listeners, to imagine that the superior being of whom Muhammad spoke used more than one messenger just as better-known "lesser" beings communicated through and to many different human beings. Perhaps those listeners who could accept the uniqueness as well as superiority of Allah still needed to be convinced that He did not operate in the same diffuse way as other communicating or inspiring beings had been imagined to. Even if Muhammad successfully argued that Allah had commissioned him to accomplish a special purpose for the people to whom he had been sent, he might still need to convince them to imagine "people" in an unconventionally broad way. After all, the *sha'ir* was an inspired figure associated with the defense and interests of a particular kin-group, but each group had its own *sha'ir.*

In the midst of this complex environment, the unifying dimensions of Muhammad's activities as *hakam* and *rasūl* began to mirror each other. Gradually, he also assumed more and more of the attributes of a *shaykh*, but in this case a *shaykh* of a new kind of "kin-group" that was forming around him in Medina. Now he assumed the military and economic protection of the town, obliged to do so by the continuing hostility of the Meccans. Simultaneously, he began to identify the practices he taught to his followers with the real *sunnah*, implying that the existing *shaykhs* were articulating a *sunnah* gone astray.

In a region containing diverse shrines associated with different locales, peoples, and clienteles, Muhammad focused on "restoring" and foregrounding a single shrine, the Ka'ba, and on returning it and its associated rites to their authentic, "archaic" condition. By encouraging all to orient their worship to the same site and to the being who had founded it, and to participate in pilgrimage to it in a uniform way,

---

31. Dale F. Eickelman, "Musaylima: An Approach to the Social Anthropology of Seventh Century Arabia," *Journal of the Economic and Social History of the Orient* 10 (1967): 17–52.

Muhammad defined as potentially one individuals and groups previously fragmented from each other. Since traditional practice had strayed from original practice, what Muhammad taught was not new but lost. It had been "recovered" only as a result of communication from a particular being who had been neglected and ignored, but who had played a critical role in the region's past.

In this rediscovery of lost authenticity, Ibrahim became the author of authentic practice (e.g., the Ka'ba and its associated rites), and also a primary member of a series of *rasūls* of which Muhammad was the latest. In a single stroke, this recovery explained why "Jews" and "Christians" had become different from their "Muslim" ancestors, and also how they might be reincorporated into a reconstituted community. All hearers, then, were both previously and potentially connected with each other.

After Muhammad incorporated Mecca, he began to attract the allegiance of groups from all over the peninsula. At his death from natural causes, in 632, various forms of personal loyalty had made him the focal point of a new but still unstable network of relationships. Many groups that affiliated with him after 630 withdrew their allegiance upon his death. Other similar figures continued to emerge, and to use privileging communication from a superior being as an important resource in organizing their own groups. Military force was required to deal with both problems, and to maintain the enlarged community with Muhammad alone as its focal point. The various practices and rules Muhammad had introduced were also not yet stabilized, and underwent further development for at least several centuries. At the time of his death, he seems to have co-opted the privileging communication of the *kahins* and *sha'irs*, and of family leaders in Mecca and Medina, but not yet successfully to have monopolized the authority associated with the role of *rasūl* on which he himself had focused. However, in the course of displacing all these other loci of authority, a number of new sources of potential authority had emerged: the uniqueness of qur'anic language, the coherence and unitary source of privileging communication, and an extension of the roles of *nabī* and *rasūl* to the wider array of powers Muhammad had assumed and integrated.

STRATEGIES OF COMPARISON

Even these very limited accounts of Alinesitoué and Muhammad suggest many avenues for comparison. However, since our focus is change,

we should center our comparison on the way in which each of our
figures presented as "lost" that which appeared to be "new," and understood the *adoption* of something different as a *recovery* of something
prior but abandoned. This observation is not novel; it was made, for
example, by Max Weber in his discussions of charismatic authority,
and it is frequently reiterated by neo-Weberian scholars of charisma or
"prophecy." Neither is the phenomenon itself uncommon, associated as
it is with many other figures who might fall into our catchment.[32]

However, well known as the occurrence of "innovation through
renovation" might be, it is rarely emphasized in studies of the individuals who invoke it. If, though, we do foreground this feature, we will find
our attention drawn in new ways to the kinds of competition it presumes
and to the kinds of social remapping it is capable of producing. In turn,
we will become much more attentive to the personal and circumstantial
qualities that make some individuals more effective than others, for
the outcome of a particular individual's use of oppositional privileging communication has an aesthetic dimension—an ability to produce
an especially appealing and harmonious conjunction of ideas, social
arrangements, praxis, identity, and material well-being.[33]

Translating into language introduced at the beginning of this chapter, we would say that the very appearance of an individual who uses
privileging communication in an oppositional way creates a disjunction
that can in time generate many other disjunctions. The most effective
oppositional figures seem able to open, and close, disjunctions, tangible
and intangible, in an especially flexible and creative way, producing a
"picture" that both explains a new-found commonality among insiders
and justifies the exclusion of outsiders. That is to say, the most effective figures seem to be those most capable of designing, and redesign-
ing, ever more accommodating patterns into which their own ongoing

---

32. For example, Tenkskwatawa, the "Shawnee prophet" (1775–1836), who
condemned the traditional medicine bundles held dear by his kinsmen, because
they contained a medicine "which had been good in its time, had lost its efficacy;
... had become vitiated through age" and corrupted by being applied in too
individualistic a manner; R. David Edmunds, *The Shawnee Prophet* (Lincoln, NE
and London: University of Nebraska Press, 1983): 36. Another example is Joseph
Smith (1805–44), who rejected traditional (explanations for) relationships among
human populations, situating the origins of human culture in North America, so
as to recover a link, between the Israelites and the Indians, and thus between the
Indians and the Christians.
33. We are indebted to our Ohio State colleague, Sabra Webber, for leading us to a
consideration of the aesthetic dimension.

activities seem naturally to fit. And that capability arises from the situation as well as the personality of the individual.

Re(al)locating privileging communication

Both Alinesitoué and Muhammad began to engage in privileging communication in environments in which privileging communication already took a number of recognizable forms and occurred through many different individuals, some inspired by an extra-human source, some not. The sudden appearance of Alinesitoué and Muhammad as privileging communicators set them into a potentially competitive relationship with these others; but the oppositional and critical nature of their messages made tension inevitable, not only with other communicators but also with those "non-communicators" who had some other kind of stake in the objects of criticism. To speak of competition and tension does not mean that other bearers of privileging communication had necessarily to show opposition openly, but rather that the "newcomers," if they were to attract a following, had to be both recognizable through familiar paradigms and also different enough to rework, recombine, and transcend them.

The processes by which the re(al)location of credibility and authority occurred in these two cases were very subtle indeed, and entailed, among other things, the careful cultivation of the audience's powers of discrimination. Alinesitoué's Kasila shrine highlighted the difference between her public, communitarian, egalitarian style and the elitism of the other shrine specialists, but at the Houssahara shrine, she beat the other elders, as possessors of secret spiritual gifts, at their own game. Much of her strength derived from the combination of the two styles. Muhammad's special utterances initially resembled the mantic *saj'* of the *kahins* and probably helped him attract recognition. He, like them, claimed that a non-human breath spoke through him; but he distinguished himself through the clarity of his speech, the "life-or-death" significance of the content, and the unitary nature of his source. As *hakam*, he shared in the arbitrative functions of some of the *kahins*, but unlike them he arbitrated in an ongoing way among groups who depended on him increasingly for protection and intercommunal stability. Like the *sha'irs* and the *shaykhs*, he concerned himself with defining authentic group practice, but rather than reinforce the narrower identity of one particular kin-group, he envisioned a larger network focused on him. He also distinguished himself from the *sha'irs* by being just as movingly eloquent as they without using recognizable meters and without the long apprenticeship they had to serve. Unfortunately, we know less about Arabian paradigms for *nabī* and *rasūl*, but whatever they were, it is clear that the qur'anic revelations continuously analogized all previous figures' careers to Muhammad's as it was emerging.[34]

The relationship between Alinesitoué and Muhammad and other bearers of privileging communication may have remained slippery throughout each of their lives. Muhammad had at first to distance himself from communicators who seemed similar (the *kahin*s and *sha'ir*s), and later from those claimed to be just like him (e.g., Maslamah). There is no evidence that Alinesitoué was opposed by elders in the villages from which supplicants came, although it is possible that she was opposed within her own village. In her actions at her personal shrine she did not need to claim to be entirely different from other elders because her superior efficaciousness spoke for itself: it began to rain again after she began to teach. However, Alinesitoué's claim that Emitai spoke and appeared to her, and in an ongoing way, did distinguish her, since few others were claiming to receive communications from Emitai, and, until the colonial conquest in the late nineteenth century, all previous claimants had been male. Her Kasila shrine was different from any other shrine in numerous respects, especially due to her willingness to teach its "secrets" openly.

Just as Alinesitoué's need to compete aggressively with other individuals seems less than Muhammad's, the number of roles he could draw on in fashioning his response seems greater. Although "elder" of a spirit shrine was not usually an oppositional role, at the time of Alinesitoué, many *awasena* elders were already opposing the French. However, she also became oppositional in another way, not to the other elders *per se*, but to a shrine system that, since the mid-eighteenth century, had increasingly emphasized wealth, security, and maleness as the

---

34. Just as Alan Segal, in *Paul the Convert: The Apostolate and Apostasy of Saul the Pharisee* (New Haven, CT: Yale University Press, 1990), has shown that the Gospels are our best evidence for first-century Judaism, so the Qur'an contains some of our best evidence for seventh-century Judaism and Christianity. Sidney H. Griffith, in "The Christians in Muhammad's World: The Qur'an and the Doctrine of the Trinity" (unpublished paper delivered at the American Academy of Religion Boston, 1987), has argued that the qur'anic account of Christianity may have offended not because it was distorted but because it was accurate. Note that the semantic field of "*Rasūl*" in the Qur'an includes verbal idioms both for imposing or unleashing something on someone and for showering a people with riches and blessings. See Mir, *Verbal Idioms of the Qur'an*: 145–7.

sources of ritual authority.[35] So Alinesitoué expanded an ongoing role by exhibiting greater spiritual gifts than were usually associated with it, whereas Muhammad sought to fashion a new role out of old ones or perhaps to utilize a role that had become peripheral. Again this is a difference of one sort that reflects a similarity of another—that each figure can be understood only in terms of the distribution of authority in his or her respective environment and the ways in which that distribution changed as a result of his or her activities.

The comparison between Alinesitoué and Muhammad demonstrates that, contrary to many views of "prophecy," privileging communication need not be confined to or focused on verbal pronouncements. Whereas Muhammad emphasized the production of special locutions, Alinesitoué emphasized the reception of shrines. That fact simply reflects the different arenas in which their respective challenges to the status quo were situated.[36] Although songs *about* Alinesitoué played a role in the conduct of the rites she taught, and are performed to the present day, the gift of special verbal formulations was not attributed to her in a significant way.[37] And although Muhammad's reform of rites was an important aspect of his career, his credibility probably hinged more on his ability to receive *qur'an*. This difference between the two figures exposes the limitations of "prophet" when it is associated with verbal eloquence and verbal communication, especially verbal communication that is full of ethical reflection. The difference also illustrates a similarity between the two figures: their shared need to establish legitimacy over and against the numerous other existing and competitive channels of communication.

Within their respective environments, the extent and nature of these two figures' authority seems unusual. For in both cases, obedience to the communicator in a wider range of matters came to be connected with obedience to the content of the messages. However, Muhammad is said to have demanded extended obedience whereas Alinesitoué is

---

35. Baum, *Shrines of the Slave Trade*: chapters 4–7.

36. At her shrines, Alinesitoué's motions were as important as her words, and included silent manipulation of objects. For a helpful explanation of a related form of privileging communication elsewhere in Africa, see Rosalind Shaw, "Splitting Truths from Darkness: Epistemological Aspects of Temne Divination," in *Ways of Knowing: African Systems of Divination*, P. Peek (Bloomington, IN: Indiana University Press, 1991): 133–52.

37. Since the Diola did not have a fixed oral tradition, except in certain praying formulae and songs, most oral performances were improvisations rather than recitations.

said to have had it extended to her without asking for it.[38] It should not
go unremarked at this point that both were helped enormously by their
ability to improve their followers' material situation. In this regard they
could claim or be perceived to be more *efficacious* than other bearers of
privileging communication.

However, they also differed from other communicators in their effort
to turn special and private gifts into public resources. Each figure offered
to everyone uniform and personal access, through a single individual,
to a superior being who, paradoxically, showed concern for all by communicating with only one. The existing non-oppositional bearers of
privileging communication in both societies seem to have emphasized
the secret private nature of their gifts more, and to have taught or acted
on behalf of much more limited audiences and on behalf of beings who
had much more limited scope and concern. For example, the ability to
receive *qur'an* was, according to Muhammad, limited to him, but its
recitation was publicly available to all, as was his personal, face-to-
face, teaching and guidance. Performance of rites at the Houssahara
shrine, and the ability to "see" its spirit, were limited to Alinesitoué,
but her teaching, especially in connection with Kasila and Huyaye, was
publicly available to all. In both cases, where "students" could not come
to them, their emissaries could carry the teachings to the students' own
locales.

So these figures' abilities to co-opt, recombine, and replace competitive sources of authority had to do with their ability to define and
resolve disjunctions between themselves and others. But it may also
have benefited from the current condition of alternate sources of authority and power, or in the audiences' ties to existing structures of authority. We do not know enough yet in either of these cases to be sure,
but to understand how any given individual acquires authority entails
knowing something about how and where authority was available at
a particular time. Other studies have shown that a little-used role can
take over when a major one becomes weak.[39] Conversely, even if all
existing sources of authority are strong, someone particularly good
at co-optation could draw on that strength. In Alinesitoué's area, the

---

38. In the Qur'an (43:31), certain Meccans say that they would have been more likely
   to follow Muhammad if he had come from a more influential family. That fact
   sheds some light on the difficulty of building a following on the basis of acquired
   rather than ascribed traits.
39. For example, Peter Brown, "The Rise and Function of the Holy Man in Antiquity":
   80–101.

awasena elders of her day were under attack and felt vulnerable, but nevertheless were still managing to compete with French administrators and Christian missionaries. However, their vulnerability to arrest by colonial administrators posed the continual threat of interrupted associations with their clienteles. We know little about the condition of other authority figures in western Arabia in the early seventh century, but it seems possible that Muhammad, at least in replacing the Meccan leaders as the center of a large network, drew on strength rather than weakness.

In any comprehensive study, we would also want to know much more about the current condition of the paradigm(s) through which an oppositional individual attempted to be recognized. Since an oppositional figure may need an unusual amount of room to maneuver, we might want to formulate a "Goldilocks hypothesis:" if expectations are too well-defined, i.e., "hot," the oppositional individual has too little room to maneuver and grow. If the audience has no notion whatsoever of the role that is being claimed, if expectations are too "cold," it will not engage their attention enough for the process of proving to proceed. It may also be that the existence of varied understandings of the desired role(s) in multiple constituencies establishes the potential for a wider following. Perhaps the more competition the better, too, since competition can stimulate more and more persuasive rhetoric.

As oppositional figures, both Alinestioué and Muhammad had to prove themselves to an unusual extent and in an ongoing manner. The stories of their respective commissionings are particularly meaningful in this context. Both are reported to have had a gripping experience while away from home, she in an ordinary place in a foreign locale, he in a less foreign place that had been set aside for special activity. Both experiences are reported to have involved both aural and visual dimensions, and in both cases a request is said to have been refused three times and finally accepted only out of fear of death. These experiences led both figures to perform initial activities that symbolized and explained their respective missions.

The difference between their initial activities reflects the different emphases already discussed: Alinesitoué's activity was the actual discovery of water as a demonstration of Emitai's ability to bring rain; Muhammad's, the forced recitation of a special verbal formulation that demonstrated the indispensable nature of Allah's guidance. Both are said to have postponed public disclosure even after accepting the commission, and to have appeared crazed or ill during the interval between acceptance and disclosure.

The two societies had similarly alternative paradigms for explaining mental disorientation. In both, "crazed" behavior could be interpreted as mental illness or as the reflection of a spiritual gift institutionalized in particular roles associated with privileging communication. In both societies, the calling or appointment to such roles already involved a degree of compulsion, calling, or appointment. So this type of commissioning may have established the unusual altruism of such emissaries in accepting such a heavy and frightening burden on behalf of others.

Such narratives could also reinforce the sense of urgency conveyed by both figures, a sense of urgency that may have been another major factor in distinguishing them from most other privileging communicators. Commissioning stories and experiences like those of Alinesitoué and Muhammad may have been a way of representing the *unusual* degree of compulsion necessary to justify their claim to be undertaking a special and critical mission at a particular juncture in the history of their people. For both figures presented themselves as the emissaries of superior beings who were trying to intervene at a particular time for a critical purpose, and therefore could not possibly be sending different messages through different people.

For both figures, the clear evidence of actual natural and/or social ills contributed to a sense of urgency, and both traced the concrete problems of their communities to the neglect of a superior being who was already known to be somehow translocal. Alinesitoué and Muhammad presented these already known beings as both more active in the world and more central to their groups' history, identity, and well-being than had previously been thought. According to Alinesitoué, Emitai was more than a caring being to be appealed to only in dire need, more than a being who had created the world and given it knowledge but not remained actively involved in it, and more than a being who would decide human beings' fates after death. Her Emitai was the force behind all the shrines, and would help the Diola if they would listen to and follow the instructions she conveyed. For Muhammad, Allah was responsible for more than matters that transcended the spheres of beings who belonged to narrower kin-groups. He was both Creator and Judge, actively and regularly intervening in a linear process of human history, the beginning and end of which he controlled according to a plan. Muhammad invoked well-established traditions of "end-of-the-world" speculation to underscore his point; Alinesitoué could have, but there is no evidence that she did.[40]

---

40. The Diola had a tradition of the world's being destroyed and created numerous times in a cyclical manner, so that in theory apocalyptic speculation was possible.

"Prophesying" the past: distinguishing traditional from authentic

Although English usage of "prophet" emphasizes predicting the future, figures like Alinesitoué and Muhammad are just as likely to "predict" the past. That is to say, although they usually have futuristic elements, their view of what will happen in the future is closely connected with their efforts to reinterpret the past and to identify their own time as a turning-point in history.

In both of these cases, the restoration of a neglected but superior being was crucial to the recovery of abandoned practices and lost identity. In some specifics, such as the purification of the Ka'ba, this meant recovering the true and older meaning of existing practices. In others, such as the association of the Ka'ba with Ibrahim, it involved the substitution of ideas and practices that diverged from existing custom only because they had been forgotten. Both figures, then, made a distinction between what had been authentic and what had become traditional. This breach was especially important in light of competition with other figures who used privileging communication to support existing practice as authoritative practice. In this process, Muhammad increasingly stressed his disjunction with other competing roles while co-opting them, just as he increasingly stressed his conjunction with earlier figures and roles presented as having a prior and indigenous claim to centrality (i.e., *nabī* and *rasūl*). As a result, he introduced and resolved yet another disjunction, between customary Arab practice and authentic Arab practice. According to the Qur'an, hearers were not being asked to abandon their authentic identity but rather to rediscover it in a more distant past. Alinesitoué presented Huyaye as a key practice in the worship of Emitai, but one which existed only as a pale and localized vestige of its former self.

In at least one important respect, these similar processes led to somewhat different results. Living in an acephalous society with a toleration for a diversity of shrines, Alinesitoué sought to *add* her new shrines and in so doing to reinterpret others, whereas Muhammad sought to replace all others with his. Once again, to explain the difference, we would need to know more about the respective situations, especially the differences between the relationship of the Diola Christians with the French and the relationship of the Jews and Christians with the Meccans. In the Arabian case, there is some evidence that tendencies toward greater exclusivism predated Muhammad: some of the Meccans had already begun the process of elevating the Ka'ba above other shrines, and some inhabitants of western Arabia already associated *nabī*s and *rasūl*s with a being who demanded exclusive attention.[41] Muhammad co-opted Jewish and Christian exclusivism and associated it with a shrine that already claimed some degree of wider authority.

Conversely, the Diola *awasena* were in competition with a group of people, the European Christians, who were trying through Christian Diola to substitute a foreign exclusivism for indigenous pluralism. Furthermore, Alinesitoué was seeking to distance herself from the French whereas Muhammad was seeking to incorporate the Meccans. If Alinesitoué was to counter the Diola who had become Christians, and, by extension, the French, and there was no indigenous tradition of exclusivism to draw on, she was more likely to benefit from claiming to have received the most efficacious shrine, not the only shrine worthy of attention. Furthermore, since the Diola Christians called the Christian god Emitai, the being she called Emitai needed to have a very different nature. And since Diola Christians claimed to have a greater path to Emitai, Alinesitoué had to underscore the superiority of her path by defining it as different from theirs.

Social remapping: new boundaries for old

The recovery of abandoned praxis and identity was, then, crucial to both leaders' ability to imagine a presumptive identity among disparate groups. For what was "recovered" was asserted to be equally authentic to a variety of constituencies whose "traditions" would otherwise have distinguished them from each other and kept them from acting in concert. To stress the shared responsibilities of these wider presumptive communities, both leaders also made a more central place for the economically and socially marginalized and disadvantaged, associating worship of the neglected being with charity to the weak and thus redefining the social position of the wealthy.

Insisting on such behavioral indicators of membership as charity, as well as public and communal worship, both Alinesitoué and Muhammad allowed for a more visible set of boundaries to come into being, since each leader defined as "one" all who adopted their norms. As a result of this new and wider unification, both leaders also drew a finer line between their followers and related groups whose status had previously

---

41. For lack of space and conclusive evidence, this account has left out the *hanifs*, who were not identifiably Jewish or Christian but appear to have been focused on the worship of a single being. The Qur'an's referring to Ibrahim as a *hanif* reinforces our sense of Mecca's communal fluidity.

been somewhat ambiguous. For example, Alinesitoué distinguished the true Diola day of rest—rest for the rice paddies—from the Sabbath of the Christian Diola—rest for humans. Muhammad adopted a direction of prayer—Mecca—different from that of the Banu Isra'il—Jerusalem.

Yet each leader also offered to the groups they had distanced a more authentic place in the new communities. In restoring the Ka'ba and its associated rites to their Abrahamic condition, and in orienting prayer toward that single location, Muhammad both explained clearly who the Jews and Christians *really* were and offered them a chance to rediscover their authenticity along with others. Thus everyone who heard him was both *formerly* and *potentially* interconnected; any who remained unconnected would now do so by their own choice. Alinesitoué required Diola Catholics to return to the *awasena* way, while allowing them to continue the new Christian rituals. As a result, Alinesitoué attracted some Christians, and Muhammad attracted some Jews and Christians.

Perhaps most important, neither figure was limited to an initial or natural constituency. Both sought to encourage ever wider and more diverse groups to worry about the problems they had identified, and to imagine the solutions to these problems as they did. Because both defined membership in their communities in tangible as well as intangible ways, both provoked opposition from the most powerful and aggressive centralizing elements in their environments, the French colonial administrators in Alinesitoué's case, and the leaders of some of Mecca's most influential families in Muhammad's. Muhammad interfered with the Meccans through caravan-raiding, and Alinesitoué interfered with the French through altering the production and use of critical commodities.

In both cases, opposition arose from the economic by-products of obedience to the new bearers of privileging communication. However, because Muhammad was able to win over most of his opposition and Alinesitoué could not, Muhammad benefited more from the results of persuading people to accept what they had formerly opposed. And although both used their control of a unique form of privileging communication as a focal point for a new network of relationships, Muhammad's situation allowed him to benefit more from his unusual skill in forging the actual social alliances that allowed him to overcome opposition. Both individuals appear to have been especially sensitive, flexible, adaptive, and insightful into their own cultures, but Alinesitoué's integrative abilities were, by force of circumstances, expressed primarily in her teaching network, whereas Muhammad was free to establish broader kinds of alliances.

Postscript

SUFFERING BY COMPARISON

Lindsay Jones

It is inevitable that while Marilyn Waldman is fondly remembered by many as a historian of Islam with special interests in comparison, others have felt her influence primarily as a comparativist with special interests in Islam. Bruce Lawrence's comments in the Preface remind us of the former possibility, and my comments accentuate the latter; that is, the sense in which my former Ohio State colleague's work is consequential and relevant to scholars of religion, indeed all scholars, who only tangentially share her deeply informed concerns with Islamic traditions.

As we are reminded in that Preface, there is an artificiality to this rendition of *Prophecy and Power: Muhammad and the Qur'an in the Light of Comparison* insofar as it fixes an unfinished conversation that the author was having with her colleagues, her students, and most of all with herself right up until the final months of her life. The latest versions of this book, still very rough-hewn, were heavily revised and reorganized in the context of the final course that Marilyn taught at Ohio State, a seminar entitled "Comparison as a Social Act;" to be sure, reading the present book transports me back to the countless discussions about the topic that we had both in and outside of that class. That Bruce Lawrence, along with a wide and shifting array of colleagues and graduate students, managed to fashion the messily exuberant manuscript that she left us into a smooth narrative is a wonderful accomplishment; that skillful editorial endurance ought to be heartily congratulated. Nonetheless, we can be certain that, had her untimely death in 1996 not intervened, there would have been many more and large revisions. She was relentlessly critical of her own work, and by no means ready to announce this project complete.

Though a large share of the materials for that final seminar were drawn from Islam, and focused especially on ways that Muslims have defined themselves and their tradition via comparisons to Judaism and Christianity, her interests spilled over into the more generic processes of comparison both as a scholarly method and, even more compelling for her, as a social practice. Herself a great champion of comparison, she alerted students to the plentiful hostility that has been heaped on comparative scholarship. They were apprised, for instance, that, for many scholars, comparison is akin to an infectious disease, made especially dangerous by its enduring and wide contagion. Unwilling to extricate their assessments of "the comparative method" from the work of James G. Frazer, William Robertson Smith and E.B. Tylor, many continue to caricature comparison as a kind of home-wrecking procedure: it yanks elements away from their systems of cultural or familial relations and slams them into the confines of some evaluative, probably evolutionary scheme. In this view, comparison, particularly of a cross-cultural sort that so fascinated Marilyn, either willfully or inadvertently wrenches historical phenomena out of their cultural contexts, and thus flattens and disrespects the uniqueness of individual cases. According to critics of that ilk, we must, as a matter of academic responsibility, and to the greatest extent possible, abjure comparison.

For others among Marilyn's inventory of detractors, the abuses of comparison, as a sibling to typology and morphology, are primarily of a (dis)organizational sort insofar as superficial similarities are allowed to provide the basis for catalogue and pigeonhole efforts: at best expedient, they are more often insidious and distorting. Interesting and telling idiosyncrasies thus become reduced to mere instances of broader, reified categories. For other critics, comparison amounts to an ahistorical or even anti-historical mode of judgment by analogy, an insidious form of misleading that perverts discrete and unique phenomena by seeing and assessing them in terms of something other than themselves. For still others, Marilyn mused, the transgressions of comparison are related primarily to generalization and totalizing abstraction. By this reasoning, what is comparison but a method for building, seemingly afloat in the air between concrete cases, forgettable idealizations and fictive universals that correspond to nothing other than the scholar's prejudiced imagination? Comparison must be condemned, we are told, as a decidedly "uncritical" affair insofar as it always undermines empirical rigor and usually perpetuates some form of social oppression and injustice. Finally, in her catalogue of criticisms leveled at comparisons and comparativists, Marilyn reminded students that for an even larger constituency—including many practioners of "comparative religion"—comparison is so integral to all our processes of thinking and deciding that it does not merit, nor should it receive, special comment. Explicit discussions of comparative methods like those on which her final seminar was trained are, from that perspective, both redundant and otiose, empty alike of substantive content or analytical rewards.

None of these criticisms is entirely unwarranted, and, of course, none escaped Marilyn's critical view. Specters of totalization and essentialism, evolutionism and diffusionism, decontextualization and reification, do accompany many versions of comparison. And they do pose, as she constantly cautioned us, significant threats to our critical health. She was, in many respects, a historians' historian, uncompromisingly appreciative of the uniqueness of particular persons and events, and thus incessantly skeptical of any version of generalization. Yet, notwithstanding widespread disdain for what is so often imagined as the "disease of comparison"—disdain linked in many cases with attachment to the hopeful, if elusive, expectation of prejudiceless description of isolated, individual cases—Marilyn persuaded us that no immunization is foolproof.

To the contrary, she countered these deep and wide suspicions about the so-termed comparative method by forcing others to recognize the ubiquity of comparison. In her view, while the prospect of studying specific historical phenomena strictly "on their own terms"—that is, ostensibly *non*-comparatively—might be well-intentioned, such efforts are certain to be frustrated, and for the very reason that anti-comparativists most fear: the ubiquity of the comparison virus. As she made eminently clear, even the most rigorous empirical descriptions, a goal to which she herself always aspired, always already presuppose comparative studies. She argued with equal measures of toughness and humor that strategic pleas to absolute singularity either for one's self or one's objects of study, claims that phenomena are "beyond compare" or "utterly different," are never, in the end, sustainable. Comparison, in some fashion, is unavoidable; it is a virus that can be contained but not eliminated.

Indeed—and this is the insight from which she drew her course title—Marilyn made the case that comparison is *not* simply a method of study; nor is it one academic option among many. Instead, she insisted that comparison is no less than *a fact of life*. Not just a virus it can also be, and should become, a cure for worse viruses. All interpretation, all organizations of knowledge, all understanding must, of necessity, pass through what others have termed "the travail of comparison." Accordingly, having realized early on that all scholarship, all teaching, perhaps all of life's endeavors, are to some significant extent comparative, she urged that, rather than aspiring to avoid comparison, it ought to be embraced—though, as she undertook all things, in a highly self-conscious and critical fashion. Though not an easy cure, comparison, if undertaken with rigor, can, she argued, heal a host of problems, scholarly and otherwise.

In order to heighten sensitivities regarding the crucial and ubiquitous role that comparison plays in nearly all aspects of life, Marilyn encouraged her students to reflect upon, and to take seriously, what she termed "lexical usages" in relation to comparison, that is, idiomatic, colloquial and seemingly off-handed phrases in which scholars and non-scholars invoked the language and strategy of comparison. She appraised and scrutinized, for instance, the familiar but glib phrases "comparing apples and oranges," "to compare and contrast," "comparatively speaking," "beyond comparison," "unfair comparison," "same difference," and so forth. And then, she provided her own favorite. She commented, as I recall, that of all the colloquial phrases she could summon to mind, the one that was best suited to *her* attitudes toward comparison, and best exemplified her understanding of the unique value of comparison for scholarship and teaching, was "comparing notes." That metaphor superseded all others because it implied an activity that served to open and promote discussion rather than foreclosing debate, to widen rather than narrow the range of alternatives, and to share and exchange insights rather than to hoard them. To mix two of her favorite metaphors, then, the academic activity to which she aspired required her to position herself as a "hostess" who brought together people, both live scholars and historical figures, to "compare notes."

Capitalizing on her own pedagogical ploy, I organize the remainder of this postscript by keying on some of those colloquial phrases as clues with which to summarize four of Marilyn's recurrent points about the happily inescapable ubiquity of comparison.

First, under that infamous rubric of complaints about the insidiousness of "comparing apples and oranges," Marilyn focused a spotlight on the widespread, actually prevalent, tendency to imagine that some phenomena are "naturally" amenable to comparison, while other comparative juxtapositions are simply impossible, infelicitous or somehow "unfair." In response to that charge, Marilyn impelled us to realize that *all* comparisons are artificial and contrived insofar as they require the construction a special, heuristic context in which to reflect, with special interests and perspectives, on a juxtaposition of one's own making. As she wrote in a brief e-mail message and then elaborated in her manuscript, when comparing, "it is important to pay attention to contexts—the context from which the things compared are drawn, and the context in which the act of comparison is undertaken." Consequently, she contended that no phenomena, however seemingly unparallel and irrelevant to one another, are intrinsically "incomparable" or "beyond compare." No—or perhaps, depending on your perspective, *all*—such juxtapositions are, in that sense, "unfair comparisons" insofar as they entail the relocation of discrete phenomena into some comparative arena, some heuristic comparative context, of the comparer's own making. By her critical assessment, neither so-termed "obvious similarities" nor "obvious differences" are ever so obvious, self-evident or "natural" as they might first appear.

A second, closely related and even larger cluster of Marilyn Waldman's insights about comparison arises in relation to her rejoinders to similarly common and equally pejorative objections about "idle comparison" or "insignificant comparison." Comparison, she reminded us, is too often imagined as a strictly academic procedure, an optional option with few consequences beyond pedagogy or illustration. In response to that charge, her scholarly protocol, both in the classroom and in writing—with the current book providing her most sustained exposition on this point—demonstrates over and over again that there are few if any fully disinterested, "idle comparisons." Invariably, comparison is, as she entitled her seminar, "a social act," a matter of some social and material consequence. That is to say, Marilyn persuaded us that comparison, as an always-contrived procedure, must become a pragmatic, evaluative, interested social act, undertaken with express purposes (either successfully or unsuccessfully) of changing opinions, reconfiguring socio-economic alliances, and redistributing religious and/or political power. Focusing on the social ramifications of comparison, Marilyn's work, whether in this book or that seminar, suggests that, on the one hand, someone, some institution, or some idea always "suffers by comparison." On the other hand, though, the converse is nearly always also true: virtually all comparisons are, from some perspective or slant, "fruitful comparisons" insofar as they accrue an advantage or privilege to the parties who undertake them.

In other words, where there has been boundless debate about the relative merits of *scholars* undertaking comparisons, Waldman shifted the gaze to a largely neglected version of "comparative religion" that scrutinizes the ways that historical communities and religious actors have themselves undertaken comparisons, especially as a means of winning ascendency over their competitors. Thus, instead of the familiar scholarly exercise of reflecting on similarities and differences among, for instance, Moses, Jesus and Muhammad, she brought to our attention the now-unmistakable—but previously unnoticed—sense in which Moses, Jesus and especially Muhammad were themselves "comparativists." This point is as brilliant as it is rare, as welcome as it has been, up till now, ignored. Marilyn made us see the sense in which, and the extent to which, historical religious figures as well as academic students of religion have relied deliberately and aggressively on strategies of comparison in order to make their cases, to plead their singularity, and thus to win some social advantage. She helped us to appreciate, for example, how Jewish claims to uniqueness depend upon, and are sustained by, a rhetoric of comparison; how religious leaders in Africa and elsewhere deploy comparison to legitimate their platforms of reform; and how the recasting of biblical materials in the Quran, say in the story of Joseph, supports in a comparative fashion Muslims' claims to continuity with, yet *divergence from*—and thus *superiority over*—other Abrahamic peoples. For Marilyn, it is the strategic role of comparison "in the street," as it were—comparison, most notably, in the calculated maneuvering between Muslims, Jews and Christians, or between Muslims and other Muslims—that is most interesting and revealing.

Moreover, once those floodgates were opened, recognitions of "comparison as a social act" multiplied at an alarming rate. This line of inquiry worked for Waldman and her students like one of those computer-generated designs that camouflages some image so that, at first, you do not even notice it; but then, once discerned, you cannot *not* see the formerly obscured image. Recognitions of comparison became, as she herself repeatedly noted, a kind of compulsion, even an obsession, and her enthusiasm for the matter was contagious. Yes, she not only identified the virus of comparison; she helped to spread it. Under her influence, we were slapped with realizations concerning the "strategic comparisons" that were at work in automobile and furniture advertisements, in the promotion and assessment of political candidates, in sports and sports commentaries, in comedians' monologues, in grocery shopping and grading papers, in walking through a building or in picking a television program to watch. Everywhere suddenly we were confronted with, to borrow again her seminar title, exercises in "comparison as a social act." She proved eloquently and emphatically, and often with her characteristically wry and self-deprecating humor, that comparison is hardly the sole preserve of academics.

In any event, that brings me to a third sort of observation about Marilyn Waldman's comparative preoccupations. By keying in on colloquial references to "felicitous comparison," "productive comparison," and/or "fruitful comparison" she forced us to recognize the sense in which the supposed "fruits" of comparison are far richer and more abundant than is commonly appreciated. Comparison is, or could be, in her view, far more than a means of organizing or cataloguing knowledge. The estimable and underestimated value of comparison is due to the fact that it is, in her words, "an important way of producing new knowledge." That is to say, where comparison is usually embraced by academics, either directly or implicitly, as a procedure for the "discovery" of apparently pre-existent meanings, meanings that are somehow already "out there" awaiting our acts of retrieval, Marilyn compels us to appreciate that "comparison involves the construction of *new* meanings." Comparison becomes productive, constructive and transformative in ways, and to an extent, that far too few scholars and pedagogues have been willing or able to realize. Comparison may be orchestrated by academics, religious leaders, architects, ritual choreographers, politicians, journalists or comedians, but invariably it becomes, Marilyn teaches us, among the most effective means for challenging and rearranging the status quo rather than simply replicating it. In short, comparison is not simply reiterative and descriptive of standing insights; it is a means of creatively (and, of course, strategically) generating new insights.

Fourth and finally we come back to Marilyn's preferred activity and her own professional path. If comparison is among our paramount means not only for arranging and transacting old knowledge, but likewise for producing new knowledge, then comparison could and should play an especially prominent role in educational processes. Marilyn was, above all, the consummate educator. I count myself not only as one of her colleagues but also as one of her students. And while her teaching was deliberately and aggressively comparative in innumerable respects, one sort of play of similarity and difference is especially noteworthy, namely, that which operated in her penchant for what might be termed "qualified agreement." Whether in seminars, in committee meetings or hallway conversations—that is to say, even in those occasions when she was perhaps an unwilling and overworked "hostess"—she entertained questions with patience and grace. On the one hand, irrespective of the *naïveté* of the queries, Marilyn virtually always found a way to agree, or at least always allowed her "guests" at these conversational encounters to think that she agreed. Always she combined patience, generosity, and creativity to find that *point of sameness* between what students had said and what they *ought* to have said. She had a rare facility for putting words in other peoples' mouths—for rephrasing their formulations and then returning them in much better shape than she'd found them. In those conversations, students and colleagues—as also some of us lucky enough to be both—were invariably flattered that she had discovered what had seemed to be an elusive point of agreement between their ideas and hers.

At the same time, however, Marilyn seemed always to disagree. Hers was always a qualified agreement. Along with affirming, she always challenged. She nearly always found something at least a little wrong with what colleagues and students said, *some point of difference* and disagreement. With Marilyn, it was always, "Yes, but ..." First she would affirm and strengthen your argument; then she would point out some presupposition left unexamined, some precedent not cited, some historical exception to the generalization, or some potentially insidious ramification unnoticed.

Her generosity was, then, always laced with a disputation, a contestation or a challenge, the intrusion of which in the end made her even more generous. Her very restlessness, impatience and chronic dissatisfaction with all ideas and formulations—her own included—kept us all on the move. Under her influence, "reification," which presupposed some false sense of the fixity of concepts and conclusions, became the greatest transgression while "heuristic," defined by Webster as "that which serves to guide, discover or reveal ... valuable for empirical research but unproven or incapable of proof," became the loudest of battle cries and the highest of aspirations. To love and respect ideas—others and one's own—required that one hold them softly and tentatively, rather than clutching and defending them. Always the experimental, the contingent, the provisional and that playful, ludic tone prevailed. She held us—and even more herself—to an unreasonable, unrealizable standard so that finishing anything, or laying anything to rest, was nearly impossible.

In the end, therefore, there is an ironic suitability to the peculiar circumstances that give rise to this publication of *Prophecy and Power*. Marilyn left us too soon, and she left behind a ragged, still-working manuscript, replete with self-critical marginalia, arrows, slashes, queries, and multiple versions of whole sections and paragraphs. It was quintessentially a work in progress, under construction, far from fully finished, especially in her own eyes. I realized in our conversations about this project, which, even while competing with chemotherapy and the other challenges of cancer treatment, had become ever-present on her mind, that it was impossible for her to reread the manuscript without rewriting it. Even in the final months of her life, instead of fine-tuning sentences and tracking down page references, she was rearranging and restructuring the entire argument of the book. Not surprisingly, the book itself had a new and different title nearly every time we talked about it. One wonders, in fact, how and if she would ever have been willing to announce that the work was completed. While she, of course, admired a well-polished book, she was even more effusive in her praise for the sort of cobbled, cluttered, and contingent group e-mail exchange that allowed her to "compare notes." Consequently, that this book finally makes its way to print only via the efforts of numerous students, colleagues, and friends—Bruce Lawrence and Robert Baum foremost among them—is indeed a fitting turn of events. Though we can be certain she would find reasons to dispute as well as to affirm the way that her unperfected drafts have been polished into a handsome volume, it has been just the sort of collaborative initiative that suggests we may, after all, have learned something from her and her example. Nonetheless, to recycle one of those lexical phrases a final time, engaging her posthumous manuscript has also reminded us that, where Marilyn Waldman is concerned—Marilyn Waldman as a teacher, writer, mentor, organizer, administrator, colleague, and hostess par excellence—we all "suffer by comparison."

WORKS BY
MARILYN ROBINSON WALDMAN

MONOGRAPH

Toward a Theory of Historical Narrative: A Case Study in Perso-Islamicate Historiography. Columbus, OH: The Ohio State University Press, 1980.

EDITED VOLUMES

Muslims and Christians, Muslims and Jews: A Common Past, A Hopeful Future. Columbus, OH: The Islamic Foundation of Central Ohio, 1992.

Judaism and Islam: Fostering Understanding. Jewish Education News 13, no. 1 (Winter 1992). Co-edited with Helena Schlam.

Understanding Women: The Challenge of Cross-Cultural Perspectives. Vol. 7 of *Papers in Comparative Studies.* Columbus, OH: The Ohio State University Press, 1991–2. Co-edited with Artemis Leontis and Müge Galin.

The University of the Future. Columbus, OH: Center for Comparative Studies in the Humanities, 1990. Co-edited with Richard Bjornson.

Rethinking Patterns of Knowledge. Vol. 5 of *Papers in Comparative Studies.* Columbus, OH: Ohio State University Press, 1989–90. Co-edited with Richard Bjornson.

Religion in the Modern World. Vol. 3 of *Papers in Comparative Studies.* Columbus, OH: Ohio State University Press, 1984. Co-edited with Chang Ho and Richard Bjornson.

The Islamic World. Readings in World History, Vol. VI. New York: Oxford University Press, 1973 (second edition: Chicago, IL: The University of Chicago Press, 1984). Co-edited with William H. McNeill.

SCHOLARLY ARTICLES

"Innovation as Renovation: The Prophet as Agent of Change." In *Innovation in Religious Traditions: Essays in the Interpretation of Religious Change*, ed. Michael A. Williams, Colett Cox, and Martin S Jaffee. Berlin: Mouton de Gruyter, 1992. With Robert M. Baum.

"Raising the Stakes: The Politics of Stance." *Papers in Comparative Studies* 7 (1991–2): 1–12. With Müge Galin and Artemis Leontis.

"Islam in Spain." In *The Christopher Columbus Encyclopedia*, ed. Silvio A. Bedini and David Buisseret. New York: Simon & Schuster, 1991.

"Reflections on Islamic Tradition, Women, and Family." In *Muslim Families in North America*, ed. Earle H. Waugh, Sharon McIrvin Abu-Laban, and Regula Qureshi, 241–84. Edmonton, Canada: University of Alberta Press, 1991.

"Bayhaqi." In *Encyclopedia Iranica*, ed. Ehsan Yarshetar. Costa Mesa, CA: Mazda Publishers, 1990.

"The Islamic World." In *Encyclopedia Britannica*. Chicago, IL: Encyclopedia Britannica, Inc., 1987; reprinted in abridged form in *Britannica Book of the Year*, 1987.

"Sunnah." In *Encyclopedia of Religion*, ed. Mircea Eliade, Charles J. Adams, *et al.* New York: Macmillan, 1987.

"Islamic Eschatology." In *Encyclopedia of Religion*, ed. Mircea Eliade, Charles J. Adams, *et al.* New York: Macmillan, 1987.

"Nubuwah." In *Encyclopedia of Religion*, ed. Mircea Eliade, Charles J. Adams, *et al.* New York: Macmillan, 1987.

"Traditions as a Modality of Change: Islamic Examples." *History of Religions* 25, no. 4 (May, 1986): 318–40.

"Primitive Mind/Modern Mind: New Approaches to an Old Dichotomy Applied to Islam." In *Approaches to Islam in Religious Studies*, ed. Richard Martin, 91–105. Tucson, AZ: University of Arizona Press, 1985.

"New Approaches to 'Biblical' Material in the Qur'an." *Muslim World* 75, no. 1 (January, 1985): 1–16. Reprinted in *Studies in Islamic and Judaic Traditions*, ed. William M. Brinner and Stephen D. Ricks. Atlanta, GA: Scholars Press, 1986.

"Women in the Islamic World." In *Women in Development Seminar Proceedings Spring 1982*, ed. Erika Bourguignon and Francille M. Firebaugh, 17–28. Columbus, OH: The Ohio State University Department of Anthropology and Department of Home Management and Housing, 1983.

"Islamic Resurgence in Context." In *The Contemporary Mediterranean World*, ed. Carl F. Pinkele and Adamantia Pollis, 98–123. New York: Praeger, 1983.

"The Popular Appeal of the Prophetic Paradigm in West Africa." In *Islam in Local Contexts*, ed. Richard Martin, 110–14. Leiden, The Netherlands: Brill, 1982.

"The Otherwise Unnoteworthy Year 711: A Response to Hayden White," *Critical Inquiry* 7 (1981): 784–92. Reprinted in *On Narrative*, ed. W.J.T. Mitchell. Chicago, IL: The University of Chicago Press, 1981.

"Semiotics and Historical Narrative." *Papers in Comparative Studies* 1 (1981): 167–88.

"Three Books on Sufism." *Numen* 27 (1980): 256–66.

Untitled major review article. *Religious Studies Review* 2 (1979): 22–35.

"Islamic Studies: A New Orientalism?" *Journal of Interdisciplinary History* 8 (1978): 546–62.

"The Development of the Concept of *Kufr* in the Qur'an." *Journal of the American Oriental Society* 88 (1968): 442–55.

"The Church of Scotland Mission at Blantyre, Nyasaland: Its Political Implications." *Bulletin of the Society for African Church History* 2 (1968): 299–310.

"A Note on the Ethnic Factor in the Fulani *Jihad*." *Africa* 36 (1966): 286–91.

"The Fulani *Jihad*: A Reassessment." *Journal of African History* 6, no. 3 (1965): 333–55. Reprinted in *Nineteenth Century Africa*, ed. P.J.M. McEwan. London: Oxford University Press, 1968.

REVIEWS

Translating the Message: The Missionary Impact on Culture by Lamin O. Sanneh. *Journal of Religion in Africa* 22, no. 2 (1992): 159–72.

The Political Language of Islam, by Bernard Lewis. *American Historical Review* 96, no. 5 (December, 1991): 1586–7.

Beyond the Written Word: Oral Aspects of Scripture in the History of Religion by William A. Graham. *History of Religions* 30, no. 3 (February, 1991): 313–17.

Transforming Women's History, ed. Margaret Strobel. *Journal of Women's History* 1, no. 1 (1989–90): 115–19.

Atlas of the Islamic World since 1500, by Francis Robinson. *Journal of the American Oriental Society* 107, no. 4 (1987): 802–03.

Islam in the Modern World, ed. Dennis MacEoin and Ahmed al-Shahi. *Muslim World* 76, no. 3–4 (July/October, 1986): 238–9.

Mouvements populaires à Bagdad à l'époque 'Abbasside, IXe–XIe siècles, by Simha Sabari. *Muslim World* 75, no. 2 (April, 1985): 120–21.

Sex and Society in Islam: Birth Control Before Nineteenth Century, by B.F. Musallam. *Journal of Interdisciplinary History* 16, no. 1 (Summer, 1985): 173–5.

Medieval Historical Writing in the Christian and Islamic Worlds, by D.O. Morgan. *International Journal of Middle East Studies* 17, no. 1 (1985): 144–5.

West Africa and Islam, by Peter Clarke. *Muslim World* 74, no. 3–4 (July/October 1984): 209–11.

Islam: Continuity and Change in the Modern World, by John Voll. *American–Arab Affairs* 9 (1984): 120–23.

Islam in Tropical Africa, second edition, ed. I.M. Lewis. *Muslim World* 61 (1981): 248–9.

Karim Khan Zand, by John Perry. *Middle East Studies Association Bulletin* 14 (1980): 256–66.

Islamic History: A New Interpretation, by M.A. Shaban. *American Historical Review*, 83 (1978): 405–06.

Nigerian Panoply: Arms and Armour of the Northern Region, by A.D.H. Bivar. *Journal of African History* 6 (1965): 429–30.

TRANSLATIONS AND TEXTBOOKS

IslamFiche (a microfiche collection of primary sources). Amsterdam: Inter-documentation, 1985. With William Graham.

Transnational Approaches of the Social Sciences: Readings in International Studies. Co-edited with Jan S. Adams. Lanham, MD: University Press of America, 1983.

"The Woman Who Lost Her Man," by Sadeq Hedayat. In *Sadeq Hadayat: An Anthropology*, Modern Persian Literature Series 2, ed. Ehsan Yarshater, 50–60. Boulder, CO: Westview Press, 1979. With Guity Nashat.

"Three Drops of Blood," by Sadeq Hedayat. In *'The Blind Owl' Forty Years After*, edited by Michael Hillman, 43–67. Austin, TX: University of Texas Press, 1978. With Guity Nashat.

"Dead End," by Sadeq Hedayat. In *Literature East and West*, 20 (1976): 47–60. With Guity Nashat.

NEWSPAPER, POPULAR, AND PROFESSIONAL ARTICLES

"Historical Perspectives on Christian–Muslim Relations," and "Historical Perspectives on Jewish–Muslim Relations," in *Muslims and Christians, Muslims and Jews: A Common Past, A Hopeful Future*. Columbus, OH: The Islamic Foundation of Central Ohio, 1992: 49–58 and 69–77, respectively.

"The Last Hundred Years—A Historical Perspective on the Middle East," *The Ohio Jewish Chronicle* (18 April 1991): 18, 68.

"Unity and Diversity in a Religious Tradition." In *The White Lotus: An Introduction to Tibetan Culture*, ed. Carole Elchert. Ithaca, NY: Snow Lion Publications, 1990.

"The Teacher as Citizen: The Public Face of Middle East Studies." *Southeast Regional Middle East Studies Seminar Newsletter*, (Spring 1990): 8–10.

"Understanding the Middle East." *Columbus Dispatch* (24 July 1985).

"A Report to the MESA Membership from the Ethics Committee ... Defense Intelligence Research Contracts." *MESA Newsletter* 7, no. 1 (Winter 1985): 8–10. With Dale Eickelman.

Untitled article on the Palestinians. *Columbus Dispatch* (14 March 1982).

"A Perspective on the World of Islam." *Dayton Journal Herald* (27 February 1981).

"View from OSU: Moslem Beliefs Both Unify, Divide Iran." *Columbus Dispatch*, (27 February 1980).

UNPUBLISHED PAPERS AND ADDRESSES

"The Power of Productive Paradox: An Exercise in Imagining Religion." Midwest American Academy of Religion, Kalamazoo, MI (March 1990).

"Periodization of Medieval Islamic History in the Context of World History." Middle East Studies Association, Toronto, Canada (November 1989).

"Multicultural Perspectives in Liberal Education." Curriculum 2000 Series, Purdue University, West Lafayette, IN (September 1989).

"Islamic Law and the Emulation of Muhammad in Comparative Perspective." Conference on Religious Law, University of Minnesota, Minneapolis–St Paul (Spring 1989).

"Women Leaders: Why are There More Outside the United States?" Women: Choices and Challenges, Lazarus Series, Columbus, OH (May 1989).

"Prophet Between Role and Event," Rockefeller Conference on History and Anthropology, Washington University, St Louis, MO (April 1989).

"Encounters with Europeans in Islamic Lands (Sixteenth Century)," Second Annual World History Symposium, San Diego State University, San Diego, CA (April 1989).

"Islamic History as World History," University of Arizona, Tucson, AZ (April 1989).

Commencement Address, The Ohio State University, Columbus, OH (Summer 1988).

"The Italian Renaissance from an Islamicist's Perspective," The Ohio State University Annual Humanities Symposium, Columbus, OH (April 1988).

"The Significance of Islamic Civilization in World History," St Olaf College, Northfield, MN (March 1988).

"The Meandering Mainstream: Reimagining World History," Inaugural Address, The Ohio State University, Columbus, OH (March 1988).

"Biography and Autobiography in Islamic History," Symposium on Babur, The Ohio State University, Columbus, OH (May 1984).

BIBLIOGRAPHY

Abbot, Nadia. *'A'isha: The Beloved of Mohammed*. Chicago, IL: University of Chicago Press, 1942.

Afsaruddin, Asma. *The First Muslims: History and Memory*. Oxford: OneWorld, 2007.

Al-Baydawi, 'Abd Allah b. 'Umar. *Anwar Al-Tanzil Wa-Asrar Al-Ta'wil*. 2 vols. Beirut: Dar al-Kutub al-'Ilmiyya, 1988.

Al-Qadi, Wadad. "Biographical Dictionaries as the Scholars' Alternative History of the Muslim Community." In *Organizing Knowledge: Encyclopaedic Activities in the Pre-Eighteenth-Century Islamic World*, ed. Abdou Filali-Ansary and Gerhard Endress. Islamic Philosophy, Theology, and Science, vol. 61. Leiden, The Netherlands: Brill, 2006.

Al-Zarkashi, Muhammad ibn Bahadur. *Al-Ijaba Li-Irad Ma Istadrakathu 'A'isha 'Ala Al-Sahaba*. Cairo: Matba'at al-'Asima, 1965.

Ali, Kecia. *Sexual Ethics and Islam: Feminist Reflections on Qur'an, Hadith and Jurisprudence*. Oxford: OneWorld, 2006.

Antoun, Richard T. *Muslim Preacher in the Modern World: A Jordanian Case Study in Comparative Perspective*. Princeton, NJ: Princeton University Press, 1989.

Aune, David E. *Prophecy in Early Christianity and the Ancient Mediterranean World*. Grand Rapids, MI: William B. Eerdmans, 1983.

Baum, Robert. M. "Alinesitoue: A Diola Woman Prophet in West Africa." In *Unspoken Worlds: Women's Religious Lives*, third edition, ed. Nancy A. Falk and Rita M. Gross, 170–95. Belmont, CA: Wadsworth, 2001.

———. *Shrines of the Slave Trade: Diola Religion and Society in Precolonial Senegambia*. New York and Oxford: Oxford University Press, 1999.

———. "The Emergence of a Diola Christianity." *Africa* 60 (Fall 1990): 370–98.

———. "Diola Religion." In *Encyclopedia of Religion*, vol. 4, ed. Mircea Eliade. New York: Macmillan, 1987.

———. "Crimes of the Dream World: French Trials of Diola Witches," paper presented at Conference on Law, Labour and Crime, University of Warwick, Warwick, 1983.

Berg, Herbert, ed. *Method and Theory in the Study of Islamic Origins*. Leiden, The Netherlands: Brill, 2003.

———. ed. *Development of Exegesis in Early Islam: The Authenticity of Muslim Literature from the Formative Period*. Richmond, UK: Curzon Press, 2000.

Bijlefeld, William A. "A Prophet and More Than a Prophet?" *Muslim World* 59 (1969): 1–28.

Brown, Daniel. *Rethinking Tradition in Modern Islamic Thought*. Cambridge: Cambridge University Press, 1996.

Brown, Jonathan A.C. "Criticism of the Proto-Hadith Canon: Al-Daraqutni's Adjustment of Al-Bukhari and Muslim's Sahihs." *Oxford Journal of Islamic Studies* 15, no. 1 (2004): 1–37.

Brown, Norman O. *Apocalypse and/or Metamorphosis.* Berkeley, CA: University of California Press, 1991.

Brown, Peter. "The Rise and Function of the Holy Man in Late Antiquity." *Journal of Roman Studies* 61 (1971): 80–101.

Casanova, Paul. *Mohammed et le fin du monde.* Paris: Gauthier, 1911–1924.

Cheikh, Nadya Maria El. *Byzantium Viewed by the Arabs.* Cambridge, MA: Harvard University Press, 2004.

Cohn, Norman. *The Pursuit of the Millennium: Revolutionary Millenarians and Mystical Anarchists of the Middle Ages.* London: Maurice Temple Smith Ltd, 1970.

Coulson, Noel J. *A History of Islamic Law.* Edinburgh: Edinburgh University Press, 1964.

Crone, Patricia. *Meccan Trade and the Rise of Islam.* Princeton, NJ: Princeton University Press, 1987.

Crow, Douglas S. "Islamic Messianism." In *Encyclopedia of Religion,* vol. 4, ed. Mircea Eliade, 477–81. New York: Macmillan, 1987.

Darrow, William Ronald. "The Zoroaster Legend: Its Historical and Religious Significance." PhD thesis, Harvard University, Cambridge, MA, 1981.

Davis, Dick. "Marilyn Waldman." In *Encyclopaedia Iranica,* www.iranica.com/articles/waldman-marilyn, last updated 25 July 2005, accessed 14 August 2010.

Denny, Frederick Mathewson. *An Introduction to Islam.* New York: Macmillan Publishing Company, 1994.

Donner, Fred M. *Muhammad and the Believers: At the Origins of Islam.* Cambridge, MA: Harvard University Press, 2010.

———. "From Believers to Muslims: Confessional Self-Identity in the Early Islamic Community." In *Patterns of Communal Identity,* ed. Lawrence I. Conrad, Studies in Late Antiquity and Early Islam, vol. IV. Princeton, NJ: Darwin Press, 2003.

———. *Narratives of Islamic Origins: The Beginnings of Islamic Historical Writing.* Princeton, NJ: The Darwin Press, Inc., 1998.

———. *The Early Islamic Conquests.* Princeton, NJ: Princeton University Press, 1981.

Edmunds, R. David. *The Shawnee Prophet.* Lincoln, NB and London: University of Nebraska Press, 1983.

Eickelman, Dale F. "Musaylima: An Approach to the Social Anthropology of Seventh Century Arabia." *Journal of the Economic and Social History of the Orient* 10 (1967): 17–52.

Ess, Josef van. *The Flowering of Muslim Theology.* Trans. Jane Marie Todd. Cambridge, MA: Harvard University Press, 2006.

Fahd, Toufic. "Sihr." In *Encyclopaedia of Islam,* second edition, ed. P. Bearman, T. Bianquis, C.E. Bosworth, E. van Donzel, and W.P. Heinrichs. Leiden, The Netherlands: Brill, 2010. www.brillonline.nl/subscriber/entry?entry=islam_SIM-7023, accessed 23 August 2010.

———. "Kahin." In *The Encyclopaedia of Islam,* second edition, ed. Emeri van Donzel *et al.* Leiden, The Netherlands: Brill, 1978.

Finnegan, Ruth. "The Poetic and the Everyday: Their Pursuit in an African Village and an English Town." *Folklore* 105 (1994): 3–11.

————. *Oral Poetry: Its Nature, Significance and Social Context.* Cambridge: Cambridge University Press, 1977.

————. *Limba Stories and Story-Telling.* Oxford: Oxford University Press, 1967.

Firestone, Reuven. *Journey in Holy Lands: The Evolution of the Abraham–Ishmael Legends in Islamic Exegesis.* Albany, NY: SUNY Press, 1990.

Fischer, August. "Kahin." *Shorter Encyclopedia of Islam,* ed. Hamilton A.R. Gibb and Johannes H. Kramers. Ithaca, NY: Cornell University Press, 1953.

Friedman, Yohanan. *Prophecy Continuous: Aspects of Ahmadi Religious Thought and Its Medieval Background.* Berkeley and Los Angeles, CA: University of California Press, 1989.

Gibb, H.A.R. *Mohammedanism.* New York: Oxford University Press, 1962.

Girard, Jean. *Genèse du Pouvoir Charismatique en Basse Casamance (Sénégal).* Dakar, Senegal: Institut Fondamental D'Afrique Noire, 1969.

Graham, William A. *Divine Word and Prophetic Word in Early Islam: A Reconsideration of the Sources, with Special Reference to the Divine Saying Or "Hadīth Qudsī."* Religion and Society, vol. 7. The Hague, The Netherlands, and Paris, France: Mouton, 1977.

Griffith, Sidney H. "The Christians in Muhammad's World: The Qur'an and the Doctrine of the Trinity." Paper presented at the American Academy of Religion, Boston, MA, 1987.

————. "The Prophet Muhammad: His Scripture and His Message According to the Christian Apologies in Arabic and Syriac from the First Abbasid Century." *La vie du prophète Mahomet: colloque de Strasbourg.* Paris: Presses Universitaires de France, 1983.

————. "Comparative Religion in the Apologetics of the First Christian Arabic Theologians." *Proceedings of the PMR Conference* 4 (1974): 63–87.

Gril, Denis. "Miracles." In *Encyclopaedia of the Qur'an.* Leiden, The Netherlands: Brill, 2007.

Grunebaum, G.E. von. "Idjāz." In *Encyclopaedia of Islam,* second edition, ed. P. Bearman, T. Bianquis, C.E. Bosworth, E. van Donze, and W.P. Heinrichs. Leiden, The Netherlands: Brill, 2010. www.brillonline.nl/subscriber/entry?entry=islam_ SIM-3484, accessed 23 August 2010.

————. *Medieval Islam: A Study in Cultural Orientation.* Chicago, IL: University of Chicago Press, 1953.

Guillaume, Alfred. *The Life of Muhammad: a Translation of Ishāq's Sīrat rasūl Allāh.* Karachi, Pakistan: Oxford University Press, 1978.

Günther, Sebastian. "Ummī." In *Encyclopaedia of the Qur'an,* ed. Jane Dammen McAuliffe. Washington, DC: Brill, 2010.

Hallaq, Wael B. *A History of Islamic Legal Theories: An Introduction to Sunni Usul Al-Fiqh.* Cambridge: Cambridge University Press, 1997.

————. "Was Al-Shafi'i the Master Architect of the Islamic Jurisprudence?" *International Journal of Middle East Studies* 4 (1993): 587–605.

Halman, Hugh Talat. "Al-Khidr." In *Encyclopedia of Islam and the Muslim World,* vol.1, ed. Richard C. Martin. New York: Macmillan Reference, 2001.

————. "'Where Two Seas Meet': The Qur'anic Story of Khidr and Modes in Sufi Commentaries as a Model for Spiritual Guidance." PhD thesis, Duke University, Durham, NC, 2000.

Hartman, Sven S. "Secrets for Muslims in Parsi Scriptures." In *Islam and Its Cultural Divergence: Studies in Honor of Gustave E. Von Grunebaum*, ed. Girdhari L. Tiku. Urbana, IL: University of Illinois Press, 1971.

Hodgson, Marshall G.S. *The Venture of Islam: Conscience and History in a World Civilization. Vol. 1: The Classical Age of Islam.* Chicago, IL: University of Chicago Press, 1977.

———. *The Venture of Islam: Conscience and History in a World Civilization. Vol. 2: The Expansion of Islam in the Middle Periods.* Chicago, IL: University of Chicago Press, 1974.

Hoyland, Robert G., ed. *Muslims and Others in Early Islamic Society.* Burlington, VT: Ashgate, 2004.

Hughes, Aaron. *Situating Islam: The Past and Present of an Academic Discipline.* London: Equinox Publishing, 2007

Ibrahim, Mahmood. *Merchant Capital and Islam.* Austin, TX: University of Texas Press, 1990.

Jaques, Kevin R. *Authority, Conflict, and the Transmission of Diversity in Medieval Islamic Law* Leiden, The Netherlands: Brill, 2006.

Jeffery, Arthur, ed. *A Reader on Islam: Passages from Standard Arabic Writings Illustrative of the Beliefs and Practices of Muslims.* The Hague, The Netherlands: Mouton & Co., 1962.

Khalidi, Tarif. *The Muslim Jesus: Sayings and Stories in Islamic Literature.* Cambridge, MA: Harvard University Press, 2001.

———. *Classical Arab Islam: The Culture and Heritage of the Golden Age.* Princeton, NJ: The Darwin Press, 1984.

Kogan, Barry. "Sa'adyah Gaon." In *Encyclopedia of Religion*, second edition, vol. 12, ed. Lindsay Jones, 7, 951–3. Detroit, MI: Macmillan Reference, 2005.

Kugel, James L. *Poetry and Prophecy: The Beginnings of a Literary Tradition.* Ithaca, NY: Cornell University Press, 1990.

Lewis, Bernard, ed. *Islam: From the Prophet Muhammad to the Capture of Constantinople.* New York: Walker and Company, 1974.

Lincoln, Bruce. "Prophecies, Rumors, and Silence: Notes on Caesar's Last Initiative." In *Episteme: In Ricordo di Giorgio Raimondo Cardona*, ed. Diego Poli. Special issue of *Quaderni Linguistici e Filologici* 4 (1986–1989): 59–73.

Lindbeck, George. *Nature of Doctrine: Religion and Theology in a Post-Liberal Age.* Lexington, KY: John Knox, 1984.

Lowry, Joseph E. "The Legal Hermeneutics of Al-Shafi'i and Ibn Qutayba: A Reconsideration." *Islamic Law and Society* 11, no.1 (2004): 1–41.

———. *The Legal-Theoretical Content of the Risāla of Muhammad B. Idrīs Al-Shāfiʿī.* PhD thesis, University of Pennsylvania, Philadelphia, PA, 1999.

Lucas, Scott C. *Constructive Critics, Hadith Literature, and the Articulation of Sunni Islam: The Legacy of the Generation of Ibn Sa'd, Ibn Ma'in, and Ibn Hanbal.* Leiden, The Netherlands: Brill, 2004.

Madelung, W. "'Ijma." In *Encyclopaedia of Islam*, ed. T. Bianquis P. Bearman, C.E. Bosworth, E. van Donzel, and W.P. Heinrichs. Leiden, The Netherlands: Brill, 2007.

Mark, Peter A. *A Cultural, Economic, and Religious History of the Basse Casamance Since 1500.* Stuttgart, Germany: Franz Steiner Verlag, 1985.

Martin, Richard C. "Inimitability." In *Encyclopaedia of the Qur'an*, ed. Jane Dammen McAuliffe. Leiden, The Netherlands: Brill, 2007.

Masud, Muhammad Khalid, Brinkley Morris Messick, and David Powers. *Islamic Legal Interpretation: Muftis and Their Fatwas*. Harvard Studies in Islamic Law. Cambridge, MA: Harvard University Press, 1996.

Meier, Samuel A. *The Messenger in the Ancient Semitic World*. Atlanta, GA: Scholars Press, 1988.

Melchert, Christopher. "The Piety of the Hadith Folk." *International Journal of Middle East Studies* 34 (2002): 425–39.

Mernissi, Fatima. *The Veil and the Male Elite: A Feminist Interpretation of Women's Rights in Islam*. Trans. Mary Jo Lakeland. New York: Basic Books, 1991.

Mir, Mustansir. *Verbal Idioms of the Qur'an*. Michigan Series on the Middle East No. 1. Ann Arbor, MI: Center for Near Eastern and African Studies, the University of Michigan, 1989.

Morony, Michael. *Iraq after the Muslim Conquest*. Princeton, NJ: Princeton University Press, 1984.

Mottahedeh, Roy P. *Loyalty and Leadership in an Early Islamic Society*. London: I.B. Tauris, 2001.

Mourad, Suleiman Ali. *Early Islam between Myth and History: Al-Hasan Al-Basrī (d. 110H/728 CE) and the Formation of His Legacy in Classical Islamic Scholarship*. Leiden and Boston, MA: Brill, 2006.

Nasr, Seyyed Hossein. *Ideals and Realities of Islam*. Chicago, IL: ABC International Group, 2000.

Newby, Gordon Darnell. *The Making of the Last Prophet: A Reconstruction of the Earliest Biography of Muhammad*. Columbia, OH: University of South Carolina Press, 1989.

Noth, Albrecht. "Problems of Differentiation between Muslims and Non-Muslims: Re-reading the 'Ordinances of 'Umar.'" *Muslims and Others in Early Islamic Society*, ed. Robert G. Hoyland, 103–25. Burlington, VT: Ashgate, 2004.

Overholt, Thomas W. *Channels of Prophecy: The Social Dynamics of Prophetic Activity*. Minneapolis, MN: Fortress Press, 1989.

Postman, Neil. *Amusing Ourselves to Death: Public Discourse in the Age of Show Business*. New York: Penguin Books, 2006.

The Qur'an. Trans. Ahmed Ali. Princeton, NJ: Princeton University Press, 2001.

Raven, Wim. "Sira and the Qur'an." In *Encyclopaedia of the Qur'an*, ed. Jane Dammen McAuliffe. Leiden, The Netherlands: Brill, 2007.

Renard, John. "Alexander." *Encyclopaedia of the Qur'an*, ed. Jane Dammen McAuliffe. Leiden, The Netherlands: Brill, 2010. www.brillonline.nl/subscriber/entry?entry=q3_SIM-00016, accessed 23 August 2010.

Robinson, Chase. "Reconstructing Early Islam: Truth and Consequences." In *Method and Theory in the Study of Islamic Origins*, ed. Herbert Berg, 101–36. Leiden, The Netherlands: Brill, 2003.

Rubin, Uri. "Muhammad." In *Encyclopaedia of the Qur'an*, ed. Jane Dammen McAuliffe. Leiden, The Netherlands: Brill, 2004.

———. "Prophets and Caliphs: The Biblical Foundations of the Umayyad Authority." In *Method and Theory in the Study of Islamic Origins*, ed. Herbert Berg, 73–100. Leiden, The Netherlands: Brill, 2003.

Sachedina, Abdulaziz Abdulhussein. *Islamic Messianism: The Idea of the Mahdi in Twelver Shi'ism*. Albany, NY: State University of New York Press, 1981.

Sebock, Thomas A. and Alexandra Ramsay (eds). *Approaches to Animal Communication*. The Hague: Mouton, 1969.

Safi, Omid. *Memories of Muhammad*. San Francisco, CA: Harper, 2010.

Segal, Alan F. *Paul the Convert: The Apostolate and Apostasy of Saul the Pharisee*. New Haven, CT: Yale University Press, 1992.

Segal, Charles. "Poetry, Performance, and Society in Early Greek Literature." *Lexis: Poetica, Retorica e Comunicazione nella Tradizione Classica* 2 (1988): 123–44. www.lexisonline.eu/images/archivio/2_lexis/segal_poetry.pdf, accessed 17 August 2010.

Shah, Idries. *The Pleasantries of the Incredible Mulla Nasrudin*. London: Octagon Press, 1977.

———. *The Exploits of the Incomparable Mulla Nasrudin*. London: Picador, 1966.

Shaw, Rosalind. "Splitting Truths from Darkness: Epistemological Aspects of Temne Divination." In *Ways of Knowing: African Systems of Divination*, ed. P. Peek, 133–52. Bloomington, IN: Indiana University Press, 1991.

Sheppard, Gerald T., and William E. Herbrechtsmeier. "Prophecy: An Overview." In *Encyclopedia of Religion*, second edition, vol. 11, ed. Lindsay Jones. Detroit, MI: Macmillan Reference, 2005: 7,423–9. *Gale Virtual Reference Library*. http://go.galegroup.com/ps/i.do?id=GALE|CX3424502519&v=2.1&u=duke_ perkins&it=r&p=GVRL&sw=w, accessed 22 August 2010.

Silver, Jeremy. *Images of Moses*. New York: Basic Books, 1982.

Slater, Philip. *Earthwalk*. Garden City, NY: Anchor Books, 1975.

Smith, Jonathan Z. *Relating Religion: Essays in the Study of Religion*. Chicago, IL: University of Chicago Press, 2004.

———. *Imagining Religion: From Babylon to Jonestown*. Chicago, IL: University of Chicago Press, 1982.

Spellberg, D.A. *Politics, Gender, and the Islamic Past: The Legacy of A'isha Bint Abi Bakr*. New York: Columbia University Press, 1986.

Stark, Rodney. "How New Religions Succeed: A Theoretical Model." In *The Future of New Religious Movements*, ed. David G. Bromley and Phillip E. Hammond, 11–29. Macon, GA: Mercer, 1987.

Sundkler, Bengt. *Bantu Prophets in South Africa*. London: Oxford University Press, 1961.

Turner, Bryan S. *Weber and Islam: A Critical Study*. London: Routledge & Kegan Paul, 1974.

Unal, Ali. *The Qur'an with Annotated Interpretation in Modern English*. Clifton, NJ: Tughra Books, 2008.

Vajda, G. "Isrā'īliyyāt." In *Encyclopaedia of Islam*, ed. T. Bianquis P. Bearman, C.E. Bosworth, E. van Donzel, and W.P. Heinrichs. Leiden, The Netherlands: Brill, 2007.

Wach, Joachim. *Types of Religious Experience, Christian and Non-Christian*. Chicago, IL: University of Chicago Press, 1951.

———. *The Sociology of Religion*. Chicago, IL: University of Chicago Press, 1944.

Waldman, Marilyn Robinson. *Toward a Theory of Historical Narrative: A Case Study in Perso-Islamicate Historiography*. Columbus, OH: Ohio State University Press, 1980.

Walker, Paul E. "Impeccability." In *Encyclopaedia of the Qur'an*, ed. Jane Dammen McAuliffe. Leiden, The Netherlands: Brill, 2007.

Wallace, Anthony F.C. *Religion: An Anthropological View*. New York: Random House, 1966.

Wasserstrom, Steven M. *Between Muslim and Jew: The Problem of Symbiosis under Early Islam*. Princeton, NJ: Princeton University Press, 1995.

Watt, William Montgomery. *Muslim–Christian Encounters: Perceptions and Misperceptions*. London: Routledge, 1991.

———. *Muhammad's Mecca: History in the Qur'an*. Edinburgh: Edinburgh University Press, 1988.

———. *The Majesty That Was Islam: The Islamic World, 66–1100*. London: Sidgwick & Jackson, 1974.

Weber, Max. *The Sociology of Religion*. Boston, MA: Beacon Press, 1993.

———. *From Max Weber: Essays in Sociology*. Trans. H.H. Gerth and C. Wright Mills. London: Routledge & Kegan Paul, 1948.

Weiss, Bernard G. ed. *Studies in Islamic Legal Theory*. Leiden, The Netherlands: Brill, 2002.

———. *Search for God's Law Islamic Jurisprudence in the Writings of Sayf Al-Dīn Al-Āmidī*. Salt Lake City, UT: University of Utah Press, 1992.

Wheeler, Brannon. "Moses." In *The Blackwell Companion to the Qur'an*, ed. Andrew Rippin, 248–65. Malden, MA: Blackwell Publishing, 2006.

———. *Mecca and Eden: Ritual, Relics, and Territory in Islam*. Chicago, IL: University of Chicago Press, 2006.

———. *Prophets in the Qur'an: An Introduction to the Qur'an and Muslim Exegesis*. New York: Continuum, 2002.

———. *Moses in the Qur'an and Islamic Exegesis*. Leiden, The Netherlands: Brill, 2002.

Williams, John Alden. *Islam*. New York: G. Braziller, 1961.

Williams, Michael A., Collett Cox, and Martin S. Jaffee, eds. *Innovation in Religious Traditions: Essays in the Interpretation of Religious Change*. The Hague, The Netherlands: Mouton, 1992.

Willner, Ann Ruth. *The Spellbinders: Charismatic Political Leadership*. New Haven, CT and London: Yale University Press, 1984.

———. "The Neotraditional Accomodation to Political Independence: The Case of Indonesia." In *Cases in Comparative Politics: Asia*, ed. Lucian Pye, 248–51. Boston, MA: Little, Brown, 1970.

Wilson, Robert R. *Prophecy and Society in Ancient Israel*. Philadelphia, PA: Fortress Press, 1980.

Zwettler, Michael. *The Oral Tradition of Classical Arabic Poetry: Its Character and Implications*. Columbus, OH: Ohio State University Press, 1978.

INDEX